D0759589

We *Are* the Union

We Are the Union

Democratic Unionism and Dissent at Boeing

DANA L. CLOUD

with

R. KEITH THOMAS,
Boeing Machinist, IAMAW
Local 834, Lodge 70 (retired)

UNIVERSITY OF ILLINOIS PRESS

Urbana, Chicago, and Springfield

© 2011 by the Board of Trustees
of the University of Illinois
All rights reserved
Manufactured in the United States of America
c 5 4 3 2 1
∞ This book is printed on acid-free paper.

Library of Congress Cataloging-in-Publication Data
Cloud, Dana L.
We are the union : democratic unionism and dissent at Boeing /
Dana L. Cloud with R. Keith Thomas.
p.   cm.
Includes bibliographical references and index.
ISBN 978-0-252-03637-8 (cloth : acid-free paper)
1. Labor unions—Kansas—Wichita. 2. International Association
of Machinists and Aerospace Workers. 3. Boeing Aerospace
Company—Management. 4. Strikes and lockouts—Kansas—
Wichita 5. Dissenters—Kansas—Wichita
I. Thomas, R. Keith. II. Title.
HD6519.W52 I6   2011
331.88'1291300973—dc22   2011015096

*For all of the dissidents who
are taking back their unions*

Contents

Preface

In June 1996, I attended a panel on the prospects for the labor movement at an activist conference in Chicago. On that panel was a union activist from Wichita, Kansas. His name was Keith Thomas, he worked at The Boeing Company, and he had a story to tell. The labor movement had been in a bad way through the 1980s and into the 1990s; many thousands of hardworking people found themselves with little defense against eroding union rights, falling wages and benefits, outsourcing and off-loading, and the pressure to increase productivity at all costs. Thomas, however, gave a presentation infused with optimism about the events of a strike of the International Association of Machinists and Aerospace Workers (IAMAW) against Boeing. Something incredible had happened. Boeing was ruthless in its demands during the 1995 contract negotiations for concessions. The union leadership, sluggish in its bureaucratic history and leery of a fight, prepared to take concessions. They presented two contract offers to the membership, which voted the first one down. The second contract was pitched as "Boeing's last, best, final offer." The leadership recommended a vote.

It came as a shock to everyone, except maybe the rank and file, that the membership, nearly univocally, voted it down. Thomas recounted how Boeing had been so confident that the union would sell the contract to the workers that the company had sent "welcome back" letters to thousands of strikers. The picket lines after the vote became rows of white flags as workers—still on strike—waved their "welcome back" letters at passing cars and media crews.

Thomas had been among a number of reformers inside his union struggling to jar union leadership into standing up for the rank and file. His group had been agitating on the shop floor for months, running campaigns for union office, and building a small organization called Unionists for Democratic Change. The defeat of the second contract was a sign, to the activists and to all interested in the fate of American labor, that the rank and file could become once again a force for change.

Thomas's presentation was riveting. I "fell in love," as they say about journalists who become invested in the stories they help others to tell. In addition to my being an activist in the labor movement, one reason that I fell so hard is that, as an activist and a communication scholar, the most compelling questions guiding my scholarly work and political activity are: How do ordinary people, through communication and experience, come to a sense of themselves as agents capable of radical social transformation; and how do they accomplish such transformation even when constrained by any number of institutional and cultural forces arrayed against them? Another way of putting these questions is to ask about when, how, and why ordinary people successfully craft resistance in a complex array of institutional, rhetorical, and economic forces. In a way that may speak profoundly to all scholars and practitioners of resistance, the dissident movement at Boeing promised some answers to these questions.

Focusing on the period from 1989 forward—with 1995 as a crucial turning point—this book tells three stories about the company and the union at Boeing: the history of the company, pressing workers in the name of competitiveness; the one told by entrenched union leaders, urging concessions for job security; and the one told by democratic unionists inside the union who gave voice to an already palpable rank-and-file upsurge against not only the Boeing Company but also union leaders who urged concessions and quietude. The contrast between these three stories points to how ordinary working people come to a sense of themselves as agents of their own future in spite of institutional structures that work to bind them to the past.

Understanding how working people can command their own futures has become that much more urgent today with the U.S. (and the world) economy in free fall. As the auto industry received an enormous bailout from the federal government, executives blamed unionized workers for the company's economic crisis.[1] National Public Radio's show Marketplace featured a spot by commentator Kevin Hassett, who argued that General Motors should enter bankruptcy in order to break its union because the union has "festooned the company with rigid work rules and extravagant costs." GM retiree Greg Shotwell countered this argument in testimony before the U.S. Congress. Arguing that the government should not allow the company to declare bankruptcy and gut workers' protections and standard of living, he said, "I am not here to apologize for workers who constitute the backbone of America. We have never failed. I am not here to beg on behalf of the men and women who fought the wars, built the roads and bridges, manufactured the goods, delivered the services, and transported every conceivable product from its origin to its destination. I am here to demand the respect and dignity we deserve."[2]

During the 2007 strike at GM, Alan Benchich, president of UAW Local 909, told the *New York Times:* "We're not overpaid and underworked. The fact is that the ones [other workers] who claim that are underpaid themselves. And the reason they are underpaid is because we're unionized, we're organized, and they are not."[3] In 2009, GM emerged from bankruptcy, forcing big losses on the unionized workforce. The Economic Free Choice Act (EFCA), which would have made it easier for workers to unionize, went down under pressure from corporate interests from Walmart to the Chamber of Commerce.[4]

Since the 1970s, in fact, workers in the United States and around the world have felt the consequences of neoliberal restructuring, which has included outsourcing and offshoring, attacks on pensions and health care, and the turn in management methods to lean manufacturing and worker-management teams. These pressures contributed heavily to a steep decline in union power. However, events at Boeing in 1995 (and since) demonstrated that workers could stand up to these trends. Against a profitable global company and a recalcitrant union, the rank and file interrupted the drive for concessions and defended their standard of living.

Although there have been and continue to be other examples of this sort of resistance, union representation and strength in the United States is at an all-time low. If anything, neoliberalism in crisis—since the 2007–2008 implosion of the world economy—is even more ruthless than neoliberalism in power, as corporate leaders scramble to restore profitability on the backs of workers from whom more and more is demanded in less and less time. Events in 2011 in Wisconsin have demonstrated the kind of challenge that is needed to take on sluggish union bureaucrats and politicians hell-bent on extracting concessions from workers and breaking their unions. In February 2011, thousands of Wisconsin state employees rose up to challenge Governor Scott Walker's plans to cut into wages and health care and to end collective bargaining rights in the state. Workers took over the state capitol chanting, "Whose House? Our House!" "Workers' Power!" and "General Strike!" Some 150,000 demonstrated outside the building on March 11. However, after these inspiring events, Walker pushed through legislation ending bargaining rights. On the run, official union leaders sacrificed their workers in a round of concessions to the state and teamed up with Democratic politicians aiming to supplant Walker and his cronies in the next election cycle. Meanwhile, the militancy of the rising working class—something not seen in the United States in several decades—was squandered, at least for the moment.

What if there had been a democratic union movement in place? Will we see such a movement arise in the wake of the passivity of entrenched union leaders?

It is clear that what is needed now more than ever is a revival of militant unionism. Achieving this goal is hampered, however, by an insular union officialdom used to taking concessions and reluctant to fight. Union leaders like those in the IAMAW at Boeing have embraced team-based management programs, team-based safety initiatives, and quality through training programs, putting workers in alignment with management rather than sharpening the antagonism necessary to a strong union movement. This book is about how small groups of workers have agitated for greater democracy, transparency, and fighting spirit on the part of their unions. These rank-and-file reform groups, in my view, offer a vision of a future, more powerful labor movement and a method for getting there.

I will argue that these groups should look to the history of U.S. unionism for models. Specifically, the emergence of powerful industrial unions through the 1930s shows how workers can reform existing institutions and build new ones that better serve their interests. Massive successful organizing drives among industrial workers and a series of militant and effective strikes marked the middle years of the 1930s. In particular, the creation of a fighting United Auto Workers out of the 1936–1937 sit-down strikes against General Motors signaled growing class consciousness and collective agency in the industrial workforce.

It has been a long time since those victories. This book addresses the mixed fortunes of labor in more recent struggles, specifically those at the Boeing Company. I am interested in the stories workers tell as examples of what Gerard Hauser has called "vernacular voices": the narratives and activities of ordinary people entering—and creating—an unruly public sphere to contest the terms of their own lives.[5] Union dissidents, whose arguments and activities run up not only against their employer but also against their official union, are doubly examples of bottom-up self-representation.

We Are the Union: Democratic Unionism and Dissent at Boeing uncovers the capacity of ordinary working people to take command of their own futures. In what follows, I tell the story of three dissident union groups at Boeing in the 1990s, whose purposes were to agitate among fellow workers in the International Association of Machinists and Aerospace Workers for greater voice in union affairs, to distribute contract information during bargaining, and to hold official union leaders—accustomed to a cozy relationship with Boeing management and stuck in the sludge of bureaucratic habit—accountable to the interests of the rank and file. A key moment in the history of democratic unionism at Boeing occurred in 1995, when the rank and file rejected a contract recommended to them by union leaders, staying on strike for an unprecedented sixty-nine days. The workers won their demands, and for the reformers this event signaled the possibility of bottom-up agency that could transform the union.

In this effort, the dissident unionists had to negotiate the narratives of both company and official union in order to be heard. In chapters about company history, union history, the habits and perspectives of the official union, the role of communication in activist efforts, and the stories of dissidents themselves, my analysis shows how the reformers' work reveals the paradoxical position of the "loyal opposition": having to fight the union in order to use the union to their own ends. This paradox finds expression in the workers' stories in the form of contradictions between collective organization and individual action, commitment to rank-and-file democracy and elitism, and the critique of union politics as usual alongside participation in elections as a central focus of their work.

It is my hope that labor scholars, communication scholars, and activists for workers' power all find something useful in my account. For labor studies, this book provides a rank-and-file account not only of the exploitation of industrial work but also of the possibility of union revitalization. The work done by the Boeing dissidents follows in a line of union reform efforts stemming from the militant industrial unionism of the 1930s. For the field of communication studies, *We Are the Union* demonstrates a method for situating workers' voices in the context of their economic clout. Both organizational communication studies and rhetorical studies have overestimated the independent influence of communication alone. The book surveys literature in communication studies on workers' voice, culture, and organization but offers a unique perspective that recognizes the special economic potential of workers' organization.

In the end, however, I hope that the book speaks most powerfully to today's labor movement in the context of profound economic crisis. Successful strikes at Boeing in 2005 and 2008 demonstrate the possibility of rebuilding union influence even during hard times. Crucial to that project is the work of dissident unionists pressing the massive institutions of U.S. labor to work in their own interests. Here I demonstrate how the stories of the Boeing workers offer lessons in both victory and defeat for a labor movement on the ropes.

Their stories are marked by the contradictions inherent in the central dilemma of having to fight an institution and use it as a matter of basic self-defense at the same time. Their paradoxical position of "loyal opposition"[6] is vexed with dilemmas and difficult to sustain. Thus, the stories of these Boeing workers is of importance to both activists and scholars seeking to understand the negotiation of constraining institutions by ordinary people and the stories they tell about themselves. The Boeing Company, too, has a history, as does the IAMAW. Members of the union necessarily negotiate with, and are therefore constrained by, the organizational imperatives of the company and the stories of union leaders.

However, the workers also possess resources in their own experience as workers that enable them to speak back to their organizations' dominant framing of events. Historically, unions are about marshaling the collective experiences, grievances, and demands of working people. An isolated voice has no power in the context of the corporate organization. If unions are to be truly about workers' power and freedom, workers must marshal their own voices independent of the official union to reform the erstwhile representative of their interests. In the view of union dissidents, the IAMAW should not see itself as the loyal opposition to the company. Rather, the union should simply be the opposition. When the union becomes too loyal to the company, a space is opened up for the loyal opposition inside the union. The balance between "loyal" and "opposition" is always contested and shifting.

Although I will make some criticisms of the unionists at the heart of this study, I write from a position of solidarity with their purpose and struggle. I hope that the book reveals what it is like to conduct advocacy research in solidarity with a movement, which can necessitate criticizing people toward whom one feels loyalty, respect, and affection. I am profoundly grateful to all of these activists for opening up their lives and their movement to me.

Acknowledgments

First and foremost, I thank Keith and Shelley Thomas for opening their home and lives to me. Since this project began more than a decade ago, they have become family to me, my partner, and our daughter. I offer deepest thanks to all of the union activists in Wichita and the Puget Sound—Keith Thomas, Kelly Vandegrift, Gary Washington, Sean Mullin, Arlene Hoaglan, David "Bones" Smith, Don Grinde, Tom Finnegan, Stan Johnson, Tom Jackson, Rick Herrmann, William Sapiens, David Mascarenas, and David Clay—who spent time with and trusted me despite our ideological differences. I am moved by the extent to which Don Grinde shared his personal thoughts and rich union archives with me. David Clay has been a good sport about corresponding and talking by phone with me repeatedly over the years. I also appreciate all of the other people who consented to be heard in this book.

I am incredibly grateful to Deepa Kumar, Peter Rachleff, and George Cheney for their work on labor, struggle, and democracy. They also were great readers of this manuscript. Their very thoughtful and helpful reviews were both rigorous and encouraging, helping to make it much stronger than it otherwise would have been. The standard-setting labor journalism of *Socialistworker.org*, especially that of Lee Sustar, was indispensible.

I thank editor Laurie Matheson for giving this project a second look. Carol Burwash was an extremely humane and talented copy editor. (Thank you!) Jack Getman here in the School of Law at the University of Texas has been a great friend and inspiration. His many books, from *The Betrayal of Local 14* to *Restoring the Power of Unions,* are necessary and inspiring reading.

My PhD student and teaching assistant Ashley Mack McCann lent me the benefits of her keen editorial eye and remarkable reference formatting skills. Ashley, I admire you as a scholar and a teacher. Thank you for your essential contributions to this project. I am also tremendously grateful for the unparalleled research assistance and support of Bryan McCann.

This work has received material support from the University of Texas and the College of Communication at the University of Texas, in the forms of the John T. Jones Centennial Professorship Fellowship in summer 2005, the University of Texas College of Communication Fellowship in 2008, research assistance grants in 2001 and 2010, a University of Texas Faculty Research Assignment in 2003–2004, and the Academic Excellence Fund grant from the College of Communication in 1999.

The two semesters I spent as a Fellow of the University of Texas Humanities Institute in 2001 and 2007 made for wonderful conversations about this work. I offer many thanks to Evan Carton, director of the Institute during those years, for advising me to let go of academic pretension and "just tell the story" (which he does beautifully in his own book on John Brown). I am grateful for the support and insight of my longtime friend Pat Robinson and my good friends and colleagues Karin Wilkins and Sonia Seeman. I thank my colleagues in the Department of Communication Studies at the University of Texas for their support, especially Joshua Gunn, the most generous of all scholars and most loyal of all friends. I thank my friend and department chair, Barry Brummett, for standing over my shoulder until I hit the "send" button.

As ever, I thank my beloved friend Rosa Eberly for her love and erudition, both of which have sustained me since the early days of this project.

During the time I spent researching and writing this book, my daughter grew from a child of eight into a remarkable young woman, now in college. I'm proud of the book—but I'm prouder of her. Finally, I offer my most heartfelt gratitude and love to my spouse (and extraordinary scholar) Katie Feyh, who surprised me with an early return from a semester conducting research abroad, only to catch me unkempt in my pajamas, bleary-eyed, hair standing on end, with pages of interviews strewn about me as I typed. Thanks for loving the real me.

We *Are* the Union

"To Get to Boeing, We First Had to Take on the Union"

Advocates for social change often find themselves in an ambivalent relationship to the existing institutions, mechanisms, and rhetorical norms of change in U.S. society. For example, opponents of the death penalty and the vagaries of the criminal justice system still must use the courts as an arena of contestation. Activist Cindy Sheehan is a strong, vocal opponent of the war in Iraq; even as she enacts unruly womanhood, she uses her status and maternal identity as the mother of a fallen soldier to garner credibility and public voice. Many gays and lesbians question marriage as a heterosexist institution, yet they still recognize it as a central civil right and movement goal. A similar situation faces workers who know that unions are a source of collective power yet who also suffer the injury of being tied to an often undemocratic labor bureaucracy stumbling under its own weight. Unions may be the paradigm case of the basic paradox in the rhetoric of social change: the imperative to work within existing frameworks while trying, at the same time, to undo them.

The foremost purpose of a labor union is to give workers more power in dealing with their employers. If organized workers collectively refuse to work, production of goods and services halts and employers are forced to bargain with their employees. It is only the economic clout of the strike or threatened strike that provides workers with leverage to reach agreements on their terms, rather than just the bosses.' As Lawrence Mishel and Matthew Walters explain, the advantages of being in a union include "higher wages; more and better benefits; more effective utilization of social insurance programs; and more effective enforcement of legislated labor protections such as safety, health, and overtime regulations. Unions also set pay standards and practices that raise the wages of nonunionized workers in occupations and industries where there is a strong union presence. Collective bargaining fuels innovations in wages, benefits, and work practices that affect both unionized and nonunionized workers. . . . [U]nions enable due process in the workplace and facilitate a strong worker voice in the broader community and in politics. Many observers have stated, correctly, that a strong labor movement is essential to a thriving democracy."[1] Although statistical evidence shows that unionized workers today earn more and have a higher standard of living than nonunionized workers (2008 median weekly income for the unionized worker was $880 versus $690 for nonunionized), unionization rates in the United States declined steadily from the late 1940s (when unions represented 36 percent of U.S. workers) until the present economic recession (12.4 percent).[2] Favorability ratings of labor unions fell sharply between 2007 and 2010—years of heightened economic crisis—to just 42 percent, an all-time low.[3]

There are many factors in this decline, including the postwar pact labor leaders made with American business, the McCarthyist purge from unions of the most progressive activists during the Cold War, and a relentless employers' offensive dating from the 1970s that has included rampant union busting alongside the off-loading, subcontracting, and outsourcing of previously unionized work. Alongside tax cuts for the rich, real wages have stagnated, and consumer debt (totaling $2.6 trillion) has hit record proportions.[4] The present economic crisis has sharpened the class divide, as the U.S. economy shed 2.6 million jobs in the last quarter of 2008 alone. (At the end of 2009, more than 14 million people in the United States were unemployed.)[5]

But unions themselves must bear part of the blame for the present state of labor in the United States. The history of U.S. labor is basically one of a profound reluctance to fight on the part of official union bureaucrats. Julius Getman captures the problem when he writes, "The labor movement must be not only for the people, as most unions are, but also of the people, in ways that most unions are not."[6] Getting a union to move has always been the product of pressure from below, from the rank and file, on union leaders. It is a paradox that workers in the United States have been faced not only with the glaring necessity of organizing in unions to protect their interests but also with the fact that their unions have not been strong advocates of those interests. Representing rank-and-file interests, union democracy groups are in a position to make important criticisms of union officials' partnerships with management (for example, workplace quality and team programs and joint management-union grievance and safety committees).

In this study of particular reform groups, I demonstrate how members negotiate meaning, identity, and control between and among employer, union, and union faction. In other words, management attempts to "include" workers in their stories of a firm; the union claims to represent workers in bargaining; and workers themselves—neither dependent upon nor independent of the other storytellers' efforts—produce and seek out stories that they perceive as faithful to their interests.[7]

The experiences of particular union democracy activists shed light on the successes and pitfalls of democratic union agitation. The central argument of this book is that reform groups agitating for greater union democracy, accountability, and militancy are crucial to the fight to restore the power of unions. Leaders and members of such groups create and circulate coherent accounts of their antagonistic relationship to the company and critical relationship—best captured in the term *loyal opposition*—to the union. This stance positions the activists in a series of dilemmas as they find themselves advocating for broader democratic involvement while relegating reform efforts and decision making to only a few people. Without a great deal of rank-and-file involvement, the dissidents resort to top-down tools such as electioneering and lawsuits to achieve the groups' objectives. In addition, the position of loyal opposition, as the very term suggests, entails a vexing balancing act between using the union both to target the company and to target the union in ways that seem to established union leaders potentially damaging to the union's effectiveness.

In this book, the dissidents articulate two main criticisms of the union: First, they argue that entrenched leadership of the union cooperates with management in the implementation of team programs and quality management initiatives, turning them effectively into "Boeing managers." Second, they call attention to such undemocratic practices as election fraud, routine in their union's life. Exclusions from the regular political process generate the need for reform-oriented groups to develop independent organization to organize and exert pressure on reified institutional structures. As one worker told me, "To get to Boeing, first we had to take on the union."

About the company, the subjects of my interviews explained that Boeing exerts incredible pressure on and demands concessions from workers even in times of tremendous profitability. The regular layoffs of tens of thousands of workers stand as constant threats to job security. The pressures of neoliberalism—a global economic regime characterized by off-loading, offshoring, and lean production—reach Boeing workers by way of seemingly empowering managerial partnership and employee voice initiatives. Members of established and upstart groups alike called my attention to the problems of job insecurity, on-the-job dangers, and the enduring salience of race, gender, and sexuality in their workplace culture.

While the timeline of this project stretches from 1989 to 2008, the 1995 strike of the International Association of Machinists and Aerospace Workers (IAMAW) is at the center of my book's narrative.[8] In the face of the elimination of tens of thousands of jobs, union negotiators pushed for a three-year contract that included wage increases, increases in cost-of-living formulas, new safety and health provisions, and improvements in insurance. In addition, the union sought income protection plans for laid-off workers, including continuation of insurance. Most important, the original union proposal included language that prohibited further subcontracting. IAMAW President George Kourpias gave voice to fighting words, accusing Boeing of "punching holes in America's future." The company, of course, pleaded economic insecurity and argued that outsourcing and layoffs were necessary to stay afloat. The union members approved a strike authorization vote in September after the union brought the company's "last, best, final offer" to them. The first time, the union recommended rejection of the offer, and it was voted down. The workers went on strike on September 13. Weeks passed without the delivery of a single new plane. Journalist Michael Cimini describes what happened next:

> On November 19, a [second] tentative agreement was reached between Boeing and the IAMAW. Although the IAMAW bargaining committee unanimously recommended acceptance of the pact, the rank and file soundly rejected it. Union members said that they were dissatisfied with the contract offer because it still called for increases in employee contributions towards health care and contained weak job security language.[9]

It was at the moment of the union endorsement of the second contract that the conditions for challenging a stale bureaucracy were born. In an unprecedented wave, the workers of the union slapped down the cautious recommendation of the leaders and voted to remain on strike. Worker accounts of this event are moving revelations of their sudden recognition of their own power. The rank-and-file members of the IAMAW went up not only against Boeing, but also against the unaccountable leadership of the union itself. It was a moment of profound class-consciousness, in which workers realized that they had the power to take their future in their own hands. Wichita, Kansas, union activist Keith Thomas described the mood of the rank and file:

> They just set that ass down there, they stuck their finger up there and they said I've just had enough. People out on the picket lines were waving their welcome back letters to the cameras and to the general public as folks would go by. And just how outstanding that was.[10]

The images of workers metaphorically (and, in some cases, literally) giving their leaders "the finger" and waving the arrogant welcome back letters from the company on the picket line convey the sense of agency and defiance the rank and file felt at that moment.

Everett, Washington, organizer David Clay told me that in his shop membership held lunchtime marches, banged on pipes with tools, and disrupted delivery of 777s. He said, "We shook the walls. People got the idea that this thing is theirs." By most accounts, the outcome of the 1995 strike was a major victory for the union. In the face of bureaucratic sluggishness on the part of the union and a relentless offensive on the part of the company, the rank and file stood up and used their collective strength to challenge both.

In this context and before, small groups of agitators gave voice to this fighting spirit. In order to understand this movement, I have conducted and taped more than forty hours of interviews with dissident unionists during 1998, 1999, and 2001. These workers spoke with me openly and at length about union strategy in contract negotiations; they also shared their experience of work at Boeing, their perceptions of the internal politics of the union, and the impact of race and gender on their work and union organizing. Since those initial interviews, I have talked and corresponded with several core activists through mid-2010. Along with media coverage and supplemental interviews with community organizers, journalists, and company spokespersons, these accounts are the foundation of this book.[11]

The first group of activists I encountered was Unionists for Democratic Change (UDC), made up of a group of IAMAW members in Wichita who formed the dissident caucus in 1990. Keith Thomas was the most prominent leader in this organization, putting out email newsletters over a period of several years to educate union members, leading pickets and other demonstrations, producing buttons and T-shirts for workers during contract negotiations and strikes, leafleting inside the plants, and engaging in other agitation-oriented activity. The UDC group contended that the international union had been operating undemocratically and against the interests of rank-and-file workers. Over a period of several years, they attempted to build an organization whose goals were worker education and winning elected office inside the union. In the Puget Sound, Don Grinde found himself at the head of a parallel caucus allied with the UDC. Variously called the "New Crew" and "Rank and File," this group of activists focused on challenging the entrenched political power of a union leadership hostile to its aims. It is worth noting that being a union official in District 751 (Puget Sound) of the IAMAW, comprising seven locals (A through F) and more than 35,000 workers, is no small deal. Those entrenched officials fought tooth and nail against the challenges of reformers. Arising at about the same time as this crew in Everett, another reform organization called Machinists for Solidarity/Take It Back rose under the leadership of David Clay. (Clay rejects the label *dissident* even as his group serves functions that are similar to the others.') Clay had been more or less aligned with Team 751, the established union leadership, in the early 1990s, but he broke with it as the decade wore on.

In the chapters that follow, I describe workers trying to navigate the dilemma of needing not only to use the union but also to fight its bureaucratic and undemocratic aspects. They tell the story of pushing the union toward greater victory and of marginalizing themselves and getting mired in internal power struggles that sometimes have taken precedence over a focus on the company or efforts to organize and involve larger numbers of the rank and file.

Organization of the Book

This book situates the struggle at Boeing inside broader narrative frames, one about the history of unions and movements for union democracy, and the other about the history of the Boeing Company and its unions in particular. The book thus moves from introductory chapters setting the stage into a narrative of the Boeing struggle followed by detailed discussion of the dilemmas and challenges facing the democratic unionists there. The 1995 strike is at the center of the book.

Chapter 1 introduces the arguments of the book in the context of a summary of the critique of traditional American union leadership as pro-business and dangerously invested in partnerships with management. The chapter chronicles the history of the rise of democratic unionism with particular attention to such movements in the United Auto Workers and Teamsters. The chapter traces the crisis of U.S. unions through the 2005 split in the AFL-CIO. The chapter also summarizes key instances of failures/selling out of union leadership, including Jay, Maine; Staley; and Detroit newspaper workers. The chapter argues for the importance of independent, pro-democratic voices inside of unions, like those that marked the early labor movement's willingness to fight even under prohibitive conditions.

Chapter 2 begins with the narrative frames of company and union, describing the rise to power of the Boeing Company—and of the IAMAW. Known for its militancy, the IAMAW has enacted a history paralleling the turbulence of the larger labor movement. Throughout its history (albeit with a few notable exceptions), the leadership of the IAMAW at Boeing has cooperated with concessions unless forced to do otherwise by the rank and file of the union.

Chapter 3 charts the emergence of Unionists for Democratic Change and Machinists for Solidarity in the International Association of Machinists in the period 1989–1999. Alongside this history, the chapter provides an account of the core issues of contestation between workers and the company: layoffs, health care cuts, outsourcing (both domestic and international and both outside and inside Boeing's plants) of union work, workplace safety, racial and gender-based discrimination, and treatment of retirees.

Chapter 4 goes into depth about the reformers' overarching critique, that the union engages in too much cooperation with the company. Such cooperation often manifests itself in joint safety, performance, and team-based management initiatives. As David Clay points out rather baldly in that chapter, "Jointness means the membership is getting the joint." These workers' assessment of programs like Total Quality Management (TQM) and the implementation of the High Performance Work Organization (HPWO) illustrate two arguments that I am making: First, workers possess the resources of their experience to recognize and reject ideological efforts to align their interests with those of the company. Second, scholars and labor union members alike should be skeptical about worker inclusion programs that ask the workers to give up their autonomy from and antagonism toward their employer. Such independence is necessary to the fight to defend and extend workers' standard of living during contract negotiations and grievance procedures.

Chapter 5 focuses on the 1995 strike. In this strike, the union presented two contracts to the membership, one with the recommendation to reject and the second with the recommendation to approve. However, the second contract was not significantly better; many workers among the rank and file felt betrayed by their leaders' recommendation. Although there had been a strike in 1989, both union and company expected ratification. However, the members resoundingly rejected the second contract offer and stayed on strike for sixty-nine days, winning most of their demands. These events, as this chapter will show, inspired workers with a sense of their own agency. It was an unprecedented moment of rank-and-file self-determination.

Chapter 6 explores how the dissident groups fell into disarray after 1995. Part of the blame lies within the contradictions inherent in the stance of loyal opposition and the role of democratic leader. These contradictions led burned-out reformers after the peak of struggle to employ individually undertaken, top-down methods to achieve, ironically, a more democratic union. Both UDC and Machinists for Solidarity prioritized elections and lawsuits to achieve their ends. For example, the chapter includes a discussion of Keith Thomas's successful use of the Labor-Management Reporting and Disclosure Act (LMRDA) to demand openness in his local lodge. The chapter offers some assessment of the implications of this ironic legal victory—which uses a conservative law to hold the union accountable to its membership—for the whole labor movement. The chapter also raises questions about UDC members' investment in internal union elections and the contradictions between this activity and the stated commitment to organizing and agitating among rank-and-file workers. The chapter concludes with a discussion of the ironies of individual legal and electoral action, resorted to in the absence of mass rank-and-file involvement.

In drawing conclusions about the limitations of top-down, legalistic means to achieve union democracy, I struggled with the ethics of using these activists' stories to further my own argument. In addition, the question kept reappearing: Shouldn't activists in unions use whatever tools—elections, laws, and so on—that help them reach the rank and file? I decided that my participants deserved a voice in the final product. Therefore, I invited Keith Thomas to respond to and reflect upon the observations made in the preceding chapters of the book. The exchange—laid out in chapter 7—reveals some of the real difficulties and challenges and the strains in time, money, finances, and reputation—that come along with the dissident role. Keith Thomas's observations will encourage readers to understand the limitations of the movement in the contexts of the real lives of activists set against a renewed employer's offensive and a very powerful and change-resistant union bureaucracy.

This collaborative chapter also enables Thomas's sense of my ideas and politics to become part of the project, encouraging the kind of reflexive self-critique that I believe characterizes ethical oral history work. As Linda Alcoff argued in her important essay on the problem of speaking for others, any time one attempts to speak for and with others, one risks imposing one's criteria and vision onto other people's voices.[12] I do not believe that this risk makes speaking for others inevitably unethical or untenable. Instead, I hope to use criteria derived from the workers' own goals and principles to assess their progress and to include my subjects' critical feedback. These innovations can help to make the work speak—even in its more critical moments—with and alongside, rather than for, the interviewees.

The penultimate chapter speaks to scholars in my home field of communication studies, surveying literature on organizational democracy, storytelling, and worker voice. In this context, the present study of Boeing union dissidents offers two insights: First, the study is one of the few in the field that pays attention to labor unions as a site of agency for workers. This emphasis underscores how ultimately worker agency is a function of economic clout. Second, my analysis extends research on opportunities for and constraints on worker voice. The discovery of rank-and-file attitudes toward team and quality programs in industrial work reveals profound skepticism toward those avenues of worker expression.

The proper relationship between union and company, according to the reformers, is as antagonists. Pressing the union to maintain a sense of independence and willingness to fight is their mission, which is hampered when worker stories begin too much to resemble those of the employer.

Finally, my conclusion assesses the situation of the dissident Machinist movement at Boeing today, drawing out and summarizing the dilemmas raised in interviews. There are a number of important and poignant lessons from this struggle for democratic reformers inside unions. These lessons speak to how reformers can push their official leadership while staying focused on the company, prioritize long-term organizing and contract cycle agitation above electoral bids and legal strategies, and recognize that unions—and dissident movements inside of unions—are only democratic and vital to the extent that they involve large numbers of their members and represent their demands. The final question that I raise is whether one can speak legitimately for the rank and file without their active involvement in the movement from a dissident position any more than one should do so from a business union position. The credentials and, more important, the power of a dissident union movement depend upon taking advantage of critical rank-and-file consciousness to build an organization that restores a balance of power between union leadership and the rank and file in the longer term. Only then can the rank and file become ready, when the time comes, to make their own history.

1

Business Unionism and Rank-and-File Unionism at the Turn of the Millennium

It was the folks down at Boeing who were the ones who had to pull it off. Not anything the AFL-CIO did. If we could get them to do something besides just give real good speeches, then we'd be getting somewhere. If they want to do something with that 35 million dollars, don't give it to the dad-gummed Democrats, so they can vote against us on bills, and give us NAFTA and give us GATT. Let's get some money out there to the line. Then let's actually do something. Let's get some actual mass picketing taking place down there. Let's stop the plant gates.

—Keith Thomas, Unionists for Democratic Change (Wichita, Kansas, 1998)

The history of labor in the United States since the latter half of the twentieth century has been, up until recently, a study in defeat. What will it take to beat back the ongoing employers' offensive? Alongside tax cuts for the rich, real wages have stagnated, and consumer debt (totaling $2.6 trillion) is at record proportions, requiring 19 percent of the average consumer's disposable income each month.[1] The economic crisis begun in late 2007 has sharpened the class divide, as the U.S. economy shed 2.6 million jobs in the last quarter of 2008 alone;[2] the official unemployment rate in the United States rose to about 10 percent by 2010.[3] According to a study by the Commonwealth Fund, of the approximately 45 million people in the United States without health insurance, more than a quarter are employed at large firms that are increasingly saddling their employees with the costs of health care.[4] Meanwhile, worker productivity has grown steadily into the economic crisis that began in 2007.[5] Workers have been working harder and harder, but for less and less in return.

Employers and politicians are quick to blame corporate overextension and layoffs on "costly" unionized workers, even though the relationship of union jobs to the economy is more complex. As Rutgers economist Paula Voos testified before the Senate Committee on Health, Education, Labor and Pensions in March 2009 on pending Employee Free Choice Act (EFCA) legislation,[6] the capacity of unions to raise the wages and benefits of employees also serves to reduce broader income inequality, thus stimulating the economy by increasing the purchasing power of ordinary people. Still, unions are weak, while the need for them is increasingly urgent.

As labor reporter Lee Sustar explains, the combined effects of tax cuts, a foundering economy, corporate ruthlessness, and the cutthroat environment of global trade agreements have contributed largely to the weakness of unions today. However, the failure of AFL-CIO unions to bring new workers into unions (despite some lip service to organizing) and to put resources into winning strikes and supporting workplace actions must also bear some blame.[7] Union leaders, rather than urge militancy, have formed partnerships with employers and politicians to avoid strikes. They have encouraged workers to accept concession after concession in contract negotiations. Perhaps part of the problem is that a great number of American workers do not regard their unions as having much to offer them anymore.

There was a time, however, when unions more faithfully afforded workers a great deal more control over their lives in the United States. In this chapter, I will describe two long waves of union development, the first beginning with the Knights of Labor and the struggle for the eight-hour workday in the 1880s and ending after the Great Depression and America's entry into World War II. This early period is marked by the rise of the Congress of Industrial Organizations (CIO) as a militant and democratic corrective to the exclusive craft unionism of the American Federation of Labor (AFL). The second long wave of union history has lasted from 1945 to the present and is marked by increasing bureaucratization and conservatism in the mainstream union movement. However, recent dissident struggles inside the mainstream unions have challenged entrenched leaders and demanded a return to a more activist role for unions.

It is not my purpose in this brief chapter to survey the entire history of the American labor movement.[8] Here I describe the two manifestations of labor: the stagnant, recalcitrant sludge of the traditional union bureaucracy and the energetic movement that has risen out of the muck over and over again to assert the power of ordinary workers. The historical narrative I present suggests that American labor needs a new progressive push akin to the formation of the CIO in the 1930s if we are to see ordinary workers make real gains against the current employers' offensive.

The chapter is organized as follows: First, I chronicle the two waves of the American union movement, telling the story of the rise of democratic unionism with the CIO and its subsequent decline in the postwar years. Then the chapter provides some examples from the 1990s and 2000s of instances in which conservative unions led workers to defeats, primarily because of the failure to prioritize rank-and-file action in favor of more administrative, legalistic, and consumer-oriented strategies. These examples include the defeat of paper workers at the Jay, Maine, paper plant in 1987, at Hormel in 1985–1986, and at A. E. Staley in 1994–1995. In contrast, the Boeing victory in 1995, the Teamsters' victory at UPS in 1997, and the United Auto Workers (UAW) victory against automakers in 1998 show that democratic unionism can once again demand and win real gains for workers. The chapter concludes with a discussion of the changing situation of labor today. My overall argument is that the story of the rise of the CIO provides an inspiring model of the birth of a fighting labor movement out of a period of fragmentation, exclusivity, and weakness in existing labor institutions. I mean to suggest that present conditions of economic crisis and the stirrings of a new militancy are ripe for a similar transformation.

From the Knights of Labor to the CIO

Although strikes are a fact of life whenever some people toil on behalf of others, the story of labor organizing and action in the United States begins in earnest after "wage slavery" replaced chattel slavery in the South and industrialization accelerated across the country. Spurred by industrialization and its attendant growing class polarization, workers on railroads and in factories began to recognize their collective interests and their collective power. Reeling from four years of economic depression, railroad workers across the nation struck in 1877 for higher wages in what has come to be known as the Great Upheaval. Although state and federal forces crushed these workers, their insurrection marks the beginning of large-scale industrial unrest in America. In 1886, railroad workers moved again. Led by the Knights of Labor (and the reluctant Terence Powderly), founded in 1869, the workers struck Jay Gould's Southwest system and brought Gould to the bargaining table. Sharon Smith argues that the Knights fell apart after this victory, however, "because the power of American capital placed unendurable stress on the fragile movement, and because of the creation of an AFL eager to take labor in a narrower direction."[9]

Nearly 500,000 U.S. workers struck in 1886 against nearly 10,000 employers in more than 1,400 separate actions. The strike wave culminated on May Day, 1886, in near-general strikes for the eight-hour workday in major cities across the United States. In Chicago during this struggle, the Haymarket bombing and subsequent unrest led to a wave of reaction against the movement. Even so, many thousands of workers won their demand for a shorter workday, and May 1 became an international workers' holiday.

From the defeated Pullman strike of 1894 to the strike wave of 1919 among miners, dockworkers, railway workers, ironworkers and steelworkers, and many others, workers built organizations and learned lessons of strategy that would take them into the next decades. Not all of those lessons were happy for the workers. As David Montgomery argues in his classic history *The Fall of the House of Labor,* the period between 1865 and 1925 witnessed the rise of class-consciousness and worker militancy out of diverse groups and situations.[10] Frederick Winslow Taylor's scientific management methods took hold concurrently with efforts of municipal, clerical, employer, and political organizations (including the Socialist Party) to institute labor peace through managerial science, union partnership with employers, wartime jingoism, state intervention, and corporate welfare-ism, all enabled by union officials increasingly operating as company mediators (and, notably, consistently opposed by the rank and file of the International Association of Machinists and Aerospace Workers). As a result, by the mid-1920s, labor organization as the home of working-class militancy had collapsed. The window was open for the formation of a more radical industrial unionism in the wake of the economic crash of 1929.

The Great Depression of the 1930s witnessed huge steps forward for labor. President Franklin Delano Roosevelt formed the National Recovery Administration, and section 7(a) of the National Recovery Act of 1933 granted workers the right to form and join unions. (Workers used this gain to argue that "your President wants you to join a union"; FDR would not have gone so far.) From 1934 until the entry of the United States into World War II, there were unprecedented strike waves among longshoremen, textile workers, autoworkers, truck drivers, and many others. Socialists, Communists, and anarchists were involved in organizing these strikes and pushing a resistant union leadership to more militant action. Farrell Dobbs and Philip Korth describe how Trotskyists were instrumental in the organizing of the successful Teamsters strike in Minneapolis in 1934. Korth quotes one worker as saying, "These people moved in gradually from the Socialist Workers Party to help, and I say without them there wouldn't have been no victory."[11] Korth summarizes the openness and commitment to widespread solidarity that made this strike successful: "In many ways Local 574 offers a model of how to organize a strike. Several tactics proved central to its success. Leaders recognized the importance of communications and of rank and file involvement. Frequent public meetings helped counter employers' propaganda and newspaper accounts. . . . The strike demonstrated the efficacy of organizing industrial unions, undermining conservative labor traditions that relied on craft organization alone."[12] Likewise, Steve Early notes that in the 1960s, radicals shifting from campus to labor activism were key to union strength in that decade.[13] As I will argue in subsequent chapters, democratic reformers in the labor movement today often call on their unions for the tasks noticed by Korth: open communication, rank and file involvement, open and regular meetings, consistent production of counter-employer propaganda, education of workers in labor relations and history, and mass organizing.

Among the victories of this time period, the sit-down strikes in the auto industry were among the most effective, since employers and their armies cannot fire on workers sitting on their valuable machinery. And because workers were sitting in the plants, replacement workers could not take over production. The sit-down strike against General Motors in Flint, Michigan, in 1936–1937 marked the emergence of the Congress of Industrial Organizations (CIO) as an alternative to the conservative AFL unions, many of which played a strikebreaking role in the sit-down strikes. The CIO, founded by John L. Lewis in 1935, aimed to organize the unorganized in basic industries rather than abiding by the conciliatory and largely craft-based unionism of the AFL.

Genora Dollinger, a key activist in the Flint sit-down strike, describes conditions before the strike in the unorganized plant: "The plants were notorious for their speed-up systems. They had men with stop watches timing the workers to see if they could squeeze one or two more operations in. . . . The men just couldn't take it. They would come home at night and they couldn't hold their forks in their swollen fingers. . . . Combined with the bad conditions on the outside: poor living conditions, lack of proper food, lack of proper medical attention and everything else, the auto workers came to the conclusion that there was no way they could ever escape any of this injustice without joining a union."[14] She describes the process of organizing and fighting in the union as profoundly transformative, opening the doors for women and black workers to be involved in the struggle. And it was the successful occupation of the plants that was the key to victory:

> When we got there we saw some big fights. Union men were throwing out the scabs and some of the foremen, and they said, "Hold that gate. Hold it, don't let the police come through here!" We strung ourselves across that gate, and it was only a matter of a telephone call before the police were sent down. They wanted to push us aside. We said, "Over our dead bodies." . . . The successful occupation of Plant 4, which joined the occupations at Fisher 1 and 2, broke the resistance of General Motors and negotiations began in Detroit. . . . On February 11 they signed a peace agreement recognizing the

UAW as representative for the autoworkers. And on March 12 the first labor contract was signed.[15]

The victory at Flint won recognition for the new United Auto Workers union alongside improvements in workers' wages, benefits, conditions of work, and hours and pace of work. It made the UAW the gold standard of the labor movement in the United States. By World War II, most large industrial companies recognized unions and their right to bargain collectively. As historian Sidney Fine writes:

> The GM strike was really more than a strike. It was not only the "most critical labor conflict" of the 1930's and perhaps in all of American history, but it was also a part, the most dramatic and important part of a vast labor upheaval that *Fortune* described as "one of the greatest mass movements in our history." The successful outcome of the strike helped to determine that the decision-making power in large segments of American industry where the voice of labor had been little more than a whisper, if that, would henceforth have to be shared in some measure with the unions.[16]

Historians of the CIO are agreed that the CIO's emergence and leadership from 1935 to 1955 was an impressive achievement for labor in the United States. Robert Zieger credits the CIO with focusing the huge waves of working-class activism that erupted in the 1930s, making labor an effective force in politics, creating permanent, industrial labor unions, and embracing the tasks of organizing black workers and women.

The CIO was founded by United Mine Workers leader John L. Lewis, who broke from the AFL in 1935 over the question of industrial unionization. In the 1930s and 1940s, the CIO and its unions, including the United Auto Workers (UAW) and United Steel Workers of America (USWA), led some of the largest, most militant, and most successful union battles in U.S. history. In contrast to the exclusive trade unionism of the AFL, which denied participation to black workers and women, the CIO was for inclusive democratic unionism. Where the AFL failed to organize workers into strong, industry-wide units that could repel strikebreaking attempts, the CIO was for industry-wide action to win industrial democracy.

Many scholars and activists think of the period following the Great Depression as one of unmitigated decline for the CIO and its unions. However, contrary to popular memory and despite attempts by President Roosevelt (aligned improbably with labor leaders and Stalinists) to command production for wartime, the war years were not a quiescent time for labor. In his history of the CIO, Art Preis notes:

When the war came to a close on August 14, 1945, the American workers had chalked up more strikes and strikers during the period from December 7, 1941 to the day of the Japanese surrender three years and eight months later, than in any similar period of time in American labor history. During the war period there had been a total of 14,471 strikes and 6,774,000 strikers. These were far more strikes and strikers than during the whole first four years of the CIO—1936–1939. These strikes were largely isolated and quelled with little gains, but the belief that the war achieved 'national unity' of capital and labor, or negated the class struggle, was proved false. The immediate postwar upsurge of labor resulted in the most powerful strike wave ever known; the class struggle in America rose to a new peak.[17]

And, according to Jeremy Brecher, "The first six months of 1946 marked what the U.S. Bureau of Labor Statistics called 'the most concentrated period of labor-management strife in the country's history.'"[18] The grievances and demands suppressed during the war years came to the fore as workers demanded their cut of the postwar economic pie. However, in the postwar period, a long period of economic expansion, increasing partnership between unions and management, and the purging of radicals from unions during the Cold War all made for a decline in union membership and strike activity in the decades to come.

Two prominent accounts of this history, those of Art Preis and Robert Zieger, differ substantially with regard to what happened in and to the CIO during and after World War II. Preis, who was a Socialist (though, importantly, not a member of the Stalinized Communist Party), observer, and participant in these events, argues that the CIO ambivalently pioneered both class struggle and class collaboration. His narrative of the history of the CIO is one of a decline from the militant heyday of 1930s sit-down strikes into the anti-Communist witch hunts, deal brokering with politicians and employers, and recourse to influence peddling as opposed to mass organizing in the 1940s and 1950s. Most significant for Preis was the uncritical support that the top leaders of the CIO provided to the Democratic Party. Even when Democrats betrayed labor—for example when Roosevelt sent the National Guard to crush strikes or enforced wage freezes and no-strike clauses during the war—the CIO leadership continually derailed the movement among rank-and-file workers for a separate labor party. During the war, the Stalinist Communist Party, which had important influence in the large CIO unions, sided with CIO leaders in demanding uninterrupted production for the war effort.

After the war, President Harry Truman continued Roosevelt's pattern of strike-breaking, proposing to draft strikers into military service and proposing antistrike legislation. In 1947, Truman signed the Taft-Hartley Act, which outlawed the closed shop, expanded the powers of the National Labor Relations Board to prosecute unauthorized strikers, mandated a sixty-day cooling-off period in labor disputes, empowered the president to intervene in labor disputes, and made secondary boycotts (sympathy strikes) illegal. In addition, the Act prohibited strikes by government employees, surrounded dues checkoff rights with red tape, and required an oath of non-Communism from union members.

The Truman Doctrine, which in 1947 announced U.S. commitment to defeat anticapitalist movements around the world, fueled the anti-Communism inside the labor movement during this time. Between 1947 and 1950, under the leadership of Philip Murray and Walter Reuther, the CIO raided Communist-leaning locals and purged eleven unions from the CIO. The 1949 CIO convention passed a resolution to ban Communists from holding CIO office. One CIO officer at that convention is quoted by Preis as saying, "Dump the aliens and kick out the reds!"[19] Reuther's granddaughter Sasha Reuther commented in June 2010 that the seventy-fifth anniversary of the UAW offered an opportunity to "take a hard look at the past and decide which parts to embrace and which to reject. . . . To start with, the union needs to become more democratic."[20]

With the McCarthyist purge of radicals from the movement, the way was paved for a quieter, less militant labor movement that over the next decades would put its resources into building the Democratic Party rather than mass organizing for workplace struggles. Against a great deal of rank-and-file opposition, the CIO backed the war in Korea and conceded to wage freezes and no-strike clauses. In 1955, the AFL and the CIO merged into one monumental organization on the basis of shared commitment to industrial unionism.

Even though Preis is critical of Lewis, the Stalinists, and subsequent leaders of the CIO who struck deals with employers and discouraged strikes, he celebrates the CIO as "labor's giant step." He writes, "Young workers must be armed with the lessons and traditions of the CIO as a powerful weapon for the further advance of the American labor movement."[21] Among those lessons, Preis stresses the importance of mass pickets that actually stopped replacements from entering the workplace, the efficacy of the sit-down strikes, the importance of mass strikes that can paralyze entire industries, and the key role of solidarity across industries in winning strikes. His emphasis is on maintaining rank-and-file militancy as a check against leaders' tendencies toward conservatism and passivity.

Zieger draws different lessons from this story. He argues that the CIO's transformation from the 1930s into the Cold War was not a decline, but rather a maturation.[22] He defends the purging of Communists and other radicals from the unions, emphasizing the productive and friendly relations that obtained thereby between the CIO and the U.S. government. On the one hand, Zieger recognizes that "the overall record of Communist-influenced unions with respect to collective bargaining, contract content and administration, internal democracy, and honest governance was good" and that the Communist-led unions were better than most with regard to racial and gender integration.[23] On the other hand, he denounces the Communists as doctrinaire, calling the purge "necessary," lamenting only that the CIO in the postwar years failed to increase racial integration in unions or stress mass organizing.[24] An additional consequence of the denunciation of Communists was the purging of any radicals, condemned by association, who advocated militancy and racial justice.

Ironically, it had been, in large part, the Communist and other leftist influences in the first place that had made racial justice, mass organization, and rank-and-file action the centerpieces of the industrial struggle. It is true that the Communist Party members in the CIO shifted with every directive of the Comintern and therefore made a number of traitorous mistakes.[25] However, Zieger appreciates the Communists most when they betrayed their anticapitalist and anti-imperialist principles in support for the war against fascism and denigrates them when they regrouped as a principled leftist voice inside the unions.[26] Among other things, the Communists after World War II opposed labor's conscription to constant production for the war in Korea and steadfastly argued for the formation of an independent labor party.

Zieger acknowledges the CIO's retreat from an emphasis on rank-and-file organizing and striking, noting, "Pursuit of basic collective bargaining goals primarily through channels of governmental bureaucracy leeched power from labor's grass roots and often made rank and file workers spectators in their own drama."[27] Yet he defends the ouster of elements in the movement who were pressing for less bureaucracy and more grassroots involvement. Contrary to all of the evidence presented by Preis, Zieger asserts (without backing), "I do not believe that there was a leftward-tending working-class militancy in the 1930s that the CIO bureaucracy defanged or diverted. . . . Furthermore, I find little evidence that industrial workers had much stomach for the kinds of root-and-branch confrontation with the American state that a more radical program would have required."[28] Here, Zieger seems to forget all of the confrontations with the forces of the state—workers confronting police, militias, the National Guard—that were the condition for the formation of the CIO in the first place.

He goes on, "I believe that the pro-union activities of the federal government in the 1930s and during World War II were absolutely crucial for the achievement of permanent industrial unions and that union behaviors that accommodated themselves to this circumstance were in general appropriate and necessary. Moreover, working within the Democratic Party was an obvious necessity to all but a handful of doctrinaire activists."[29] I am not sure how Zieger can credibly reduce the Communists to a "handful of doctrinaire activists" after acknowledging their profound influence on the CIO in earlier chapters. More important, he seems to forget that the New Deal and war years were marked by more antiunion legislation and union busting on the part of the federal government than prounion activities, with the strong exception of Section 7(a) of the National Recovery Act, which legalized workers' organizations.

I recite this debate at some length because its lessons are crucial to labor activists today. Clearly, what the CIO became had a profound influence on the labor movement as it stretched across the second half of the twentieth century. The CIO began as an expression of radicalism and resistance to labor conservatism. Yet the leadership of today's unions is, generally speaking, uncritically wedded to the mainstream electoral process and the Democratic Party, mired in bureaucracy that stifles rank-and-file voice, hampered by lingering anti-Communism that ostracizes radicals who otherwise would be strong activists in the movement, reluctant to prioritize mass organizing and loath to challenge the provisions of Taft-Hartley that have hamstrung labor. Racism has also had a devastating divisive impact on the labor movement, especially in the South. (Even so, the New Orleans general strike of 1892 and the struggles of Alabama miners and sharecroppers in the early part of the twentieth century demonstrate the capacity of rank-and-file workers to fight racism in a united struggle.)[30] The result has been the slow erosion of workers' influence in society, standard of living, conditions of work, and job security.

Instead of welcoming the bureaucratic, top-down version of the AFL-CIO that emerged from the 1950s, we should take to heart the lessons of the CIO in the years of its formation, years in which masses of striking workers confronted the law with their economic power and won both the right to organize and a better life for themselves and their families. Zieger concludes his book by noting that we need another Walter Reuther, anti-Communist bureaucrat of the 1950s CIO. In my view, we could do without another Reuther (labeled by historian Nelson Lichtenstein "the most dangerous man in Detroit").[31] What we need is another militant push like the one that gave birth to the CIO. The union democracy movement is where that push must come from if labor is to revive from its doldrums.

Postwar Business Unionism and the Employers' Offensive

From the Cold War to the present, the trend in American labor has been toward ever greater concessions in contracts, ever greater bureaucratization of the unions, and ever greater reliance on politicians, especially Democrats, who with ever greater boldness betray every promise they have made to U.S. workers after union money helped them get elected. Brecher notes that since the merger of the AFL and the CIO in 1955, the proportion of workers in unions has gradually declined. "Most employers accepted unions as part of the system, while unions made few attempts to challenge the status quo."[32]

Labor scholars Michael Schiavone and Paul Buhle have called attention to the problem of undemocratic and probusiness union organization since the merger of the AFL and the CIO in 1955.[33] According to Buhle, the roots of this conservatism lay not only in the tendency of union leaders to secure and protect their own bureaucratic privileges, but also in the acceptance of union leaders of the tenets of "American exceptionalism," the idea that American unions should avoid class struggle and support the postwar, defense-industry-driven social contract that, for a time, produced secure jobs and a high standard of living for a large proportion of American industrial workers.[34] However, in the 1970s and 1980s, that contract fell apart, exposing the limits of worker-employer partnership and cronyism. Offering one case study on this point, Steve Early profiles the Service Employees International Union's (SEIU's) international executive board, the majority of whose members are "completely beholden to the union's top officers. As such, they can't easily question leadership decisions or prevent costly organizational mistakes."[35] The result was a culture of political conformity and fear of retaliation.

The composition of the leadership of the largest unions in the United States is a recipe for disaster in the context of neoliberalism. The last few decades have witnessed a relentless employer's offensive characterized by declining standards of living, mass layoffs, and union busting. The ravages of neoliberal priorities—cutting social spending, privatizing public sector work, intensifying global competition, pressuring workers in regimes of lean production, and busting unions—were most potently signified by President Ronald Reagan's busting of the air traffic controllers' union in 1981. Corporate globalization has further undermined the legitimacy of unions and enabled employers to rationalize exploitation and threaten workers into making damaging concessions. Under this pressure, the labor movement has suffered a series of failures of imagination, of, in Nelson Lichtenstein's words, a "deficit of ideas necessary to insert working America into the heart of our national consciousness."[36]

However, there are some notable exceptions to this pattern, most occurring alongside the radical movements of the 1960s and early 1970s. One notable case in point is the organizing of the United Farm Workers (UFW), whose organizing drives among the most-difficult-to-organize migrant workers and community-building efforts are inspiring.[37] Brecher notes that workers' action at this time became increasingly independent from official uniondom, including wildcat strikes and the organization of rank-and-file dissident caucuses. For example, in 1970 postal workers went on a national wildcat strike, risking jail and fines to demand higher wages. Although President Richard Nixon sent armed forces personnel to replace the strikers in sorting and delivering mail,[38] the strike ended in a huge victory for the workers. Likewise, a 1970 Teamsters wildcat brought wage increases for the drivers. Steve Early documents other challenges brought by rank-and-file unionists to leadership complicity with employers in what he calls "the civil wars in U.S. Labor."[39]

One of the most inspiring struggles of the late 1960s and early 1970s was that of the Detroit Revolutionary Union Movement (DRUM), which lasted from 1967 to 1974. In the only book-length history of this movement, Dan Georgakas and Marvin Surkin describe how militant black autoworkers formed the League of Revolutionary Black Workers at Chrysler in the wake of the urban rebellion in Detroit in 1967.[40] Georgakas and Surkin note that in the postwar years, the UAW had made a number of deals with Chrysler, allowing greater managerial control of the pace of work on the shop floor.[41] "The union acquiesced to company demands and was rewarded by support in dealing with its own internal problems."[42] They add, "Such cooperation found further expression in three- and five-year contracts with which the mutual interests of company and union were insulated from annual crisis. . . . There would be no work stoppages of any kind. Any unauthorized (wildcat) strike could be punished by the courts as a breach of contract, pitting the offending workers against the union as well as the company."[43]

The auto industry had begun to hire black workers in growing numbers in the 1960s, but "all the better jobs were dominated by whites," and black workers were barely represented among foremen, superintendents, and skilled tradesmen.[44] "Organizations like DRUM emphasized how the company deliberately cultivated institutionalized racism in order that white workers and black workers would face their workaday lives in racial conflict with one another rather than in class solidarity."[45]

In response to these conditions—intensifying exploitation, institutional racism, and UAW detachment from its mass base—black workers like John Watson and James Johnson organized DRUM, not as a caucus inside the union but as a separate organization for black workers. In 1968, black and white workers held a wildcat strike, which resulted in harsh management crackdown, especially on black workers. DRUM held pickets, boycotts, and protests, culminating in a strike of 3,000 black workers at Dodge Main later in 1968. Although the strike, which won sympathy from other workers, effectively halted production for a brief time, it was also directed to the officers of the UAW local. Specifically, DRUM presented the UAW with demands for greater representation in the union structure.

DRUM also published leaflets and a newspaper, combined labor action with antiracist action in the city and on the campus of Wayne State University, and made a film about their struggle called *Finally Got the News*.[46] Combining the cultural strategies of the New Left with traditional class-oriented workplace action, DRUM challenged the Detroit labor movement. Even though the group's racial separatism in organizing eventually hampered their effectiveness, its understanding of the need for work stoppages and of the significance of race in the regime of American corporate exploitation provides a model for democratic unionists today.

Despite such high points, the emblematic moment of the period from 1955 through the 1980s in American labor was the tragic PATCO strike in 1981. The long boom of the postwar years ended in 1973, when the United States entered deep recession. Amid the intensification of international competition and falling profits, American corporate executives began a decades-long offensive against workers. Although many antilabor offensives occurred during the Jimmy Carter administration, under President Ronald Reagan these measures grew sharper teeth. Reagan cut social services and gutted agencies that protected workers' rights, such as the Occupational Safety and Health Administration.

In 1981, the air traffic controllers' union, PATCO, went on strike. The already weakened union movement was struck a killing blow when Reagan permanently fired all of the striking workers and replaced them with permanent new workers—an action not taken since the Great Depression. The result was a drastic shift in the balance of power between unions and corporations, workers and management. During the 1980s, the number of strikes fell as management demanded more and more concessions. A series of disastrous strikes at Greyhound, Eastern Airlines, and other workplaces created a deepening sense of pessimism about the effectiveness of conventional strikes. According to Brecher, the proportion of workers in unions fell from 27 percent in 1978 to 15 percent in 1996.[47]

Brecher notes that suburbanization, racial division, U.S. economic decline on the world stage, and government and corporate attacks on workers' bargaining power were all partially to blame for the long-term decline of the labor movement. Certainly, the ratcheting up of exploitation under the regime of neoliberalism pressured labor leaders to become more cautious. Furthermore, the dependence of labor on the Democratic Party—despite repeated betrayals, intervention in labor disputes on behalf of corporate power, failures to introduce or advocate for legislation benefiting workers, and so on—has seriously undermined labor's power since World War II.[48] However, as Brecher writes, "The long term decline of organized labor was also due in substantial part to internal characteristics of the labor movement itself. . . . Top down control created a gulf between most union leaders and the rank and file."[49] This top-down control has its roots in the postwar labor movement's conservatism, led by leaders who, in Paul Buhle's words, were "taking care of business."

The AFL of Samuel Gompers and the AFL-CIO administrations of George Meany and Lane Kirkland firmly established what has come to be known as business unionism, defined as "running unions like a business or corporation, with dues payments as the bottom line and assorted perks normal to executives of the business world."[50] Founded on the postwar boom-time social contract between employers and unions, business unionism is also characterized by fervent anti-Communism, passivity and concessions in the face of employers' demands, and the suspicion of radicals inside the union movement. Unlike European labor movements, American business unionism refuses egalitarian and inclusive progressive agendas in favor of "American exceptionalism"; instead of seeing the world divided by class internationally, business unionism operates in a framework of nationalist support for U.S. economic and geopolitical hegemony around the world. Buhle calls union leaders' lip service to workers' power and union democracy "pseudo-egalitarian rhetoric" that contradicts consistent anti-Socialist and antidemocracy measures inside the AFL-CIO.[51]

For example, even though Samuel Gompers, the founding president of the AFL in 1886, began his adult political life as a socialist, as head of the American labor movement he privileged white, male, skilled workers to the exclusion of blacks, foreigners, and women. He blamed immigrants for loss of American (white, male) jobs. He threw his support behind the United States in World War I and invited government repression of radicals in the movement. In the 1920s, he attacked the left-leaning Trade Union Education League and played a role in stopping the movement for an independent labor party. Gompers faced challenges first from the Industrial Workers of the World and later from John Lewis and the CIO, but the legacy of business unionism was in place when Meany took the helm in 1952. Buhle writes, "Inflated salaries, large expense accounts, nepotism, and ostentation indicated and reinforced, from Gompers' time to the Meany era and beyond, the wall that divides union officialdom from the rank and file. A bureaucratic, self-perpetuating ruling group within trade unionism, with its own ideological pretensions, interests, and rewards, had expanded rapidly and fattened measurably. Below, members grew steadily more alienated not only from the 'efficient' and 'automated' corporate workplace but also from what was theoretically 'their' union."[52] Prejudiced against unskilled workers, people of color, and women, Meany felt a tremendous animosity toward the CIO. He abhorred strikes and pledged during wartime his support for business and government. After the AFL-CIO merger in 1955, he led the charge against Communists in the movement with resolutions forbidding former Communists from holding union office and upholding the anti-Communist provisions of the Landrum-Griffin Act even after it was found unconstitutional by the Supreme Court in 1965.[53] He collaborated with the CIA in the overthrow of the elected Jacobo Árbenz government in Guatemala in favor of the dictator Col. Carlos Castillo Armas, who murdered thousands of workers and peasants. In addition to participating in covert undermining of Communist regimes in Latin America, Meany's administration often looked the other way at mafia and other union entanglements. When the Landrum-Griffin Act became federal law in 1959, Meany approved of all the legislation's antiunion provisions but rejected the union members' Bill of Rights provision, which was the one part of the act with democratic potential for the rank and file. No champion of civil rights, Meany refused to integrate AFL-CIO conventions. Likewise, his administration fought tooth and nail against the student movements, peace movements, and women's movements of the 1960s and early 1970s. Meany supported Nixon and then Carter, whom Buhle describes as "offering symbols rather than substance" to labor amid increasing arms spending.[54]

Lane Kirkland took over the AFL-CIO in 1979, having been an indispensable assistant to Meany. He excelled at Washington politics, and like Meany he was a foreign policy hawk whose international programs emphasized a critique of labor repression in Communist regimes even as the United States financed, trained, and installed many worse regimes guilty of horrible violations of labor and human rights. The AFL-CIO did support the Solidarity movement in Poland, but only alongside support for repressive dictatorships in Latin America and Africa. Kirkland and his cronies attempted to displace Nelson Mandela in favor of Mangosuthu Buthelezi in the ANC because of Mandela's embrace of the South African Communist Party. Buhle describes Kirkland's reign as "globalism, combined with a pallid and increasingly nominal domestic liberalism."[55] As the AFL-CIO sank in influence and membership into the 1980s, Kirkland suppressed all dissidents. After the collapse of Stalinism in 1990, the AFL-CIO–funded Free Trade Institute set out to undermine indigenous Russian and Eastern bloc unions in favor of new organizations that would accept the new privatization of Eastern European markets.

Rank-and-File Movements
"Scare the Hell Out of" Their Leaders

As noted previously, the regime of global capitalism and its attendant pressures on the labor force emerged snarling from the 1970s. Four decades of concessions and austerity, of speedup and overtime, of outsourcing and subcontracting, of cuts in benefits and pay generated both motivation to fight again and fear of defeat in the 1990s and 2000s. Many workers feel they have little to lose in struggling, since they are losing by not struggling in the first place. The late 1980s and early to mid-1990s witnessed a series of heroic fight-backs that might have won if not for the pessimism, passivity, and inaction of the unions' official leadership.

In Austin, Minnesota, in 1985, meatpackers and members of United Food and Commercial Workers (UFCW) Local P-9 struck Hormel in the wake of layoffs and wage cuts. The strike, which was initially sanctioned by the UFCW nationally, increasingly met with resistance from union officials. The UFCW failed to support the strike financially. In 1986, the president of the UFCW ordered P-9 workers to take concessions and return to work, even with the national outpouring of support for the local. Peter Rachleff names Minnesota Governor Rudy Perpich (a Democrat), the National Guard, schools and bankers who supported Hormel, and private union-busting firms among the enemies of the P-9 strike. However, he adds that "The United Food and Commercial Workers Union leadership and the entire superstructure of the AFL-CIO were instrumental in crushing P-9. In the end, their role was probably the crucial one. Had they stood with P-9, as the United Mine Workers and its labor leadership did with the Pittston miners later in the 1980s, it is entirely possible that the combined forces of Hormel and the state might have been turned aside. This was not to be."[56] Further, Rachleff explains that the P-9 militancy threatened the entrenched bureaucrats of the International, who had been acquiescing to corporate demands for concessions for more than a decade. Rachleff writes, "P-9 quickly came to symbolize democracy and membership participation, a willingness to oppose corporate demands for concessions, regardless of international union agendas or strategies, and a form of 'horizontal' solidarity that threatened the vertical, bureaucratic hold that international unions exercised over their locals."[57]

Similarly, Julius Getman describes the ways in which union officials were complicit in the defeat of a 1987 strike of 1,200 militant, democratic paper workers against International Paper in Jay, Maine.[58] In this struggle, national union officials undercut the decisions of the local by refusing to build solidarity among other paper workers at other plants or to build a multiple-plant bargaining unit, failing to cover the strike in the union newsletter, failing to support the strikers' boycott of International Paper, rejecting the local's employment of the Corporate Campaign, and failing to support a dues supplement for the strike fund. Local leaders were prohibited from speaking at the national union convention to get support. Finally, national union leaders called off the strike and decertified the local. The workers were left worse off than when they began, despite their best efforts and heroic sacrifice.

Union officials behaved similarly through the first half of the 1990s. For example, at Staley Manufacturing in Decatur, Illinois, locked-out members of the United Paperworkers International Union (UPIU) sought AFL-CIO and UPIU support for their struggle. Dan Lane, a leader in the rank and file of the Staley struggle, traveled during a prolonged hunger strike on his part in 1995 to the AFL-CIO executive council meeting. Activists Steven Ashby and C. J. Hawking's moving oral history describes how, despite a surge in militancy and involvement among members, a successful work-to-rule[59] campaign, and inspiring acts of civil disobedience, the Staley struggle foundered on conservatism in local factions and national leadership. The AFL-CIO refused to back the local and scoffed at activist Dan Lane's hunger strike of more than two months.[60] Ashby and Hawking write: "Instead of welcoming the Staley fight as a model for the labor movement, [AFL-CIO President Lane] Kirkland viewed local 7837 as a threat to their passive, accommodationist strategy and top-down leadership. Only a handful of national labor leaders saw the fight as a crucial moment in labor history. The Staley fight, declared Communication Workers of America vice president Jan Pierce, was a "rank and file fight that really did have the potential of revitalizing the union movement. Which just *scared the hell* out of national union leaders."[61]

In the end, the UPIU forced a vote on a contract thirty months after the beginning of the lockout. The contract was no improvement over the offers the workers had been rejecting, including unlimited subcontracting by the company, twelve-hour rotating shifts, mandatory overtime, no amnesty for workers fired for union activity, and a loss of two-thirds of the plant's jobs. In the end, only one-fourth of the locked-out workers got their jobs back. The Staley defeat is perhaps the most poignant of the "War Zone" (Decatur struggles including Caterpillar and Bridgestone-Firestone) defeats of 1994 and 1995. Workers who had proudly declared themselves warriors against Staley at the beginning of the strike ended up victims of the company and of their international union.[62]

A few words are in order here about the Corporate Campaign strategy, which I believe exacerbated the ineffectiveness of many of these struggles. In moments of desperation, workers facing losing strikes or lockouts have turned to the strategy of targeting an employer's subsidiaries, financial backers, and customers in order to put moral pressure on these secondary targets to stop supporting the employer in question. I believe that the Corporate Campaign is, especially in the absence of production-oriented action, costly and, when used as the only line of attack, ineffective.[63] Most often led by Ray Rogers, who founded Corporate Campaign, Inc., the Corporate Campaign costs striking or locked-out workers hundreds of thousands of dollars. For example, in the Jay, Maine, struggle, workers paid Rogers $800,000 for an ultimately losing strategy.

The reason the Corporate Campaign can be a weak strategy is that it diverts the focus of struggle away from where workers have real power. It other words, it assigns *too much weight* to the role of moral suasion in the process of labor struggle. Historically, the most effective tactics are designed to stop production and cost the employer directly through real pickets aimed at keeping replacement workers from entering facilities.[64] I am skeptical that large firms such as Miller Brewing, Pepsico, and the other companies targeted by the Staley workers (again, in a losing, expensive strategy) can be moralized into supporting workers' rights. These firms also exploit laborers in the attempt to extract as much work as possible from them at the lowest possible cost. Why would they feel shamed into cutting off business ties with a firm like Staley or International Paper? Labor scholar Jane Slaughter concurs with this analysis, adding that the Corporate Campaign can be unnecessarily complex and abstract, asking workers and the public to identify and pressure targets remote from the workplace and employer.

Getman responds to these charges, arguing that while ineffective when used by itself, in conjunction with pickets and demonstrations, the Corporate Campaign can help publicize and win sympathy for a struggle, raising public awareness and creating a kind of indirect pressure on the employer.[65] In the Jay, Maine, struggle, he contends, the Corporate Campaign, called for and funded by the rank and file without the support of union leaders, was transformative of workers' consciousness, giving them a sense of their creative agency. He also notes that the Corporate Campaign often brings in more money than it costs. In any case, the 1990s were off to a demoralizing start for ordinary workers.

The Struggle for Democratic Unionism in the 1990s

However, alongside the War Zone defeats of the mid-1990s there arose a countervailing trend. The election of reformer John Sweeney as president of the AFL-CIO in 1995 marked an opening in the fortress of business unionism. Sweeney had been head of the Service Employees International Union (SEIU), which had grown in membership and had encouraged new practices in organizing janitors, health care workers, and office workers. Sweeney's New Voices coalition put "the most inept leadership in labor history" out of business, indicating the possibility of movement renewal on more progressive grounds.[66] However, Buhle concludes that despite this opening, in the Sweeney era "the distance between the bureaucracy and ordinary union members has not been meaningfully lessened, nor has the historic dependence upon the Democrats been reconsidered."[67] Even so, there were other signs that labor may be on the verge of rediscovering its progressive and powerful past.

Teamsters for a Democratic Union (TDU) had played a determining role in propelling Sweeney's slate to power in the union. With the support of the TDU in 1997, reformer Ron Carey (who himself had risen from the rank and file) would lead the Teamsters in the most momentous strike of the 1990s, the strike of drivers against UPS for full-time jobs. From July 30 until August 18, 1997, 200,000 UPS drivers in the United States were on strike. There was remarkable solidarity on the picket lines, with less than 5 percent of the workforce crossing the line. UPS lost an estimated $30 million a day in profits. In the end, UPS agreed to create 10,000 full-time jobs and to limit their use of subcontracted labor. Both part- and full-time drivers won a significant pay increase. The allegations of and investigation into fundraising misconduct and improper use of union funds by Carey unfortunately tarnished the credibility of the reformers, and the strike's gains have eroded over the last decade. The victory at UPS signaled the beginnings of a return to the militant unionism and solidarity that characterized the 1930s sit-down strikes. Although the old guard of the Jimmy Hoffa era now runs the Teamsters and UPS never fulfilled its promise to create all of the full-time jobs that the 1997 contract obligates them to, the UPS strike and the public's support for the workers offer some hope and confidence that labor can still fight and win.[68]

In more recent years, a number of labor actions—from the 2005 strike at Boeing, the Transit Workers' strike in New York in 2005, the mass protests for immigrant workers' rights in 2006, the screenwriters' strike in 2007–2008, the strike at Boeing in 2008, to the sit-in at Republic Windows and Doors in 2009—indicate a new militancy and budding confidence on the part of rank-and-file workers (if not their unions). Lee Sustar recognized sparks of a new militancy at the end of a "grim" year in 2009, as strikes by Philadelphia transit workers and University of Illinois graduate workers, a UAW upset at Ford, and election victories by reformers indicated the possibility of an upturn.[69]

We cannot know the future, of course. However, we can learn something from the past. In this chapter, I have narrated a particular history of the U.S. labor movement, one that calls attention to the rise of the CIO as the defining moment of workers' power. Postwar business unionism and the Cold War interrupted the potentially revolutionary trajectory of events so that today rank-and-file forces must mobilize from below to push staid and even corrupt bureaucracies into action. In the context of economic crisis and rising class-consciousness, the period to come may rewrite that history with a new ending. Events at Boeing can help us better understand the current obstacles to—and the emerging possibilities of—to the project of union democratization.

2

Not a Smooth Flight for
Boeing and the Union

Robert J. Serling's history of the Boeing Company describes Boeing as "a corporate Horatio Alger," growing from a tiny manufacturing company into one of the nation's largest industrial firms.[1] Serling's narrative emphasizes the engineering innovations and the personalities of the corporate leaders and engineers at Boeing, omitting stories of the tens of thousands of workers who actually built the planes. In reality, the story of Boeing is not that of a smooth flight, but of a turbulent history marked by the pressure of competition with Airbus and other firms and the presence of fighting unions: the Society of Professional Engineering Employees in Aerospace and the International Association of Machinists and Aerospace Workers (IAMAW).

Between them, these unions organized in 1995 more than 50,000 workers at Boeing plants in Seattle, Washington, and Wichita, Kansas, and have held combined national memberships in the millions. In the workers' story, turbulence between workers and management at Boeing has involved both necessity and risk. In response to layoffs, outsourcing of work, and cuts in benefits, these unions have been an antagonist to Boeing's attempts put profits above people, reminding the corporate leadership that the workers are among the people—and, in fact, are the key people—who make Boeing an industrial giant.

Even though the unions have a fighting history, this chapter will show that union officials often performed in concert with corporate imperatives. For example, in 1977, Al Schultz, the IAMAW negotiator, took management's side during the forty-day strike of the Machinists and vowed that there would be no controversy. Union members proved him wrong. Serling relates one story about a union member refusing to shake hands with IAMAW President William Winpisinger, saying, "You're not president of my union."[2] Even Serling, in his glowing account of Boeing's history, noted that Schultz was "a great one for maintaining the union party line," which was conservative. Despite a reputation for being a progressive unionist,[3] Winpisinger even went so far as to praise company outsourcing of 757 and 767 programs to Japan: "If I was in Boeing's shoes, I wouldn't do it any other way."[4]

In response to the conservatism that has contributed to the decline of workers' standard of living, workers in the IAMAW at Boeing have rebelled at key moments in the union's history. Since then, dissident factions inside the union (also known as caucuses) have created more turbulence for both the company and the unions, and while turbulence is not healthy for an airplane in flight, it is a necessary component of democracy and progress.

Boeing's corporate history is marked by an increasing and predictable prioritizing of shareholder profit over product quality and workers' well-being. In any huge industrial corporation, of course, profits are the central concern; however, through the 1970s, the company led workers through an ideology of familial care, which was displaced steadily through the 1980s and 1990s with a strategy of lean production requiring an ideology of competitiveness and sacrifice. Substantiating this narrative, this chapter provides a brief chronicle of the company's history, overlaid with a history of the unions' fight to preserve jobs, wages, and benefits.

The Company: From "Family" to Giant

The Boeing Aircraft and Aerospace Company got its start in the 1910s, when Bill Boeing built his first plane, incorporated his company as the Pacific Aero Products Company, and won a series of Navy contracts during World War I. Changing the company's name to The Boeing Company, Bill Boeing and his engineers built their first plant in Seattle, where they designed and produced the historic seaplanes the Bluebill and the Mallard. Following World War I, the company was forced to diversify into building furniture, but in the 1920s, a new fighter plane and the Model 40A (which was used to fly mail) were successes that laid the ground for future development of passenger planes. The Boeing 247 was the fastest multiengine transport plane, and TWA and American Airlines purchased forty-seven of them.[5]

Boeing's progress unfolded in tandem with competition from rival aircraft manufacturer McDonnell Douglas, which manufactured the DC-1 and DC-2 during this period, and later from Airbus. During the Great Depression, Boeing suffered a number of hits, including the Air Mail Act, which forbade aircraft manufacturers from owning airlines (Boeing had owned United), and the economic crisis that resulted in layoffs of more than a thousand workers (out of 1,700). Even so, in 1936, Boeing built its second plant. The unionization drives of the 1930s did not fly over Boeing, which recognized its first union, Local 751 of the International Association of Machinists, in 1936.

The union struck for the first time in 1948, damaging the company's program to produce a luxurious passenger plane known as the Stratocruiser. This work stoppage was a wildcat strike unauthorized by the union; it was further complicated by a Teamster raid welcomed by company President Bill Allen.[6] The unionists successfully resisted the raid but were weakened by pressures to deliver planes. At around the same time, engineers formed a separate bargaining unit from the factory floor workers; this organization would eventually become the Society of Professional Engineering Employees in Aerospace (SPEEA). The IAMAW would strike again in 1965 over the company's seniority system, which management had replaced with promotions based on supervisors' reports rather than on number of years in the plant. In the nineteen-day 1965 strike, the workers won back the seniority system.

World War II's need for military aircraft was a boon for Boeing, which had been developing not only larger passenger aircraft but also the B-17 and B-29 bombers. These planes dropped 46 percent of all bombs and shot down 67 percent of enemy fighters during the war.[7] Another large-scale social phenomenon affected production at this time: The absence of men gone to war from the production line meant that hundreds of women, more than half of the Boeing workforce, now produced the planes. After the war, the development of the B-52 bomber resulted in a plane that was in military service through the 1991 Persian Gulf War. In the 1950s, Boeing increased its involvement in the manufacture of military aircraft and missiles, including the Minuteman missile, instrumental in the arms race during the Cold War.

On the passenger side, the 1950s saw the development of the 707, contracted by Pan-Am. The 707 introduced passengers to the jet age; President Harry Truman's Air Force One was a 707, and larger and faster aircraft such as the Boeing 720 were in development. Meanwhile, the Boeing Company expanded its operations, purchasing Vertol Aircraft in Philadelphia, the eventual maker of the Osprey. During the Vietnam War, this plant produced the Chinook and Comanche helicopters. The Philadelphia plant was organized by the United Auto Workers (UAW) and was notorious for conflicted labor relations. Like the early strikes at the Boeing plants, the UAW strike at Vertol in 1974–1975 also defended the seniority system in hiring, firing, and promotion.

Importantly, management at the plant implemented the company's first quality management program (well before the 1990s proliferation of Total Quality Management, workplace team programs, lean manufacturing, and so on): the Pride in Excellence Campaign. Explicitly, this program was designed to reduce union militancy by giving workers a voice in production and by imposing an ideology of quality over workers' rights, which became a matter of individual merit rather than class interest. This strategy of implementing programs that give workers voice and control without any material gains has been key to winning concessions from the union until the present day. These programs also train workers to work more efficiently and to combine jobs—thus spelling future layoffs.[8]

If the 1950s were years of passenger jet development in the consumer age, the 1960s witnessed Boeing's increasing role in the space program. Alongside the ongoing development of the 747 jumbo jet and a supersonic transport, the company made lunar orbiters, submarines, and the Saturn V rocket that launched the Apollo spacecrafts. The tragic 1967 Apollo launch pad fire resulted in layoffs. But 3,000 737 jets were delivered to passenger airlines by 1991, competing successfully with McDonnell Douglas's DC-9. The first flight of the 747, produced in the Everett plant built for the purpose of crafting the huge jets, was in 1969, but thirty of them sat on the tarmac without engines through 1970. Boeing 707s were still being used by the Air Force, along with air-launched cruise missiles, constructed at a new plant in Kent, Washington.

Throughout this period, Boeing was rocked by economic crisis and labor conflicts. A corporate crisis in 1969–1970, during which orders dried up, resulted in the reduction of the workforce from 101,000 to 38,000. In Seattle, the unemployment rate hit 17 percent as Boeing integrated its production facilities in Washington. Despite a bounce back to profitability (based on 727 sales) later in the decade, wages and benefits for workers remained stagnant. In 1974, Boeing stock was selling at $12 per share, and it split six times over sixteen years, resulting in stockholder equity soaring from $995 million to $8 billion between 1974 and 1999.[9]

This period also marked a shift in corporate thinking, not only at Boeing, but also across the aerospace industry around the world. Labor and media scholar Deepa Kumar explains that the internationalization of capitalism during this time period was tied together with new management offensives. The shift from earlier industrial models of production to neoliberal ones included the adoption of new productivity techniques to mitigate economic instability. The restructuring of the production process resulted in models of "lean," "just-in-time" production. In turn, workers faced the exhortation to team up with management to make the production process more efficient in programs like Total Quality Management and the High Performance Work Organization. These programs accompanied pressure for concessions in bargaining, speedup of production, and increasing job insecurity.[10]

A team of researchers from Yale, headed by Edward Greenberg, conducted a study of the transformation in organizational culture from the 1990s into the 2000s, documenting the effects of organizational change on employees.[11] "Boeing leaders Carl Shrontz, Phil Condit, Ron Woodard, Alan Mulally, and eventually Harry Stonecipher changed Boeing root and branch from the mid-1990s through the mid-2000s."[12] Greenberg's project, like my own, captures one segment of workers' experience at the corporate giant during a time of massive structural and cultural change in a rapidly shifting economic context. The new exigencies of this time period included competition from Airbus, airline deregulation, investor pressure, and the neoliberal shift in the world economy toward practices of team-based, just-in-time production requiring increasingly fewer numbers of workers. It was a time of intense job insecurity. Over this time period, Greenberg et al. describe the toll in emotional and physical well-being of Boeing workers, who, the authors argue, ended up "bruised and battered" and "detached and resentful"[13] in the new lean, mean world where shareholder value "became the mantra of company leaders."[14] The authors also note that the leadership of Boeing's major unions—the IAMAW and SPEEA—largely defended managerial prerogatives and were unable to hold the line on questions of job security.[15]

In the 1980s and 1990s, Boeing maintained profitability against the trend of broader economic crisis. In the recession of the 1980s, Boeing's diversification into military and aerospace proved an asset despite some scandals in the 1980s about price gouging in foreign and government contracts. Other problems plagued Boeing during these years, however, including huge safety and health problems resulting from fiberglass, graphite, and phenol-formaldehyde resin making people sick at the Auburn plant. Doctors later dubbed the nausea, lung problems, and other symptoms exhibited by workers "aerospace syndrome."[16] Filling the business union role, IAMAW District Lodge 751 President Tom Baker called on sick workers to "calm down" while he negotiated safety improvements with the company.

In addition to safety, workers were concerned with the growing trend of mandatory overtime. In 1989, the union had 57,000 members in Seattle and Wichita. In their forty-eight-day strike in 1989, they won both wage increases and a reduction in mandatory overtime. (The company claimed that it was strapped for cash, "only marginally profitable.")[17] The strike also resulted in the second of Boeing's labor-management "persuasion" strategies: the Quality through Training Program, which according to some Boeing workers meant an institute that trained workers in how to perform multiple jobs, enabling layoffs. Also at this time, the union and management collaborated on the joint IAMAW/Boeing Health and Safety Institute (HSI), designed to reduce union grievances over occupational hazards. These measures represented a growing movement in industrial corporations into the age of consultants, quality management, and improved "communication" between labor and management in lieu of conflict and strikes. As Mike Parker and Jane Slaughter have argued, such measures offer lip service to worker empowerment while reducing real material redress for grievances.[18] In 1990, the Quality through Training Program (QTTP) was "implemented as a way of life" and a hundred Boeing executives traveled to Japan to learn how to motivate workers and avoid labor action.[19]

In the 1990s, competition with Airbus stretched Boeing's resources without cutting deeply into Boeing's market share, especially with regard to the 747, which dominated jumbo-jet passenger markets.[20] *Interavia Business and Technology* journal reported in June 1997 that, in fact, Boeing in the 1990s lived a "charmed life."[21] The charm only applied to executives and shareholders, as Boeing subcontracted 20 percent of the work and a share of profits on the 777 to Japanese firms, a trend that has continued into the twenty-first century.[22] Boeing posted record profits in 1991, producing one aircraft every fourteen hours. In 1993, however, Boeing's sales were down due to airline losses and canceling of orders. Even so, sales were at $25 billion in 1993 and net profits at $4.2 billion.[23] Boeing controlled more than two-thirds of the passenger jet market, despite declining orders. In 1994, with President Bill Clinton's support, Boeing won a contract from Saudi Arabia for a number of 777 aircraft. The 777 was unveiled in April 1994, with 147 orders in the wings.[24] That same year, Boeing was flush enough to begin talks about a merger with McDonnell Douglas. The union, however, avoided a strike in 1992 amid a serious power struggle inside the union that involved the reformers.

In this context, the 1995 strike of the Machinists is best understood as a demand for a share of the company's obvious wealth and a calling out of the company on its hypocritical claims that tight times made mutual sacrifice necessary. The strike lasted for sixty-nine arduous days and won a number of gains for the workers, which I will discuss in subsequent chapters. The business press admonished Boeing, arguing that if the company had only had a more bilateral communication style with the workers, the strike could have been avoided.[25] However, workers' accounts make it clear that communication was not the central issue and that material threats to their standard of living would have forced the strike regardless of any more talking.

The merger in 1995 between Boeing and McDonnell Douglas generated losses for the company despite record orders, and the company faced criticism in the business press for taking on more than it could handle with its outmoded production systems.[26] Thus, between 1997 and 2000, Boeing underwent major changes in the production process in order to render the production of aircraft more efficient. In 1997, Boeing reported a loss of $178 million, the first loss in over fifty years. Then the 1998 Asian economic crisis led to the cancellation of a number of orders. Yet despite falling profits, employment levels remained high, and 1998 saw a record number of jet deliveries.[27]

Boeing CEOs Phil Condit and Harry Stonecipher, former McDonnell Douglas CEO and head of Boeing's passenger division, had a relationship marked by conflict. Even so, they agreed in 1999 to shift Boeing's organizational culture away from a warm and quasi-familial atmosphere (which put a kinder face on the exploitation of the workers)[28] to a more openly "tough, lean, and team-oriented" environment.[29] Charles Bofferding, president of the engineers' union, SPEEA, commented, "They speak about changing from a family culture to a team culture, but it's really family vs. dictatorship."[30] The same year, new CFO Deborah Hopkins implemented what she called a "management for value scheme," oriented directly toward raising profits for shareholders instead of toward product quality or worker satisfaction.[31]

Indicative of this shift to a tough, lean, and value-oriented management style was the move of Boeing's corporate headquarters from Everett to Chicago in 2001. CEO Phil Condit said the move was a "strategic decision" to "maximize shareholder value."[32] A number of workers saw the move as a desertion of a community Boeing was preparing to "trash," without having to look workers and their families in the face.[33] Confirming this impression, the *New York Times* quoted Condit as saying that the headquarters of U.S. operations had to be physically separate from any of Boeing's operations so that the company could make objective decisions about where to add and cut jobs.[34]

The engineers struck during the winter of 1999–2000 for forty days, publicizing their demands among Boeing's investors and customers and causing the value of Boeing's stock to drop by 32 percent.[35] Involving 22,500 engineers, the strike won salary raises of 17 percent over three years, a signing bonus, and another contract without workers' contributions to the costs of health insurance. Greenberg et al. note, "It is rare to find professional employees going on strike and walking the picket lines. That those at Boeing did so for forty days is another powerful indication that Boeing had become another kind of company."[36] The SPEEA strike was their first in their fifty-six-year history; leaders of the union saw that in 1999 profits rose 42 percent, and the workers were not seeing their share of that bounty. Boeing laid off thousands of workers in 1999 and 2000 despite soaring profits and optimism about the development of the small Sonic Cruiser. *Business Week* hailed the layoffs and increased outsourcing: "The moves paid off. Earnings have beaten estimates. . . . Operating income climbed 14% to $3.5 billion. Stock hit $770 a share."[37] The contradiction between mass layoffs and record shareholder winnings generated anger and class-consciousness even among the strike-skittish engineers.

IAMAW negotiators avoided strikes in 1999 and 2002. In 1999, Machinists had voted to give the union the option of striking; the key issues were subcontracting, the nontraditional workweek, tying pensions to inflation, and preserving health care benefits. Boeing already had announced the layoffs of up to 50,000 workers over the next year. The *Seattle Post-Intelligencer* reported, "The multinational corporation is trying to walk a fine line between satisfying its work force and the demands of Wall Street investors, who are clamoring for a leaner company. . . . Union negotiators said they're cautiously optimistic they can avoid a strike this year."[38] While union negotiators engaged in conciliation with the company, however, 1999 was a banner year for Boeing's stocks, whose value had surged by 39 percent.[39] The *Post-Intelligencer* article goes on to quote a Boeing worker named Fred Eastland who, after twenty-five years on the job "doesn't trust either party in the negotiations."[40] Eastland said, "I know they weren't telling us the truth and Boeing isn't telling us the truth." In those years, job security against outsourcing and increasing benefits costs were central concerns of contract talks. In 2002, the IAMAW unsuccessfully demanded the restoration of 26,000 jobs and an end to outsourcing. They had a basis for these demands: Profits, productivity per worker, and quality were up; a third of jobs at Boeing had disappeared since 1999.[41] In 2001 and 2002, Boeing laid off 30,000 workers amid plans to ramp up overseas production facilities in Russia, China, Poland, and Mexico.[42] President Alan Mulally justified the permanent shrinking of the workforce and the subcontracting of formerly in-house work. This trend of ruthless cuts in jobs alongside soaring profits continued through early 2004. In the current period, Boeing has benefited from contracts with Aeroflot and the U.S. military. Between 1999 and October 2003, the number of layoffs reached 35,560. In 2003, *Avionics Magazine* forecast a "positive business outlook" for Boeing for the next twenty years based on growing percentages of business in defense and space markets. Even so, Boeing pledged to its shareholders that it will not rehire the tens of thousands of laid-off workers.[43]

Flying High into the New Millennium

Boeing's sales in 2004 exceeded $50 billion, and it has been profitable every year since. In 2008, Boeing's net earnings were $2.7 billion, down from $4 billion in 2007, its annual report says, due to "the strike that halted commercial airplane production for nearly 60 days."[44] Boeing is the largest defense contractor in the world. Yet the company justifies its ongoing efforts to strip union jobs from the company in terms of a crisis of competitiveness. The contradictions between the situation of the company and its shareholders and what they ask of their workers are stark. Throughout 2001 and 2002, Boeing engaged in mass layoffs, firing more than 30,000 workers across all of its facilities, including 11,000 in Wichita.[45] According to the *New York Times,* the lives of many Wichita families "unraveled."[46] Notably, in 2002, Boeing earned $54 billion, with net profit of $2.6 billion, the second highest amount since 1999.[47] In December 2001, Boeing Commercial Division chief Alan Mulally ironically justified both enormous executive salaries and outsourcing, saying, "We have got to get everybody to share the risk of this huge enterprise."[48]

In May 2004, Boeing implemented lean production practices in its operations for the new 787 jet (originally called the 7E7; midsize and fuel-efficient), cutting the number of workers needed for the project from 5,000 to 1,000 and off-loading most of the work to overseas and nonunion workplaces in a global supply network.[49] In February 2005, Toronto-based investment firm Onex purchased Boeing's Wichita manufacturing facility for $1.2 billion, displacing or laying off as many as 10,500.[50] During this period, the company was mired in scandals, including an investigation of a tainted 2003 Pentagon procurement purchase, which resulted in no charges being filed against the company (although CEO Phil Condit resigned as a result; his replacement, Harry Stonecipher, would resign in 2005 in the wake of a sex scandal).[51] Meanwhile, Boeing began to expand its globalization efforts, shifting most of its work to lower-cost suppliers in the United States and around the world.[52] In 2006, it purchased Aviall, Inc., an aircraft services and parts distributor, for $1.7 billion, even as it eliminated a quarter of the now-emaciated Wichita workforce, cutting 900 jobs.[53] As reported by new Boeing CEO Jim McInerny, between April 2003 and May 2006 share prices at Boeing tripled.[54] Clearly Boeing is prosperous and capitalizing on its ability to undercut union jobs and acquire key pieces of a global supply and manufacture network. With the basic relation of exploitation laid so bare, it was not yet clear whether the unions would stand up in the near future to this behemoth of profitability. The IAMAW in particular had a fighting history, but it is one obscured in recent years by the conservatism of its leadership.

The Machinists: A Little Weather Ahead

In the decades leading up to the 1995 strike, machinists at Boeing proved themselves willing to fight, walking off the job for an astonishing 140 days in 1948 over seniority, wages, benefits, and the right to have a union; for nineteen days in 1965 over performance measures and benefits; for forty-four days in 1977 over retirement and cost-of-living increases; for forty-eight days in 1989 to dispute mandatory overtime and demand wage increases; and for sixty-nine days in 1995. Thomas Talbot founded the International Association of Machinists (IAM) in 1888 in line with the dominant, conservative trade union philosophy of the time. Robert G. Rodden, in his book *The Fighting Machinists*, writes that Talbot's purpose was "not to create disorder and strikes or to antagonize capital and enterprise," but rather "to help members find jobs and raise the dignity of the craft."[55] Successors to Talbot often called off strikes, even during upheavals such as the railroad strikes of the 1890s. In 1892, President John O'Day called on workers to "obey orders" and did not support the embattled Homestead steelworkers in their ultimately defeated strike.[56]

In the 1890s, the approach of the IAM contrasted with the unions formed with the help of the Socialist Party led by Eugene Debs. The American Railway Union, founded by Debs in 1893, retained none of the class and skill divisions and exclusion from union membership that the craft unions endorsed. Sympathetic to the new philosophy of industrial unionism, a number of Boeing workers left the IAM for other groups. In 1894, IAM members walked out in support of the Pullman rail strike, even though leaders ordered them not to do so.[57]

In 1895, the IAM affiliated with the American Federation of Labor (AFL) and, although the AFL was conservative in its embrace of exclusive craft unionism, the federation forced the IAM to remove, at least nominally, its color bar against black workers. But economic crisis and upsurge in radical unionism radicalized the workers. The IAM strike in 1890 hit Chicago; Cleveland; Patterson, New Jersey; and Detroit, winning the nine-hour day.[58] These events ended the long-standing alliance of the IAM with the association of corporations employing its workers. Likewise the strikes, often led by women, in the textile industry during the 1910s challenged craft unionism, and the rise of the Industrial Workers of the World (IWW), founded in 1905, accelerated this process.

Of course, the IAM leadership was actively hostile to the IWW, which, in Rodden's words, was "at war with capitalism." Rodden condemns the IWW as an advocate of sabotage and violence; its organizers were "a reckless, brawling, hell-bent-for-leather, irreverent and singing bunch of agitators"—a lovable group from some other perspectives.[59] Despite the IAM's hostility to radical unionism, however, the popularity of Eugene Debs' Socialist Party led to divisions in the union while its president, James O'Connell, continued to seek amicable relations with management. Setting a pattern that marks all of the IAM's history, members cut against this conservatism, holding twenty-five strikes in 1907 alone and forcing O'Connell out of office.[60] Even as early as 1900, the professionalization of the IAM facilitated alignment with management imperatives. The differences in interest between union officials and the rank and file become ever more pronounced. According to David Montgomery, "The IAM's officers had come to view themselves as full-time specialists in labor-management relations."[61]

The 1920s saw both a rise in unionism and a great deal of federal legislation limiting the rights of labor. The Palmer Raids allowed conservative union officials to purge radicals from the ranks of the union, and the National Association of Manufacturers invented the open shop. As the nation entered the 1930s, however, the economic crisis spurred an outbreak of near-revolutionary union activity. Appeasing this new militancy, President Franklin Delano Roosevelt's National Industrial Recovery Act allowed union organization—but allowed big business to control the codes governing labor relations. The 1935 National Labor Relations Act created the National Labor Relations Board (NLRB), which legalized collective bargaining and defined unfair labor practices. The IAM remained conservative at the top, however, and in 1936 Lodge 284 in Oakland bucked the union and had its charter revoked. IAM President A. O. Wharton forbade IAM members from supporting the history-making sit-down strikes in the automotive industry in 1936 and 1937, which led to the biggest development of the 1930s for unions: the rise of the Congress of Industrial Organizations (CIO) and its leader, John L. Lewis. The leadership of the IAM bitterly opposed Lewis, and the IAM was left behind in the wake of industrial unionism.[62]

The IAM lodge at Boeing in Seattle (Lodge 751) was chartered in 1935, and in 1936 the union established the first contract with the company after signing up 70 percent of the employees. Due to these numbers and the resulting strength of the new union, the workers started with a contract featuring a good minimum wage, an eight-hour day and five-day week, overtime pay of time and a half, and paid holidays.[63] Radical members of the union were key to this victory, yet the influence of Communists in Lodge 751 led International leaders to suspend the union and expel fifty members. The lodge was then structured into smaller lodges (perhaps to atomize the influence of radicals), becoming District 751. The aircraft industry was booming on the eve of World War II, giving workers at all aircraft unions a large bargaining chip. Lockheed and Douglas were organized by the Machinists at the same time.

Predictably, in the spirit of wartime loyalty to the cause, there was a decline in strikes (from involving 23 million workers in 1941 to 4.1 million in 1942).[64] Roosevelt found labor's cooperation "splendid"—especially in unions crucial to the war effort. Wage increases were delayed and strikes discouraged. Even so, some locals struck on the basis that their work was making the war run; Oakland's local was notable among these. After the war, there was a resurgence of strikes alongside continued conservatism among union leaders.

Then, in 1947, the antiunion Taft-Hartley Act crippled labor, and membership declined. The 1948 strike at Lodge 751 was met with a Teamster raid; Teamsters' leader Dave Beck offered Boeing a form of "sweetheart unionism," in which concessions would be the rule. The raid was defeated, but the conflict damaged the union and its will to fight.[65] The Joseph R. McCarthy witch hunts purged radicals. The racism and national chauvinism inside the union also prevented solidarity and militancy.

Having disaffiliated with the AFL in the 1940s, the union rejoined the federation in 1950. Union presidents during the economic boom of the 1950s, however, oversaw victorious strikes and increasing internationalism. Their leadership had little to do with these triumphs; the booming economy and increasing passenger air travel put the workers into a position of strength in which they could ask for and get what they wanted. For example, during this period Boeing instituted the comprehensive health and pension benefits that would set the standard for the industry for decades. With the entry of numbers of women into the union, leaders began negotiating nondiscrimination clauses in contracts.

However, the Taft-Hartley legislation eventually cast a pall over union life. Historian George Lipsitz explains that the act "adapted existing labor legislation to the new challenges posed by rank-and-file militancy. Consistent with traditional corporate-liberal aims of stability, predictability, and security, the bill addressed itself primarily to restraining mass strikes, to ensuring management control over production, and to preventing rivalries within unions from leading to excessive demands on management."[66] The act endorsed open shops in which workers could be employed without joining the union, thus reducing the possibilities of unity among the workers during a strike. In such an event, employers can use the nonunion workers to replace striking unionists, thus breaking the strike. This so-called right-to-work legislation spread to seventeen states by 1957 (including Kansas, where the Wichita plant was located). But Lodge 751 organized to fight the open-shop referendum in Washington State—and won, again signaling skilled workers' unique strength in one of the most powerful corporations in the U.S. economy.[67] The other major piece of labor legislation of the 1950s was the Landrum-Griffin Act, which granted some new rights to union members—but also emphasized in the law's Union Members' Bill of Rights the right of workers *not* to join unions. Interestingly, Rodden criticizes not the law's limits for the rank and file, but the act's encouragement of workers to act independently of their union leaders. Rodden writes:

> [Then President Al Hayes] knew that in the unequal and never-ending struggle between labor and capital the survival of the group must sometimes take pre-

cedence over the rights of individuals. He believed that a democratic union, like a democratic nation, must be able to protect itself against internal spies and saboteurs. Intellectuals, academics and organizations such as the ACLU and the so-called Association for Union Democracy applauded when the Landrum-Griffin Act curtailed union [leaders'] rights. But the experience of America's unions since 1959 proves that Hayes was on target when he accused Landrum Griffin backers of "attempting to encourage irresponsible minority dissent as a means of obstructing effective action on behalf of the majority."[68]

This conservative critique of the Landrum-Griffin Act stands in stark opposition to the leftist critique of the law as weakening union solidarity—solidarity conceived as the unity of rank-and-file workers (sometimes in collective rebellion against a recalcitrant leadership), rather than as blind obedience to the union officials.

Despite the workers' new bill of rights (which ostensibly empowered workers to challenge their unions), the official union remained staunchly business-friendly into the 1960s, focusing more and more on electoral politics, especially the presidential campaign of Lyndon Johnson. Union leaders raised their own salaries, produced a radio show featuring disputes settled without strikes as models, froze death benefits for workers, tried to raise the retirement age, pushed and passed a resolution to allow changes in the union constitution without a referendum (which continues to prevent members' vetoing union leadership decisions), and intervened to stop several strikes.[69] Johnson, having won the votes of the union members, did not work to repeal right-to-work laws as he had promised, but he did cap industrial wage increases at 3.2 percent a year during the Vietnam War. Yet a strike of IAM machinists during the war shut down 230 airports nationally, wining a 6 percent wage increase and demonstrating the ability to fight back against blind patriotism and complacent leadership.

The union was actively hostile to the explosion of other social movements during the 1960s. In the antiwar demonstrations in 1968 at the Democratic National Convention, union leaders regarded Chicago Mayor Richard Daley as a hero.[70] Despite the union's increasingly disciplinary stance regarding the rank and file, there were a number of militant strikes, including a wildcat strike (a strike undertaken by the rank and file without official union approval). In 1969, a slightly more progressive union member, Floyd "Red" Smith, was elected president and oversaw the 1969 strike at General Electric, which won its demands.[71]

However, the economic crisis of the early 1970s led Boeing to abandon the development of a supersonic transport jet and to lay off 60,000 workers in Seattle. As President Richard Nixon enacted a program of systematic strike breaking, the IAM came out in favor of wage increase limits and asked members to report themselves if they received too large a raise. On the other hand, the formation of the Occupational Safety and Health Administration (OSHA) allowed workers to voice their safety concerns. The union campaigned for Democrat candidate George McGovern in 1972, despite his antiunion record in the Senate (a record that he has maintained following his retirement from government; in August 2008, McGovern came out against the Employee Free Choice Act in the *Wall Street Journal* and in October recorded a television ad against it).[72] The pattern of defensive unionism, taking concessions and accepting the lesser evil during a time of perceived labor weakness, became entrenched even as the IAM lost members and businesses laid off millions of workers, increasing weakness rather than holding the line.

The new union president elected in 1977, William Winpisinger, declared a new era of noncooperation with management at Boeing. Rodden writes, "Winpisinger believed the labor movement was losing ground because too many young people saw unions as part of an establishment supporting military adventures overseas and the status quo at home. He felt the need for leadership that would put as much emphasis on social protest and reform as collective bargaining."[73] Other sources confirm Winpisinger's new approach to union organizing. In the front matter to John McCann's history of Local 751, Winpisinger wrote, "Labor's blood is in the water. Even the most gentle of management fish are becoming sharks."[74] Winpisinger described himself as an advocate of disarmament (even as he led a union dominant in the aerospace industry), opponent of anti-immigrant unionism, and "seat-of-the-pants socialist."[75] He favored the formation of a Labor Party in the United States and focused a great deal of attention on union public relations and politics outside the workers' struggle, inaugurating all-IAM NASCAR races and other public events.[76] Against unionists who have felt that concessions were necessary in the era of globalization, Winpisinger claimed to endorse a new class war and railed against labor-management teams and quality circle initiatives.[77] On the other hand, union activists on the shop floor perceived Winpisinger as just another business unionist: Unionists for Democratic Change (UDC) activist Keith Thomas commented, "He was just like the rest of them."[78]

Clearly, how one regards the relationship between union leaders and rank-and-file members depends on one's perspective. Even as Rodden's history of the union claims it for the conservative, conciliatory trade union tradition, McCann locates this history in the more radical traditions of the IWW and the CIO. Thus, his book emphasizes different events that support a vision of the union as militant and restive. His history begins with the charter of Lodge 751 in 1935 during a "revolution from below" heralded by the rise of the CIO.[79] In 1937, the IAM at

Boeing was recognized by the NLRB, and, according to McCann, this particular lodge ran against International's lead, criticizing bosses, unions, and government alike for using the war to hamper unions during World War II.[80] During the war, workers worked ten-hour days without rest breaks at subsistence wages, leading one worker to comment, "We were the working poor."[81] Alone among the IAM lodges, 751 struck to win wages over and above the wartime cap, even as union leaders "sought to prevent rank and file strikes and walkouts to curb growing anti-labor sentiment in Congress and the armed forces."[82]

From a point of view opposite McCann's celebration of the Red Scare, Rodden describes how Lodge 751 opposed the purging of Reds, exonerating workers charged with Communist leanings. International stepped in, suspended the lodge's charter, and expelled fifty people, including the progressive unionist Hugo Lundquist, who had tried to organize the union into the CIO.[83]

McCann also hails the belated opening of the lodge to women and black workers, which was driven in part by complaints from the NAACP. As the war neared its end, Boeing laid off 40,000 workers. The 1948 strike was aimed at enforcing a seniority system in the rehiring of some of those workers. At the time, Boeing President William Allen sought to end the seniority system.[84] Weakened by lack of International support, the Teamsters raid, and the provisions of the Taft-Hartley Act, the longest strike in 751's history up to that time was broken; the NLRB ordered Boeing to reinstate striking workers, but under the company's terms.[85]

As Rodden's book also notes, the 1950s saw a fight against right-to-work legislation; workers won the closed shop in 1962 after President John Kennedy's intervention in that year's strike. Through the 1960s and 1970s, what had become District 70 in the Puget Sound won a series of gains in health benefits, wages, and retirement.[86] The employers' offensive in the 1980s interrupted this string of victories. In 1989, the union conceded to the formation of joint health and safety institutes. In the late 1980s and early 1990s, concessions continued even though Boeing experienced a surge in profits from $15.5 billion in 1987 to $30 billion in 1992. The 1989 strike took place in the context of $7 billion in outstanding orders. And despite Boeing's victory in bidding wars over other companies and its purchase of the profitable McDonnell Douglas in 1995, the company laid off 40,000 workers, resulting in speedup and panic.

Boeing's profits before the merger were $732 million; those of McDonnell Douglas were $695 million. The merger combined 105,000 workers at Boeing with McDonnell's 63,000, which were concentrated in the defense and space areas.[87] Thus, in 1995, the scene was set for a major labor-management confrontation. The 1995 strike still holds the record for the longest strike in the union's history, lasting from October 6 to December 13, 1995. The strike involved 26,000 workers in the

Puget Sound area, 7,400 in Wichita, and 1,200 in the Portland area. In addition to health care costs, job security was the largest issue in the face of increasing trends toward off-loading work to other countries and subcontracting production to nonunion shops inside the United States. Union leaders recommended that the first "last, best, final offer" of the company be rejected on October 2, and it was voted down. The second offer and the workers' response to it demonstrated the militancy of the rank and file in opposition to the union leadership.

On November 19, the IAMAW bargaining committee recommended acceptance of a contract not significantly different from the first offer, which gave concessions on wages, increased health insurance premiums and higher deductibles, and the right to off-load and outsource. Despite the union's recommendation of the contract, union members soundly rejected the proposal. The final contract that was accepted by workers was a "victory on every major issue."[88] In 1998, SPEEA followed the IAMAW's lead, walking out in the Puget Sound area and winning wage increases over merit-based raises and the maintenance of current health care benefits.

The rest of the 1990s, however, progressed as a sobering denouement to the 1995 strike. Boeing's income was uneven during these years, and industry analysts diagnosed the company with a "big problem" of production inefficiency.[89] It is worth pointing out, however, that Boeing still had a great deal of money on hand. According to reports filed with the Securities and Exchange Commission and Boeing Annual Reports, Boeing's net earnings during this period were as follows: 1993, $1.2 billion; 1994, $2.3 billion; 1995, $1.9 billion; 1996, $2.2 billion; 1997, $2.5 billion.[90] In response to industry perceptions that Boeing's production line was inefficient, stock prices dropped by 30 percent in 1999. Boeing laid off 50,000 workers that year.

The union, citing the threatened layoffs, made proposals to increase productivity and lower costs, despite clear evidence that Boeing continued to be profitable. These plans were rejected by Boeing, which was operating from a position of strength. In 1999, in response to "cost-cutting pressure from Wall Street," Boeing restructured under the leadership of President Phil Condit and CEO Harry Stonecipher. The official union was on the run. About the 1995 strike, union President R. Thomas Buffenbarger (otherwise known among workers as "Buffy") commented, "The strike never should have happened."[91] The union under Buffenbarger adopted the attitude that workers should cooperate with management, becoming centrally involved in reengineering production (thus allowing for the elimination of union jobs). A joint IAMAW-Boeing team traveled to China to understand why Boeing needed to off-load work to Shanghai and Xian. The union agreed that the solution to this problem was not fighting to retain jobs in the union, but to provide retraining programs to help laid-off workers to find new jobs.[92]

The trend toward labor-management cooperation continued into 1998, when Boeing initiated plans to start an assembly line in Long Beach, California. Boeing gave the union some assurances that the Long Beach plant would not siphon off union jobs from the Puget Sound area. Boeing's strategy coming into 1999 contract negotiations was to offer symbolic gestures toward joint interests and job security. The business press emphasized that after the stinging defeat at the hands of workers in 1995, Boeing was operating at a disadvantage. Workers held the upper hand but did not press it.

At a powwow in 1998 on the direction of the company, Boeing Chairman Phil Condit and Machinists President Tom Buffenbarger expressed the desire to "shift the focus to shared interests" during the run-up to contract negotiations.[93] Though appearing to play nice, however, Boeing turned around and announced huge layoffs in late 1998. Once again outraged, the unions accused the company of pandering to its shareholders.[94] However, union officials quickly recovered from their state of shock. Suffering apparently from short-term memory loss, the leadership of the union again pressed the strategy of conciliation.

The IAMAW did not strike in 1999, despite threatened additional layoffs, soaring Boeing stock value, and the production of a record number of planes. Bloomberg reported, "Boeing's machinists have a history of unpredictability. After striking for 47 days in 1995, the rank and file defied the recommendation of the union leaders and turned down Boeing's sweetened contract offer. By prolonging the strike for 22 more days, the machinists won higher wages and more concessions on health-care premiums."[95] In 1999, worker anger at Boeing management was high. A worker named Rick Beldon articulated this feeling: "We're cutting to the bone and they don't want to listen. The only thing they are listening to is the stockholders."[96] Keith Thomas made special buttons for that contract negotiation period: "Happiness is waking up and finding [Boeing President] Harry Stonecipher's name on a milk carton."

It was during this contract cycle that the IAMAW sought to appoint a member to the Boeing board of directors; IAMAW President Buffenbarger called every employee a shareholder. "Such an appointment would help resolve the tension between the union and Boeing over the company's practice of outsourcing union jobs to low-wage domestic and foreign contractors."[97] These strategies speak to the conciliatory "team" stance the union was adopting toward negotiations with the company. Dick Schneider, head of the IAMAW's bargaining team, expressed admiration for Boeing CEO Phil Condit. "Union leaders appreciate Condit's efforts to solicit their opinions on recent production problems," commented

Business Week.[98] "We're here to negotiate a contract, not a strike."[99] Schneider approved of the company's offer to protect 3,000 jobs—in the context of layoffs of more than 40,000 in the offing; Boeing had planned in 1998 to eliminate 48,000 of 238,000 jobs over a period of two years.[100] Yet this meager agreement was hailed as a "landmark agreement" by District 751 President Bill Johnson. "This is a good example that shows that no matter how difficult the task, we can sit down together and resolve our differences."[101] Suspicious of Harry Stonecipher, next in line to become CEO, the union adopted a conciliatory stance with Boeing in 1999, adapting joint management-union committees to study why the company might really need to outsource after all. In a position of strength, the union retreated from their fight for job security.

The SPEEA workers showed this strategy to be unnecessarily concessionary when their forty-day strike in 2000 won raises, maintained the closed shop, and preserved health benefits. Meanwhile, the business press celebrated the joint management-union institutes for "uniting labor and managers on worker safety." Boeing manager Robert Gentry and paid IAMAW official Bill Stanley became "teammates whose work transcends such divisiveness. . . . They stress that they work side by side as administrators for the independent IAM/Boeing Health and Safety Institute."[102]

Negotiations over the 2002 contract between Boeing and the IAMAW began contentiously in fall 2001, with union negotiator Dick Schneider proclaiming that the members would strike rather than take more concessions. Boeing was cutting production, and there had been 30,000 layoffs in the previous twelve months, leaving the union relatively weak in comparison to 1999 and 1995. The company's contract made no guarantees against overseas outsourcing and pay increases below the rise in the cost of living. Even given the usually recalcitrant union negotiators' recommendation to strike, members narrowly voted not to strike (although they voted overwhelmingly against the contract).[103] One reason for the vote may have been that Boeing demonstrated bravado, claiming in the business press that they wanted the strike and could profit from a work stoppage in a period of declining orders.[104] As noted previously, the confusion and sense of betrayal around the union's discounting of the first vote was a source of division and anger among the rank and file.

The resulting 2002 contract was a major defeat for the workers, symptomatic of increasing fear among the rank and file and an ever-hardening line on the company's part regarding outsourcing and off-loading. An article in *Business Week* summarized, "Now, Boeing can count on lower costs to keep it in the running [in competition with Airbus]. Indeed, the new pact with the International Association of Machinists could cut Boeing's total labor bill, adjusted for inflation, after years of steady increases. . . . 'This is why Boeing's popping champagne and not returning our phone calls,' says one union official."[105]

Another result of this defeat was weakened morale and company loyalty among workers, and when production picked up into 2003, management sought improved relations with the union. In December 2003, Boeing CEO Harry Stonecipher agreed to keep the production of the new 787 jet at the unionized Everett plant and promised union President Thomas Buffenbarger to grant workers greater voice on the shop floor. However, these gestures, understood in the context of the 2002 takeaways and the layoffs of more than 17,000 workers between 2002 and 2003, exemplified lip service to workers' rights in an effort to bolster productivity (and thus reduce the number of workers necessary to the production process). The High Performance Work Organization initiative, like the earlier Pride in Excellence Campaign, ostensibly offered workers control over their productivity. However, like other similar initiatives past and future, it asked workers to become more productive without reciprocal assurances of job security, health care stability, and wage increases. During negotiations with Stonecipher, Buffenbarger agreed that "outsourcing is a reality," and that "as Boeing plants become more efficient, there will be fewer jobs."[106] Arguably, the friendly offers made by Stonecipher to Buffenbarger were a Trojan horse whose goal was to produce more willing cooperation of workers with the possible elimination of their own jobs.[107] As Jane Slaughter has pointed out, "When they grant concessions, union members risk financing their own future job loss."[108]

The contrasts between the 2002, 2005, and 2008 contract struggles demonstrate how concessions can be beat. The union faced a strong and ruthless company in 2002, when contract negotiations concluded controversially (without a strike)[109] with the workers making deep concessions on subcontracting. In contrast, according to the *Wall Street Journal,* the twenty-four-day 2005 strike was "a test of labor's mettle"—a test that the workers aced.[110] Costing Boeing billions of dollars in backlogged orders, the workers won a contract providing significant bonuses and the protection of health care and retirement benefits. In 2008—during a profound economic crisis—workers once again waged a successful strike.[111]

In the context of the current economic crisis, these struggles are momentous in their lessons: If an organized workforce can win even in the here and now, the realm of possibility opens up for other workers facing the harsh reality of recession. Thus, this project is ultimately about how regular people use—and criticize, and condemn, and negotiate with—their often problematic institutions to garner agency and voice in the unfolding of the conditions of their lives. Unions are only one such vehicle for human self-determination, but the story of one group of workers in one union over a period of nearly two decades may speak to all of our aspirations, not least among them the desire to have some control over our destinies as individuals, families, and workers.

Summary

I asked the IAMAW's education directors, Virginia Roberts and Sue Moyer, about the perennial threats and execution of mass layoffs. Knowing the history of the company and the workforce well, Roberts said, "There were thousands of layoffs at that time as well, similar to this year. *But then that is the story.* Boeing . . . You go back to the history, it just goes like this."

The moral of this story is clear: The company will press its advantage during lean times and will offer symbolic "gains" to appease workers when it faces labor challenges in addition to fiscal hardship. Rather than recognizing their power in these moments, union officials have time and again accepted lip service and job-eliminating joint programs instead of pressing their advantage. Boeing has used the short-term cycles between productivity and profit on the one hand and decreasing stock prices on the other to threaten and cajole the union into ever-greater concessions. The lesson of 1995 was largely lost—at least for a time. As a result, up until 2005 the company had nearly complete license to export jobs, lay off workers anywhere in the United States and around the world, route safety grievances through joint management committees instead of traditional union process, and ask more and more of workers as they take back the hard-won gains of previous decades.

Denise Harris, a Boeing worker in Wichita and representative of Local 834 and District 70, described to me the steady erosion of her quality of work life:

> I've watched it steadily decline. When I hired in, in 1975, I felt like the people were treated with more respect then than they are now. I don't care what their QTTP management working lists, combining and joint programs—I'm not a big supporter of that because I really think they're just soft-soaking us into taking more cuts in our contract. I had better insurance coverage ten years ago than I have now. I've watched that decline. Probably I have a more bitter attitude about what's going on there because I did hire in on the upswing and I've watched it swing down. Some of these guys who have only been out there ten or fifteen years, they did not see things peak, and now I'm watching it steadily decline. Due to my age it's scary to watch it decline like that, because I wonder what it's going to be like when I go to retire, which is a long time off still. So I want to see everything go up, and I see people taking concessions and watching it go down. Where am I going to be when I get sixty years old?

Am I going to be worse off than I was if I'd retired ten years ago, fifteen years ago? So I don't like what's going on at Boeing at all. People have got to stop accepting that.[112]

In *Concessions and How to Beat Them,* Slaughter notes that companies often blackmail workers into accepting concessions.[113] Alongside direct threats, companies conduct an ideological offensive stressing commonality of interests rather than the idea that the interests of workers and employers are at odds. If accepted by union leadership, this ideology of shared interests generates a tendency toward accepting devastating concessions. The IAMAW is certainly not alone in adopting this stance. Since the 1980s, the partnership philosophy has been dominant across labor unions in the United States. Not coincidentally, during the same time period we have seen union membership in the United States drop to its lowest levels since World War II. To provide necessary counterforce to concessions, Slaughter recommends that unions know the economic situation of their employers, demand and use relevant financial information, educate the membership in the reality of the economic situation and the consequences of accepting concessions, and build solidarity with other unions.[114] Throughout labor's history, striking has been any union's strongest weapon against concessions.

Throughout the union's history (with a few notable exceptions), the leadership of the IAMAW at Boeing has cooperated with concessions unless forced to do otherwise by the rank and file of the union. At key moments, such as the 1995 strike at Boeing, rank-and-file workers can push their leaders from below, putting out educational flyers, petitioning against concessions, and organizing union members into an anticoncession caucus. The next chapter explores how union dissidents took on these tasks at Boeing during the 1990s and began to realize a vision contrary to business unionism and the steady erosion of workers' livelihoods.

3

Enter the Dissidents

Keith Thomas is a tall, pale-haired, loud-talking, sturdy dynamo of a man. He is the kind of person who leaps to his feet to be useful before you realize you needed something. In July 1999, we were in his basement workshop getting ready for a picket at the Wichita, Kansas, International Association of Machinists and Aerospace Workers (IAMAW) union hall, which is right across the street from the Boeing plant. The goals of the picket were twofold: to warn the company that unionists were ready to strike (with the slogan "Get Ready for the Long One") and to protest the inaction of the union local in preparation for the contract fight. All the while talking to me about the history of the local and its representatives and about the likely terms of the coming contract, Thomas was using templates projected on a wall to paint posters with slogans like "We *Are* the Union," "No More Offload," and "Remember '95—We Can Do It Again!" Using a circular saw, he cut lengths of lumber into pickets and stapled the signs neatly front and back to the posts with a staple gun. At the picket itself, he (with megaphone) led the small group in chants, spoke earnestly with fellow activists and reporters, and, it looked to me, had the time of his life. He was wholly in his element. But it had not always been so. Surprisingly, when he hired on at Boeing in Wichita in 1978, he actually refused to join the International Association of Machinists. Yet after joining almost ten years later, he would become a strong voice in his union for democracy and militancy. His reasons for not joining the union in the first place were not antiunion. He was reluctant primarily not out of disregard for the workers' fight against the company, but out of skepticism that the union was the proper vehicle for that struggle. About his distrust of the union, Thomas said:

Folks need to understand there is no good reason for not joining a labor union, so any reasons that I give, they're not excuses and they're not good reasons. I don't ever want to be on tape somewhere and somebody saying, Keith Thomas gave a real good reason for not getting in, because there isn't a good reason for not getting in. And I'm gonna say that I said the typical things, made the typical rationalizations that you can't make a difference, it doesn't make a difference, the leadership is terrible. I did the same things that people will do with organized religion sometimes. There'll be some preacher out there who just commits some heinous acts and we will brand an entire religious group according to what this particular individual does. It can happen. And from the union leaders I'd seen, I wasn't very impressed.[1]

Eventually, Thomas made a distinction between the institution of unions as the necessary organization of workers in capitalism and the behaviors and ideologies of particular labor leaders. This passage demonstrates his point of view: It is necessary to use the union and to build the union while at the same time questioning its leaders and institutional practices.

Fellow activist Sean Mullin—a slight man with brown hair and keen, expressive eyes—also tried to convince people to both use and fight the union:

I had a scab tell me the other day, I don't have any power. I can't make any changes in this union. I said, you know, the funny thing is the exact complaints that you have with my union are the exact complaints that I have with it. And it's the exact complaints that every other scab out here has with the union. You know what, my vote they can count on being against them every time. They can count on your vote not counting because you can't vote. Here's the deal. If you and every one of the rest of you scabs would get in the union, get together because you all have a common opinion, use your one vote [so you] have way more votes than they have. But you are the silent majority who refuse to get up off your asses and do anything about it.[2]

Mullin's argument is that one can join *and* dissent; a worker can't control what the union does by refusing to join it. Once in the rank and file, a skeptic can challenge the organization's m.o. from within. One purpose of Unionists for Democratic Change was to offer disgruntled potential unionists a home where they could fight the company and be on the right side in contract struggles without suspending criticism of the union itself.

After he joined the union, Thomas never gave up his vigilance regarding the tendencies of some leaders of the IAMAW both locally and in the International. Thus the structure of his relationship with the union was essentially dilemmatic:

From an entirely prounion stance and knowing he and his fellow workers had to use the union, he still wanted and needed to question and challenge—and hoped to displace—the union's leadership. This dilemma is at the core of democratic unionism today. It is necessary to negotiate that dilemma in order to make unions democratic if they are ever again to win over working people to their ranks and to be powerful forces in social relations.

Keith Thomas is just one example of a unionist who has tried to navigate the paradoxical relationships that dissidents inside unions have with the union itself. He and some of his co-workers formed a dissident caucus in the IAMAW in Wichita in the early 1990s in order to challenge the inherent conservatism at the top of the union and to educate other workers more fully about contract issues and their rights. The organization was called Unionists for Democratic Change (UDC). Eventually an allied organization sprang up in Everett, Washington, variously called the New Crew or Rank and File. In the Puget Sound area, another organization called Machinists for Solidarity (MFS) was initiated by David Clay, another longtime Boeing worker who set himself against the entrenched leadership of District 751 while remaining steadfastly on the side of the union in contract struggles with the company.[3]

Clay was, at the time of my first interview with him, in his thirties, clean-shaven, compact, and graying at the temples. He was direct and soft-spoken. Like Thomas, Clay sees the union as a tool against the company and the caucus as a tool to make the union more accountable and militant. He calls the entrenched union leadership a "dynasty" and, like Thomas, insists that he is not the founder of his group. "I'm not in charge," he said. "The people are in charge." And, like Thomas, he has faced attacks from the union establishment. At one point, the union put out thousands of pink flyers denouncing Clay, but these only served to attract supporters who questioned why the union would attack someone who was putting out the issues.

In his interview with me in 1998, Clay talked about the caucus he and others formed in 1989:

> Well, there's probably about two hundred people from throughout Puget Sound that came together and came to me because this isn't the first time in the contract that I've organized people behind issues. And, you know, by trade I'm a toolmaker, and they came to me because they needed a tool to get a job done. You know, my experience with the legislative process and the governmental affairs position helped in that, in this day, we have an initiative process where the citizens, if they want to get a lobby for the citizens to vote on, you can sign on to an initiative and that brings it before a vote before the people.

So we decided that we'd do the same thing with this. The group thought that it was a good idea to gather the items that we want to see improved in the contract and get the membership to sign on to them, and we would deliver that to the negotiating table as well as to the company.[4]

In 1995, Clay and his group gathered several thousand signatures on a petition demanding a better contract. They delivered the stacks of petitions to IAMAW negotiator Dick Schneider during the contract negotiation. And during the vote on the contract at the Kingdome, MFS distributed leaflets, buttons, pins, stickers, and flyers with the group's Web site address. In order to raise awareness of contract issues among workers, they participated in county fairs and small-town events. The slogan of MFS is "You are the union—take it back. Fight for the future, respect the past." In this theme, he says, they tried to encapsulate a commitment to union democracy and gains for both new employees and retirees.

Neither the UDC nor the Puget Sound groups are very active today, although members of each made meaningful interventions into discussions during the 2005 and 2008 strikes. Some activists instrumental in starting those groups have drifted away from grassroots organizing, tapped out financially and burned out emotionally and intellectually. The experience of these organizations, especially that of the UDC in Wichita, raises important questions about the democratic union project. Most important, we have to ask how and under what conditions might the dissident caucus have been sustained into the contract battles of the late 1990s and early 2000s? What did the UDC members do that was effective in mobilizing the rank and file and democratizing union business? And what did the members of the UDC and other organizations do that might have undermined their efficacy and staying power?

In subsequent chapters, I will address three ways in which the actions of dissident unionists contradicted their motivations and ideals and helped to undermine their ability to sustain progressive organization. These contradictions are the tendency to celebrate rank-and-file participation while substituting a small group's activity for that of a broader collective, the habit of criticizing the Administrative Caucus (or established union leadership) for their electioneering and inattention to shop-floor organizing while at the same time engaging in heated and all-consuming election fights themselves, and the belief in democratic progress and the capacity of ordinary people to act in their own interests alongside pessimism about whether the rank and file would have the will or the interest in democratic organizing. These tendencies led the UDC to underestimate their own potential and to burn out highly dedicated individual leaders without building the support for the movement from the ground up.

However, in this chapter, I will introduce more fully the activists and their organizations and relate their stories about the origins and purposes of the caucuses as they told them to me. In addition to these introductions, this chapter lays out the agenda and perspectives of these activists regarding the company and the IAMAW and its leadership. The themes of these stories include the rejection of cooperation with management in the form of joint programs, the identification of union leaders as "Boeing managers," the desire to retain and restore labor gains of previous generations (which they view as having been squandered by union leaders), and the recognition of the ways in which race, gender, and sexual orientation influence the working experience. The overall goal of this chapter is to understand more fully the critique, resounding in these accounts, of the practices of both the union and the company.

In Memory of Joe: Unionists for Democratic Change

The UDC was formed in 1990 in the wake of the confidence-building 1989 strike and out of the felt need to build on rank-and-file militancy. Activists also saw the need for a voice from below in the union to call attention to issues of safety, job security, wages, and contract struggles.

The ability to connect personal experience to collective experience and oppressive structures characterizes this discourse. Keith Thomas remembers his motivation for being among the founders of the UDC in a tragedy striking a close friend in the plant:

> Joe Cauley was one of my best friends. I lost him in 1988. They carried him out of the plant and he never came back in. On our particular process line, we had a lot of acid tanks. There were various chemical processes that took place. Our exhaust system for these various tanks weren't functioning properly. And what happened to Joe, and he was only thirty-four years old, he developed a hole in his lung. Essentially, chromic acid anodize, the mist off that, it's an acid that attacks mucous membranes in the nasal passages and of course in the lungs. I had been handling a complaint. I had come back in and Joe was already in trouble. To make a long story short, Joe was loaded into an ambulance. And I just can't forget it for the rest of my life. It's hard for me to talk about the last time I saw Joe was waving goodbye in that ambulance. Saw that sweet Joe smile. And never saw him again.
>
> And some company manager moron the whole time was yapping at me that I couldn't go with him in the ambulance because I'd asked Joe if he wanted me to come along. And this fucking nitwit from the company was, "Oh Keith, I don't know if we can allow that, you know, we've got insurance concerns." I

didn't give a crap what he was talking about. And if Joe had wanted me in the ambulance, I would've been there. Joe obviously didn't know he was dying. And neither did I. And so I missed that part, being with him.

Joe died in the emergency room. His wife Beth had to file a workers' compensation suit against the company. She won the first time; she also won the appeal. The company kept dragging this out in court because they don't pay any interest or penalties on a workers' compensation suit. And that's all you can sue them for; you can't sue them for criminal negligence or the other things in Kansas, so that's all she had at that point was the workers compensation suit. And he had two children, Alex and Jessica, left two small kids behind. And that had a profound impact on me.[5]

Thomas's personal experience translated into a desire for more power in and on the part of the union against a company that neglected workers' safety. The company's disregard is distilled in his narrative down to microcosmic moments, when the company representative would not let Thomas accompany his friend in the ambulance and when they fought Joe's widow in court. The personal stories became political when Thomas became a fighter in his union.

In the same passage of this interview, Thomas immediately connected his experience to the broader corporate reality and need for collective, organized struggle:

Figure 1. Keith Thomas, 1989, Wichita, Kansas. Courtesy of Keith Thomas.

You can only make corporate America respond to pressure; they fix these things because they're made to fix these things. They didn't take the kids out of mines until they were forced to take children out of mines. They didn't change factories like the Triangle factory fire in 1911 until a whole lot of workers died and the [others] organized and fought back. They turned right around in Carolina and did the same damn thing. Corporate America. I talked to some safety inspectors where they locked those folks in that chicken factory . . . and what they found when they got the fire out and back into the plant there were footprints in the steel door because the door was locked and people had jumped and tried to kick the door open and they actually had human footprints in a steel door because these people were trying to get out.[6]

In this conversation, I was struck by how Thomas's desire to fight and his knowledge of how workers in New York had fought contrasted with a sense of despair and hopelessness: We have to keep fighting the same battle, and the horrific tragedies of capitalist exploitation go on, generation after generation. It is out of such motivation that militancy springs. The UDC in Wichita and groups in the Puget Sound were expressions of outrage and the desire to take action to make unions more effective.

The UDC: Taking the Lead in Wichita

The drive to organize a reform organization comes out of workers' capacity to connect the personal to the structural, to understand the principle of solidarity as necessary to agency, and to embrace antagonism as a source of democratic change. As I noted in the preface, I first met Keith Thomas at a political conference in Chicago in 1996. On a panel with other labor activists, he spoke eloquently about the 1995 contract struggle and the radicalization it generated in union activists. He talked quickly and peppered his speech with gestures. He seemed the epitome of the energy and dynamism vital to any movement. As he explained, he was just one among a number of activists fed up with business as usual at the union and willing to put in many hours and dollars to see if they could make a change. Thomas credits an anonymous woman, an activist in another union, with the idea for and success of the caucus in its initial stages. She had shared her experience as the target of established unionists and given UDC-ers a sense of what to expect. Based on those ideas, Thomas searched out other activists— "the people who are being outspoken and taking a position other than that being espoused by the Administrative Caucus."

The UDC was founded as a caucus in 1989. A caucus is an organization inside a union that can rally support around itself, run candidates for elected office in the union, and agitate for or against particular policies or union strategies. A dissident caucus usually finds itself at odds with what is often called the Administrative Caucus, which represents incumbent union officials tied to prior generations of union leadership. Thomas describes the events leading up to the solidification of the caucus:

> We just took really a terrible beating in the 1989 strike, and not only at the hands of the company and of the community, but also really from our own so-called labor leaders as well. The union leadership was practically nonexistent for the folks out on the line, and their main concern when they came down here—when I say they, I'm talking about our International reps, when they came down—was to get the strike checks to people. Pretty much that was their main source of involvement from our perspective on the line, anyway.[7]

Thomas had been active in the union as a shop floor steward but felt that the union leadership was becoming increasingly ossified. Rather than form a caucus immediately designed to run candidates for office, Thomas and the others decided to come together to "represent the interests of the people" in a new caucus organized to educate the rank and file about events in the labor movement and to "open lines of communication with anyone that we could." The UDC was especially interested in the rise of dissident organizations inside unions, including the Teamsters for a Democratic Union, Paperworkers for Reform, and the New Directions movement in the automobile industry. The UDC caucus tried to learn the lessons of these other groups' experiences in democratic organizing and to build solidarity with them.

Kelly Vandegrift is one of the original UDC group. Here he summarizes the purpose of the UDC:

> And we saw this [undemocratic practices, cooperating with concessions] going on over and over again and saw our leadership not disseminating information to the members. In '95 the UDC was very instrumental in getting the membership the opportunity to have a three-day look-ahead at the contract before we voted. That's something we've never had. We've always been presented a contract right then and there, and, "It's time to vote. Here it is, go vote." You don't get the opportunity to go sit with your family and talk it over and think about what these things are going to mean to you until the next three to four years. The company would disseminate a little information through little management bulletins a day or two ahead of time, but you never knew how much of that was accurate and how much of it wasn't. So I think the UDC has done some really good things in that area. But basically in 1990 we were pretty fed up with the way our local was being run and, for that matter, the way the

International was run. But we knew we couldn't have an effect on the International right away. We had to start somewhere, so we started with the local.[8]

In addition to articulating the function of the caucus, Vandegrift's narratives explore the theme of solidarity and power. Vandegrift (who, at the time of this writing, was vice president of Local 834 in Wichita) took pride in his work at Boeing as an A operator, "which means I move all the big stuff. Studied hard, took big tests, and I move fuselages, do rail switches, drive 50,000-pound forklifts, all the big equipment you see moved around Boeing, we do it." He is a ruddy-faced, bearded man whose animated humor and energy were central to the formation of

the UDC. Enthusiastic about all things union, he embraces what he calls the "wolf pack theory" of solidarity: "It's nice to be a lone wolf. Everybody respects that. But do you know what a lone wolf dines on? Rats, crickets, grubs, stuff like that. And in the dead of winter, when there's no other wolves around, no crickets or rats to catch, it eats bark off trees. And usually it doesn't make it till springtime and it

Figure 2. Kelly Vandegrift in Wichita, Kansas, July 14, 1999. Photo by Dana L. Cloud.

dies. Now, however, you have a pack of wolves. We eat caribou, we eat deer. And everybody gets a share, everybody gets to eat, and everybody survives till spring." For Vandegrift, the power to take down the "big game"—that is, gains from the company—comes only from bonding with and struggling alongside others. This metaphor suggests that organizing not only in the union but also in challenge to established union leadership is a matter of sheer survival.

Again, there is a clear connection between personal experience and the collective fight. Vandegrift became emotional discussing his role as a founding member of UDC and his love for Thomas and the rest of the crew:

> The first time I met Keith was during the 1989 strike. And they said there's this nut outside and he's just going berserk, he's got all these issues and he's passing out papers. And I went out and I met with Keith, and Keith had some real concerns. And I said, Why do you call him a nut? This guy is true blue and concerned, and you know what? He's a dues-paying union member. He's got a lot of points. Well, I learned through the political way. I didn't know too much about it, because I just assumed that if you were part of the political

in-party that that was fine. That they controlled everything. And they tried to control and shut this man up when this man had legitimate concerns. Well, I always said that Keith turned me up and I turned him down. I brought calmness and legitimacy to Keith, and he brought radical, new ideas to me. And so we've worked together as a team to carrot-and-stick a lot of folks. We've been a good team at it, along with Dave ["Bones" Smith, a UDC member] and Gary [Washington] and an old guy by the name of Jack Johnson, who bowed out of the organization a long time ago and just decided to go blasé. Between all the guys, we have great camaraderie, great love for one another. And I know that sounds corny, but that's exactly what it is, great love for one another and each other's families.

Vandegrift's insight that the language of mental illness was used to discipline Thomas and mute his effectiveness is important. As authors Dana Cloud, Robert Whitaker, and Jonathan Metzi each has noted, labeling dissidents as mentally ill is a form of discipline that operates in the service of established power.[9] This passage also reveals Vandegrift reflecting upon the adversarial role Thomas was taking with the union. At first, Vandegrift said he liked being "one of the bad boys, one of the rebels. It was like joining the union in the first place, we were the bad boys, or the militants, or the ones that stood up for what was right for people's rights, to help folks, to make sure that they got the knowledge, the education. And that's what the UDC did." To foster antagonism and to welcome confrontation with the union leadership were, for the UDC, necessary to standing up for people's rights. Rank-and-file education operates in this context not only to arm workers in the struggle with the company, but also to make demands on their union leaders in service of the larger fight.

The adversarial stance did not win friends among those leaders. In response to the UDC's activism, the union leadership ridiculed and threatened Thomas, trying to dismiss him as a "nut" who was making noise for noise's sake. Yet Vandegrift and a number of others recognized that Thomas had "legitimate concerns" conveyed in a very energetic style. Vandegrift also describes how the formation of the UDC gave people who could have "gone blasé" about the union a political home, a site for voice and agency beyond the traditional avenues. This passage illustrates how love is a key theme that pervades the discussion of UDC activists. Identification and solidarity with one another cultivated the desire for collective action benefiting everyone.

The 1989 strike motivated Vandegrift to take union work more seriously. Although the company and the economy in general were experiencing a boom, Boeing demanded concessions. Vandegrift described what was at stake for the workers in the 1989 strike: "At stake there for me were ideals and principles.

Simply, it wasn't for wages; they wanted concessions. And we were in a boom. We weren't about to give concessions. [They wanted] concessions in insurance, in benefits that we had earned. And you know you get told you earned an eight-hour day. But they wanted things like the irregular workweek. They wanted folks to work irregular hours. Swap a lot of things that we never had to do before." Importantly, Vandegrift highlights in this discussion how crucial it is to have a movement inside unions that will resist pressure to give concessions. Striking is often as much about holding as it is gaining hard-won ground. It was an offense that the company wanted to take away what generations had struggled for—the eight-hour day and insurance benefits—when the company was profitable. The union's collective strength meant that *we*, all of the workers, would not have to give up ground. In this conversation, Vandegrift also discussed the dispro-portionate effects of a bad contract in 1986 on new hires who were relegated to the lowest pay grades for the term of the contract. The experience committed Vandegrift to future struggles: "I said to myself there I would never take a new person and ask them to join my organization and then put my thumb on them to hold them down." The group sought to organize across grade, job description, seniority, and age, enacting the principle of solidarity.

When the new caucus formed, the Administrative Caucus was, in Thomas's words, incensed. The caucus had its coming out, so to speak, at a Labor Day picnic in 1990. The caucus focused on elections, occasionally winning offices, but also emphasized educating members regarding contract issues and union democracy. Thomas said:

> We knew that that flow of information to the membership had to start taking place all the time. We already knew based on what happened to us in '89 that we weren't going to get correct information, and if they did get us correct information it wasn't going to be in a timely manner, enough actually to do us any good in contract negotiations. In the 1989 strike, we weren't often told about letters of understanding [agreements between company and union with-out membership approval that form addenda to the contract; often regarded as creating loopholes for the company in holding to the contract agreement]. We wouldn't find out a lot of our contract language that really was causing us trouble until it was signed and we agreed to and gone back to work.[10]

Thomas added that information was especially crucial when workers had "been taking steady losses, making concessions mainly in the area of medical benefits and job combinations."

In the 1990s, Thomas began to put out newsletters (precursors to his Weblog; in 1998, they went to email) called *Floormikes*. Each of these ran many pages and contained Thomas's witty analysis of information gleaned from contract proposals and existing contracts, from union leaders, from the newspaper, from Boeing financial documents, and from the Securities and Exchange Commission to put together a bigger picture: The company sought concessions and threatened jobs despite profitability, and the union leadership cooperated with the company in negotiating concessions. An example from *Email Floormike* #2:

> BOEING CEO PHIL CONDIT ADDRESSED IAM AEROSPACE CONFERENCE: IAM International President Thomas Buffenbarger said that he was pleased and honored (twice) to introduce CEO Condit to the conference and in comments made later said that Condit was a "regular" guy. He also mentioned that Condit was not afraid to come onto the shop floor and discuss the issues. (Well come on down!) Condit gave the typically smooth polished presentation that one would expect from a CEO at his level. He had a video shown during his address that was really quite nice.
>
> Condit talked about the usual things: Teamwork * Globalization * We're in this together * People are important * Boeing sells in a global marketplace * It's important that the Boeing mission statement uses the word company and not corporation (Like, I give a big rats ass what the Boeing mission statement is.) * We live in a complex time * Blah, Blah, Blah * Blah, Blah, Blah.
>
> When Condit entered I did stand with the rest but I didn't clap. I waited until the others sat down then turned around and showed him the back of my union shirt that has the slogan "Contract '99 Get Ready For The Long One." Then I sat down. I did NOT stand up and clap when he left even though I WAS glad to see him go.
>
> The IAM has changed all right. They've gone even more company.

This email indicates multiple dimensions of the reformers' activity and arguments. The reformers challenge the company; "Get Ready for the Long One" is a reference to a threatened strike for 1999. Thomas's comments describe the glad-handing and apparent goodwill between the union leadership and the company, concluding that the union had only changed to the extent that it was even more conciliatory with the company. Thus the UDC's role was to challenge the existing leadership in the union and to provide not just specific contract information but also broader political analysis and debate about the overall scene for labor in today's workplace.

In Everett, the UDC-like group Rank and File/New Crew formed at about the same time as did the one in Wichita. A few key activists and longtime Boeing workers were in contact with Keith Thomas and decided that some local agitating was within their capability. Don Grinde, a leader of the Everett group, described

Figure 3. (Left to right) Tom Jackson, Don Grinde, Keith Thomas, and Alan Harteland, in Seattle, 2005. Courtesy of Keith Thomas.

its purpose: "With a small group of dedicated people, who believed in what they were trying to do, who'd share their message or concerns over the issues, whether it was something wrong with the union or wrong with the contract. We published flyers, we blanketed the factory with flyers and tried to make as many contacts as we could, and develop an email list, a mailing list, phone list, whatever it took, to try to build an organization."[11] Grinde, Tom Finnegan, David Mascarenas, Tom Jackson, Rick Herrmann, Stan Johnson, and Bill Sapiens were the core group in the Puget Sound organizing the dissident caucus. As future chapters will clarify, much of the Everett group's efforts centered on electioneering inside the union. They were also quite hostile to the other democratic union activist organization in Seattle, the Machinists for Solidarity, and the feeling was mutual.

Machinists for Solidarity: Taking It Back in the Puget Sound

The story of the Machinists for Solidarity (MFS) in the Everett plant is quite similar to the narrative of the creation of the UDC. Despite the sometimes-heated rivalry between the two groups, there are strong resonances between not only the groups and their purposes but also their leaders and strategies. David Clay is a longtime unionist who, in the 1990s, decided that the Administrative Caucus in District 751 was not representing the rank and file as fully as it could be. Breaking from the Administrative Caucus (after holding office in their name off and on for over a decade), he began the MFS to organize ordinary workers. In 1999, his group involved about fifty core people; they criticized the establishment but used its resources. In 1999, Clay came within a hair's breadth of wining the union presidency, and his running mate won the position of secretary-treasurer. He ran on the promise of membership education.

Clay is a consummate politician, whose strategy for leadership is one of inclusion: "Our idea is this is a union, it's not the cowboys and the Indians or the Democrats and the Republicans, but after an election, if somebody comes within five hundred votes of me, he has a constituency and he's going to be included in. I'm going to give that person something to do and include those people in."[12] Contrary to the portrait of him painted by some members of the UDC, Clay says he is not interested in a career union position. He lives in a middle-class suburb in a very nice house, as does Thomas. We sat in his kitchen to talk in 1999, with children playing in the yard behind us. He had a wall of buttons and stickers proclaiming support for union democracy and other liberal and progressive causes; Thomas also has a large collection of such items, including a quilt that his wife, Shelley, made for him out of the dozens of union T-shirts he had.

Somewhat younger than Thomas, Clay is of medium build with brown hair. When he speaks, his affect is calm and measured. He told me:

> For the 1995 contract, two hundred people in Puget Sound came together. I organize people behind issues. They needed a tool. I'm a toolmaker. I have experience with the initiative process and the electoral process outside the union. We decided to use initiative process, gather items to be improved in contract, and get members to sign onto them. We got 3,000 and gave them to contract negotiator Dick Schnieder. We handed out petition packets, pins, stickers, pens. We would go to fairs and parades to get signatures. We have been raising the consciousness of the membership because the information handed out by the union is incomplete. We wanted to raise the expectations, share issues of concern to membership. Our theme is Take It Back, Machinists in Solidarity. You are the union. Fight for the future; respect the past.

It is natural that both groups would talk about their roles as "tools," since machinists make the tools that get enormous things, like jumbo jets, built. Their vocabulary shows how their organizing flows from their identification with their work.

Just as the UDC went to the Labor Day picnic, the MFS attended fairs and other public events to get their word out. Like the UDC, the MFS emphasized organizing the rank and file and the distribution of information to union members. Clay makes many of the same arguments as Thomas: The union's information is incomplete, and the workers deserve more. "The people that are in there, the incumbency, are out of touch with the membership, they're self-serving. They're a very small, select group that has held onto power through threats, intimidation, and other methods."

However, Clay goes to pains to distinguish his group, which was larger and somewhat more effective at achieving its aims (which themselves were less antagonistic to the Administrative Caucus), from the UDC:

> We're not dissident. With the level of support we have and the tack we're pursuing, we're in the mainstream. [The UDC] is taking a completely different tack: Overturn the whole applecart. They don't have experience to run the union. They are adept at pointing the finger. We need to work toward something, get something accomplished. We have. Here we have gotten the bylaws changed. We are getting the membership involved, engaging the membership. We're not pointing the finger. Educating the membership allows them the ability to make a difference. After this is all said and done, we have to run things. I'm not going to take out the International. What we're after is to have a voice and a say in our own destiny. TDU [Teamsters for a Democratic Union, a reform caucus] and UDC are about dismantling structure, when they don't understand how the structure works. Don't derail the train and blow up the tracks. Take over the train.

Clay's group made the antagonism with the union less pronounced than did the UDC. Interestingly, we can see in his remarks that his organization is not founded on the interpersonal relationships that were the backbone of the UDC.

IAMAW librarians Sue Moyer and Virginia Roberts appreciated Clay's orientation toward confrontation with the company rather than the union: "'Take It Back' is essentially people who opted to get involved in leadership. The other group is more extreme."[13] This sentiment may explain why in the lead-up to the 1999 contract, Thomas and UDC activists in Seattle believed that while Clay positioned himself as the voice of the people, he also took advantage of his mainstream credentials. Meanwhile, Clay brought together, on his account, two hundred people to agitate around that contract.

Of course, Clay's rhetorical identification with the mainstream could have partially aligned his objectives with those of the official union. And UDC members are quick to point out that they also have long experience in union office, that they have the same goals as Clay—to educate the membership and take over the union—and that, no matter who undertakes the task, taking over the union is a fairly radical demand requiring dissent from the way the union is currently operating. Clay explained that the issues with the UDC stemmed from their targeting him for not breaking soon enough, or cleanly enough, from the incumbency. To him, UDC members in the Puget Sound got too personal in their attacks. "They don't forget. They're not willing to work even if there is common ground. There is no middle ground. I've tried." He claimed that he did not take it personally. He respected Don Grinde but felt that his leadership lacked democratic process. He objected to talking dirt about the union and its leadership to the media. With regard to the outside world and the company, it was important to present a united front. In other words, Clay's negotiation of the position of "loyal opposition" leaned a little farther toward the loyal than did the New Crew's.

Clay's remarks also gesture toward a mistake that he and the UDC both made in not banding together for more strength and solidarity. Perhaps the greater resources of Clay's organization would have allowed the New Crew to continue past 1996 in Everett; and perhaps the strong propaganda skills of the New Crew there would have aided the MFS in their campaigns. In fact, in 2005, the two groups did collaborate around contract education and agitation.

In any case, both organizations set as their goal to gather and distribute as much information as possible about a range of contract and union issues. These include warnings against offshoring, off-loading, and layoffs; the necessity of defending workers' standard of living; the critique of the union's failure to act consistently in that defense, and the experience of race, gender, and sexual orientation as dividing lines among workers.

The Issues Targeted by Dissidents

It is important to get a sense of the big picture: Boeing throughout the 1990s and into the 2000s enacted the imperatives of neoliberalism, defined cogently by Joel Geier as the

> 25-year long period of economic growth based on the neoliberal model—a model that was for years a great boon to capital but a great misery for the working class. Neoliberal measures were enacted a generation ago—after the long post–World War Two boom and the onset of crisis in the 1970s—to restore capitalist profitability. Those policies involved something called supply-side economics, which included tax cuts for the rich, economic deregulation and privatization, cuts in social welfare, union-busting, and wage-cutting. These policies led to a tremendous buildup of debt. Monetarism subsumed fiscal policy, and cheap credit came to be seen as the solution to economic downturns.[14]

David Harvey similarly explains that neoliberalism is characterized by "deregulation, privatization, and withdrawal from the state," the destruction of former modes of labor and social relations, the valuing of market exchange on the belief that "the social good will be maximized by maximizing the reach and frequency of market transactions," and the bringing of "all human action into the domain of the market."[15] Elsewhere, Harvey argues that neoliberalism was the extension of national and corporate power through finance: "Capital markets. . . . had to be forced open to international trade. . . . Financial power could be used to discipline working-class movements."[16]

Mass layoffs are characteristic of such a regime. In 1997, the Boeing Corporation as a whole employed 234,850 workers. In 2003, that number had dropped by more than 75,000 workers to 159,161. At the time of this writing, that number is just over 150,000.[17] This rapid attrition resulted from Boeing's relentless offensive against the union in contract negotiations in 1999 and 2002. The company had learned from the 1995 strike to offer conciliatory gestures to stave off strikes while at the same time putting forward provisions that undermined job security.

The 1995 strike is the subject of chapter 5. Here I want to lay out in broad strokes the critiques of the Boeing Company and the union put forward by the dissidents across the last two decades. These are that the company, on the neoliberal model, has outsourced more and more work to nonunion shops and temporary workers on-site; it has off-loaded many manufacturing tasks and jobs to overseas plants where the cost of labor is incredibly cheap compared to paying union workers. The resulting layoffs and loss of job security are the biggest complaints and fears of the workers. Declining health benefits and retirement benefits have also been on the table. In each area, the union has resigned itself to losses and concessions. Furthermore, racism and sexism are ongoing problems in the plants, though they are not often discussed. Finally, Boeing had moved shift organization at plants to the irregular workweek, in which employees might work two shifts three days in a row and then have three days off (not necessarily on the weekend). This arrangement is incredibly difficult for workers with families.

Handing Safety Over to Management Teams

There are two areas in which democratic unionists hold the union leadership responsible for cooperating with management: The formation of a joint union-management safety committee and the creation of the High Performance Work Organization (HPWO). Alongside the HPWO, Boeing initiated a Continuous Quality Improvement program designed to streamline production and put pressure on workers to monitor the quality of their product with fewer people on the floor. The joint safety committee replaces the traditional union grievance process, in which a union member would file a complaint to the company about a safety issue in a process governed by the Occupational Safety and Health Administration (OSHA). In this scenario, the company is responsible for correcting the safety problem and workers can sue the company for injuries sustained as a result of uncorrected safety problems. In the team program, union officials and management get together to oversee safety on the shop floor. If a worker is injured, the company no longer bears sole responsibility. Many democratic unionists see this development as a betrayal of traditional union rights and corporate accountability. Thomas describes having to go around his own union safety committee to call attention to the hazards of the shop floor:

> On some of the first OSHA complaints that I filed, I actually had to fight my own union safety committee. I was a steward at the time; I represented the people on the floor. The people working in the manufacturing process facility had some serious safety concerns, and they were right. There were openings where people could actually fall through to a second level; it was a two-level building, and there were just openings and you could just walk right off. There were elevated workstations out there that had openings in the railing, and people could step right off a four-foot drop. There was equipment malfunctioning; there was a serious problem with cranes falling. Of course, the company was saying everything is OK, everything is fixed. And of course, things continued to fall.[18]

When Thomas contacted OSHA, he found himself at odds with the union safety committee. Taking vacation time, Thomas accompanied the OSHA inspector, indicating safety issues and describing his members' complaints. Management demanded that he leave the plant voluntarily or with an "escort," and he left rather than risk losing his job. Subsequently, the company and the union safety committee began a campaign of harassment against him. Several more conversations with OSHA and a costly freedom-of-information request later, Thomas discovered that it was his own union business agent who had asked the company to remove him from the plant during the inspection. "So," he concludes, "the tagline on all of this is that the union safety committee gets you killed on the job."

Administrative Caucus representatives had a different perspective. Roy Moore is a talkative health and safety systems manager at Boeing in the Puget Sound. He had been president of Lodge 751 and clearly represents a mainstream union perspective. A defender of union head Bill Johnson, he finds it productive to negotiate concessions with Boeing to reduce domestic labor costs and avoid offloading. His take on the joint safety program is that, like the HPWO, a safety committee involving both union and management representatives can enforce the contractual obligations of the company and provide safety training to employees. When, in 1999, there was a fatal accident involving a falling crane in the Everett plant, Moore said that the health and safety committee enabled quick investigation, response, and communication with workers on the floor. At the same time, he recognized the benefit to the company in keeping employees— whose work time and skills are valuable—alive and healthy. The company, he said, estimated the cost of injured workers to be hundreds of thousands of dollars (Moore estimated $300,000) per aircraft. He expressed enthusiasm about the "aggressive communication plan" the union was developing with the help of an outside public relations firm.[19] As I will describe in the next chapter, joint safety committees are like HPWO and the Quality through Training Program (QTTP) that seek cooperation between labor and management about core issues, overlooking the fundamental conflict of interest. In particular, reformers are concerned that union cooperation with managerial imperatives undermines the ability to protect jobs in an era of corporate globalization.

Outsourcing, Off-loading, and Layoffs

The danger of mass layoffs predated and has persisted beyond 1995, of course. A 1999 phone conversation with a Boeing public relations spokesperson provides a sense of the company's interests as antagonistic to those of workers. I was traveling in my car in Everett and was just then moving past the Boeing plant. I asked the executive about the recently announced layoffs of more than 40,000 workers. Cheerfully, he replied that the layoffs were good for his stock options. He told me that Boeing's ability to make production leaner made Wall Street happy. (I had queried the company's public relations office to schedule an in-person meeting but did not receive a reply.)

Clearly, the workers at Boeing, fearing if not undergoing layoffs, have interests that are antagonistic to those of the executives and shareholders. Sean Mullin expressed his anger at layoffs pending before the 1995 strike:

> They were taking employees with ten years of seniority and more and putting them out on the street. But what happened, the way I see it, they started inflicting a lot of fear into people through this strike. They were making record profits when they were laying people off. Well, when they decided it was time for the contract to roll around, they hired a bunch of people back: "Well, these people are hungry. They're gonna want to stay at work. They're gonna take what we throw them. Any bone we throw them, they're gonna

take it." Well, the main issues, at least the main issues for me, were on-site subcontracting, subcontracting in general, but on-site was one of the big issues. And our insurance benefits.[20]

Mullin explains well the company's threatening of layoffs in order to negotiate concessionary contracts, ones in which "bones" were thrown to workers frightened of being hungry.

In addition to having fears about the outsourcing of work to outside companies both at home and abroad, Mullin describes how Boeing had begun to bring nonunion employees on site to do the work that previously had been done by union workers, thus undercutting union strength and members' wages. Much of this work was and is performed by temporary workers, as Mullin explains:

> Well, what that would lead to is a situation like they have here in Wichita at the Coleman factory. And they have small . . . temporary service agencies will hire people off the street for five bucks an hour, just anybody they can . . . any *body* they can get in the door, and they'll send them in there. And they'll work them for a while and then they'll send them out the door. Well, they're making five, six dollars an hour. The temp agency's probably making five, six dollars an hour on top of that. Nobody's getting any benefits. Boeing's making all the money, because instead of paying a new hire ten dollars an hour, plus all the benefits and all the FICA matching and all that, all they're paying is straight ten bucks an hour, and they're not having to worry about the workers' comp insurance, because the temps are picking that up, so they're making out like bandits. And then eventually they won't even need any permanent employees.

Keith Thomas described the effects of layoffs and threatened layoffs on morale and productivity in 1999:

> The stress level's phenomenal right now. Everybody's doing everybody else's job. We were threatened on a regular basis up until a few weeks ago. I did a newsletter which actually talked about it to Phil Condit when he was at the aerospace conference. Phil Condit is the CEO of Boeing. One of the things I said at the aerospace conference is we hear all these things about teamwork: Why is it that at our crew meetings we were regularly threatened with losing our jobs by having our work off-loaded? And after a long drawn-out answer on Phil's part, he said well, that's not an effective way to manage, and they shouldn't be doing that. . . . That company is sending work to other plants every day. They're sending it overseas every day. There's entire shops dedicated to off-loading work out there. Their threat's a hollow threat to people because it's already taking place, and people know that. The company's already

announcing layoffs. The company's already taking the same actions they've taken historically since the last decade.[21]

Thomas noted that the pressure had increased since the 1996 merger with McDonnell Douglas.

From 1996 into 1997, Boeing took an increasingly hard line with workers. Thomas and others complained that the company had shifted its management style, from a family-oriented company in which generations of workers could feel secure about having a job for life to one in which rounds of hirings and layoffs followed one another without apparent reason and in which Boeing sought to extract the greatest possible concessions from remaining workers. Thomas described the new "lean and mean" Boeing, emphasizing that the numbers of layoffs had been 40,000 to 50,000 "during the best of times":

> How could you expect management that's gonna do that to its own workers when times are good, how are they gonna treat their workers when times are bad? And times are bad now, and we know how they're gonna treat their workers; they're gonna do the same things they've always done, they're going to lay people off. They're going to destroy families. People are going to lose their homes. People aren't going to be able to do the things for their children that they want to do, that's how the company's gonna take care of it, the company that's got this good image out there.

Union representative Mike Burleigh explained that in future contract struggles, workers need to "be clear on issues, not on heart" to see through company pleas of financial hardship.

> A lot of people want to look at the contract as a heart issue. Boeing really thinks all they have to say is, well, we're broke or we'll ship it somewhere else. And you know they're not broke. Anytime you go out and buy other companies, sure you're going to spend a lot of money and the stockholders are gonna kind of look around and see. But they actually went out and bought almost everything. Like I tell people, if Boeing felt that they had to go out and buy all the furniture factories in the world so everyone will come to them—that's kind of what Boeing has done.[22]

Sean Mullin was also skeptical about the programs that build community image as "having nothing to do with the workers at all. . . . They are a company union-type tactic. It's kind of like quality teams. At Boeing, quality teams are not about quality. They're about playing games and creating charts to justify things that you've already done." I mentioned to Mullin that I saw a lot of charts at the plant, to which he responded, sardonically, "They're chart heavy." Mullin, like all of the other activists I interviewed, is deeply concerned with protecting past union gains. No chart can rationalize the erosion of pensions and health insurance of unionized workers whose parents had fought to preserve them.

Hard-Fought Gains: Pensions and Health Insurance

Part of Boeing's "good image" as a worker- and community-friendly corporation has depended upon the excellent health and retirement benefits it has historically provided its workers. Wichita Local 834 Treasurer Mary Johnson stressed the importance of keeping those benefits: "I'm the type of person who enjoys insurance. I enjoy getting my teeth cleaned."[23] Johnson is a single parent whose commitment to the union is demonstrated in her willingness to negotiate time for her son, her job in the plant as a material processor, and her union participation. A gently spoken black woman with short, reddish hair and very long, well-manicured nails, Johnson noted that her pay grade was only a five when the men around her were sixes, to her boss, who was a ten. She told me that because she had been a dedicated employee, the company owed her the same dedication. She was terrified of layoffs and resentful of threats to her health care.

But Boeing's new approach to management included increasing the cost to the workers of employee health insurance. As Sean Mullin explained at some length:

> They were wanting to cut benefits in areas and add a ten-dollar per office visit co-pay. Well, to a lot of people who don't have as good insurance as we have, or who don't even have insurance, that was a great deal, but to us, we had struggled and fought to have that insurance for a long time. We didn't feel like we should have to give it up when they're making record profits. And Boeing's forecast ever since I hired in there was for this large increase in production—exactly what they're going through. So we knew that they were going to build more airplanes, we knew they were going to sell more planes, but at the same time [they] were willing to tell us that they were gonna cut our benefits off, and that's not acceptable.

Two issues are striking in this commentary: First, Mullin's outrage comes from the fact that workers were becoming more and more productive and Boeing was incredibly profitable. Thus, Boeing's take-backs on insurance seemed unreasonable, an ironic punishment for increased productivity. A second key point is that insurance benefits were something that the union had struggled for, the product of victories in strikes conducted by generations past to be defended in the present if those past struggles were to remain meaningful.

In a sense, the opposition to cuts in insurance is an expression of resistance to the changing corporate culture from a secure and rewarding work environment to a 1990s lean production model. In this context, cuts in even very good benefits signaled the beginning of the end of the gains that had been made in past struggles. Undoing that work is, for union members, unacceptable. Mullin also noted in this conversation that the 1989 strike had prevented changes in the insurance plan. And the plans for reduced benefits were part of what motivated the 1995 strike, a full discussion of which follows.

Likewise, slashes in pension benefits and in cost-of-living increases in those benefits for retirees sparked anger among Boeing workers, whose own future retirement is also at stake. David Clay explained:

> The retirees all have told the International, "This is what we want with the negotiators, we want cost of living for retirees, we want to retire early, and we want more money." And they've come across and said, "Oh, you want the National Pension Plan." No, we didn't say that. We said we want more money, retire early, cost of living for retirees. And they say, "You want the National Pension Plan." No, we don't. That's what they want. I mean, they spent a lot of money, they sent everybody in the bargaining unit a $3.25 priority mail package with a videotape trying to sell us that pension plan.

Clay distrusts both the company's and the union's bids to control the pension plan. In the eyes of union democracy activists, workers could have some control over a company-sponsored plan negotiated in the contract. Clay told me in 1999 that he did not want the International to impose its universal plan on Boeing workers. However, neither did Boeing want to maintain consistent cost-of-living increases for retirees.

Another set of complex issues arises for Boeing workers from the divisions of race, gender, and sexuality. Although instances of discrimination are grieved through union procedures, differential treatment persists.

(Not) Speaking of Gender, Race, and Sexuality

The growing scholarship on race, gender, and sexuality in the labor movement has focused on how these divisions may split the working class and impair solidarity,[24] on how the meanings of work and struggle shift across variously gendered perspectives,[25] on those moments in which divisions are overcome in interracial struggle and unity between men and women,[26] and on the role of militants and radicals in attempting to organize class solidarity while respecting the self-determination of specially oppressed groups.[27] At Boeing, it is clear that these issues need to be addressed. Workers are reluctant to speak about issues of racial and gender-based discrimination in the plants. According to those I asked about it, forms of discrimination are subtle, involving the placement of women in lower-skill and lower-paying jobs and of black men in the more physically arduous jobs such as the paint shop. I was able to speak with a number of Boeing workers about these issues.

At the time of my talk with her at the District 751 lodge in Seattle in 1998, Jackie Boschok was the district recording secretary and had worked at Boeing in Airline Logistical Services for nineteen years. She is a leading member of the Congress of Labor Union Women (CLUW) and the State Labor Council Women's Committee; gender equity is important to her. At the time of the interview, Boeing was facing a lawsuit for racial discrimination. Boschok said, "And the sex question is right there too. . . . I don't think that Boeing overall is as blatant as some companies, but I think that it's there and it's everywhere."[28] She went on:

> I had a girlfriend who, she was a tool-and-die maker, an area in which there were not very many women, and she was hassled with the lead, and she said she didn't want to be a forty-year-old junior person with an eighteen-year-old lead, or a twenty-five-year-old lead, and so she bailed out, and they did incredibly terrible things to her, and Boeing's typical attitude is to punish the victim. They'll move the person or they'll . . . that's typically what Boeing does to women who are having trouble, they move them somewhere else, so they never really, and there's enough places they can move you to.

The subtle placement and treatment of women is part of the organizational culture at Boeing. Boschok recalled that it was not easy joining the Machinists as an activist in CLUW in the 1980s, because many people feared that she would be too radical. She did defy convention by getting an education and finding a job for herself rather than marrying and settling down. "I've always been the unacceptable alternative." It is not only the company, but also the union that needs to change "to make women and minorities more welcome and respected."

Sherri Hood, a petite, round-faced woman in a brown ponytail, had worked at Boeing nine years when I interviewed her, in the area of electrical and sheet-metal assembly. She was a district delegate from Local 894 to District 70. A member of the women's committee, she noted that "Boeing is a man's world, and the union has always been a man's world. And now they're trying to get women more involved."[29] When asked about whether she experienced any discrimination, she said:

> I don't know if I'd say really so much discrimination. But if they have a choice between a man that does something the same way as a woman, chances are

they're probably going to pick the man. I've seen a lot of harassment go on. I've had to fight against that. I can do my job just as good as any guy I've worked with. And if a guy's standing around talking at work, everything's fine with that. But if a woman stops, everybody notices. Women are just more noticeable.

Actually, Hood had laid out a textbook definition of discrimination. On the question of union democracy, Hood acknowledged that the union officials sometimes railroaded outspoken individuals. She expressed hope that the women's committee would help, "because a lot of times, when a woman stood up at a meeting and wanted to say something, that's when the guys would turn to talk to their buddy beside them. I think it's changing."

Madeleine Mueller, a pseudonym, is a slight, soft-spoken, brown-haired woman who said she supported the work of the UDC, although she was not an active member. When I interviewed her in 1998, she was somewhat bitter about the situation for women in the plant: "I think there's going to be real issues with the women because you know they have to file grievances to get their upgrades. And most of the managers don't want to deal with giving women upgrades. And it's like on our union executive board, you have no minorities at all. And I think that's a major issue with them." Mueller notes gender and racial inequity with regard to both the union and the company, both examples of a "good old [white] boy" system.

Historically, the tensions between work, family, and activism have been felt acutely by women, who, as scholar Mary Triece argues, must find ways to negotiate their competing roles.[30] This negotiation is difficult, however, placing enormous burdens on women who want to support their families and be involved in their union while also being responsible for their family in the domestic realm. The good-old-boy system at Boeing has not been very forgiving of women who get pregnant. Denise Harris told me that she had been put on medical leave when she got pregnant:

> Back in those days, women didn't have babies at Boeing. Well, mainly, women didn't work at Boeing, and women my age for sure didn't work at Boeing. I had to go to an arbitration with a lady who was returning from a leave of absence—I mean, returning from layoff—and they asked her if her medical condition had changed, and she said, "Well, yeah, I'm pregnant," and they said, "Well, you can't come to work here." So we had to go to arbitration. It was discrimination.[31]

Harris's co-worker won "lots of back pay. It was a really good win. I haven't seen many things like that happen." I asked her whether there were still issues like that in the plant. She replied, "They would rather you weren't pregnant, they would rather not accommodate you if you are pregnant. They accommodate people all the time for all sorts of reasons, and they should have to accommodate someone who has a pregnancy." She doesn't see this issue as only a women's issue, explaining, "Men will get the ultimate benefit from all of this." A manager said he wanted her fighting for him because "the women's issues are becoming their issues. They're worried about health care, they're worried about day care, they're worried about the things they weren't worried about before." Harris is an optimistic fighter who goes after opportunities to hold union office and to speak out against injustice.

Others have been more effectively beaten down. Arlene Hoaglan, for example, described herself as supportive but "not enamored" of the UDC and its ideas. She spoke of the complex interaction of pay grades, seniority, and gender when it came to being promoted. She had been angry when, as a grade two employee, she was doing grade four work without the accompanying upgrade in pay. Then, when she did demand an upgrade so she would be paid what she was worth, she was put on third shift, despite having a family. She said:

> It was awful, awful. It was the worst. Of course you know my family means a lot to me. I was about ready to quit the job, because—but my dad, I called him and talked to him, and he said I was just tired. And I agree. I was very tired. I had to keep my job. I had to go to third, with less senior people on first. And I was very angry about that. And I think it all came around because I was hollering about, make me a grade four or get somebody else to do the job.[32]

Regardless of her seniority, management would not promote her without making her work nights. Hoaglan did not indicate directly that her shift assignment was designed to punish her for demanding an upgrade or that the choice of shift was made knowing full well that she had family responsibilities. However, both the delay in promotion and the shift assignment are likely indirect forms of gender discrimination. Hoaglan's simple statement, "I was very tired," resounds with the fatigue of all women working the double shift—factory and family—with the added burden of night work.

The union has made efforts toward inclusion of women and minority workers in the union leadership. For example, Mary Johnson was effusive in her excitement about having been chosen to speak to the assembly of the AFL-CIO at its convention held in New York City during the 1995 strike. She felt that her situation as a working single parent touched the crowd and that her inclusion at the podium indicated a sense of solidarity that moved her to tears: "It was such togetherness that made me really know why I was part of a union. See, I'm a real proud person. I'm really proud of being a union member. If you don't stand for something, you'll fall for anything. And I believe in what I do."

Even so, she had noticed some injustices in the plant. Although she herself had not had to file any grievances on race or gender issues, she described the situation of a friend:

> There are patterns of discrimination. Yes. What I notice is when it comes to promotion. You know. They tend to be looked over. I work with a lady, and I know that she's put in for management, and you know she was told that being black and this is what she was told, if you are black and there's a white lady, if she scored higher, the white lady would still get an extra point over her. Because she was white. And we didn't understand that part of it. But this came from management's mouth because she is filing a grievance against it. And it's just like a lot of times they say, well, you need more minorities, and to them, you know when we say minority, we want to say, well, do you have any more blacks because what I noticed during the time they were laying off is they weren't retaining any blacks and they could retain so many, and even though I had as much time as I did and I had a—cause it got so close to me—I had trained so many people, I knew I didn't stand a chance at being retained. The reason is, too, a lot of times is I feel a lot of times blacks and especially women I think, if you speak up and you tell it like it is, that's a no-no.

Again, discrimination at Boeing takes the form of a subtle overlooking of women, black workers (especially women), and outspoken agitators against injustice. In the context of constantly threatened layoffs, there is pressure not to complain about being passed over for promotion. Johnson's emphasis of "Yes," after acknowledging the presence of discrimination, and her repetition of "a lot of times is I feel a lot of times" suggest both hesitancy (building up to an observation through repetition) and emphasis in discussing this delicate topic.

Gary Washington, one of the founding members of the UDC, described how difficult it had been for him as a black man to break into being a robot operator.

> One guy said, "Hey, you've got to let him because we have no black robot operators." So he [another guy] said (he wasn't really thinking on that level), "You're kind of right. There's no Hispanics in our area." But they call me [Gary] the black Mexican. I'm half Mexican, as a matter of fact. You see I look Puerto Rican. They say you're going to have to include at least some minorities in over there, so since I stepped in I think we have four or five now.[33]

According to Washington, Boeing did not have a formal affirmative action policy or clear criteria for hiring and promotion, making the process somewhat arbitrary.

Evidence for claims of antigay discrimination at Boeing is also anecdotal and scarcer, emerging from the interviews with experienced workers and union activists. And there is little research regarding the intersection of gay oppression and rights and the labor movement.[34] A gay union member at the Everett plant spoke with me candidly in a diner in Seattle about the heterosexist culture at Boeing.

Figure 4. Gary Washington, July 14, 1999. Photo by Dana L. Cloud.

A blond man in his early thirties, Joe (who asked me not to use his last name) was angry at his treatment by both the company and the union. He had been a mechanic at Everett for twelve years, but due to mental health problems (some of which stemmed from the stigma of being gay in a predominantly [presumably] heterosexual work environment), he had taken a leave of absence. At Boeing, he was not provided domestic partner benefits, nor did the union include this demand in contract fights. "A lot of people don't talk about the issues; we avoid arguments about this issue."[35]

As Krupat and McCreery argue, most gay and lesbian people are working class, and rank-and-file activism has made progress toward better conditions in both the workplace and the union.[36] Therefore, it is essential that gay and lesbian unionists become involved in the struggle. However, doing so can be uncomfortable, if not outright dangerous, to "out" gay workers involved in union reform. While women and people of color are represented in union governance and among activists, gay and lesbian visibility is low.

Because of routine harassment of gay men especially, Joe felt stressed by the need to maintain a low profile at work. He had been the target of "fag" jokes and commented, "I've been outed several times, and it was tough. There were no threats on my life or anything, but Christians telling me I'll burn in hell, etc. If I'm going to get them to work with me, I have to educate them and be a good boy. But I don't have time to reeducate the whole Boeing Company." He explained that the diversity classes offered through the union did not help and in fact "led to a backlash." (Such backlash is common in corporate diversity training.) He also had noticed stereotyping when the company placed gay workers in jobs. Gay men, he said, were primarily employed in customer service jobs. He was the only gay man working as a mechanic. Lesbian women, stereotyped as more butch, could get jobs on the factory floor more easily than gay men. He concluded the interview on an optimistic note, saying, "I'm trying to get my marbles together. The time off has been good for me. I'm up in the air right now. But I'm thrilled to see women and gays get involved in labor. I've worked with union benefits and union wages, and it has gotten me quite a bit. It's good."

Along with Johnson and Boschok, Joe recognizes the incredible importance of the union to their power and voice at work. All three have been active and outspoken in the union and in criticism of it. To different degrees, they represent the dilemma of criticizing an institution that has done them a great deal of good, with Boschok and Johnson weighing in with more enthusiasm. Illustrated here and throughout the interviews, there is a spectrum of positions along an axis of support for the Administrative Caucus and institution of the union, anger and criticism, and oppositional organizing.

Summary

In this chapter, I have sketched the basic arguments of dissident activists at Boeing. With regard to the company, Keith Thomas, Kelly Vandegrift, David Clay, and others are concerned with providing union members with information and arguments about the real practices and priorities of the Boeing Company as opposed to its stated values and justifications for concessions. An analysis of corporate profitability, antagonism with workers' interests, and routine discrimination against women, minorities, retirees, and new workers is a rhetorical resource for a rank and file organizing itself in its own interests.

In the next chapter, I turn to the dissidents' critique of the union itself. Central to their case is the argument that the union cooperates too much with management, which often takes the form of team and quality programs. In addition, reformers find the union often undemocratic in its practices and unaccountable to its members. Consequently, Thomas, Clay, and the others see their role as motivating others to become more involved in the activities of the union, to mistrust union representatives in contract negotiations, and to develop an independent workers' perspective that can inform their struggles in the long term.

4

The Problem with "Jointness"

In keeping with the traditional union philosophy, the International Association of Machinists and Aerospace Workers' (IAMAW's) vision has been one of maintaining credibility through negotiation with Boeing rather than antagonism. There is perpetual hope that this method will result in job security and other gains. However, time and again, conciliation has been just that: agreement to concessions and the maintenance of friendly team relationships with management at the expense of workers' power against the company through antagonism. As Steve Early and Paul Buhle have each pointed out, the adoption of a posture cooperative with the interests of employers is common among established union leaders.[1] As this chapter will demonstrate, union activists at Boeing have regarded the union as cooperating with management in both the bargaining process and the creation of and participation in joint management safety programs, quality efforts, and productivity programs. Unionists for Democratic Change (UDC) activists label certain union leaders and workers seeking promotion into quality or safety team management positions as "company union" spokespeople and/or "Boeing managers." Technically, workers with jobs in the company management programs remain in the bargaining unit and are not managers, but the labels serve to emphasize the cooperative roles that some officials and workers seek to fill. The union's behavior during the 1995 contract negotiations is a case in point.

Sean Mullin, for example, discussed how union leaders tried to sell the flawed second contract in 1995. Like other UDC members, he recalls seeing the local's president, David Eagle, on television repeating, "This is a good contract. He's holding it in his hand. This is a good contract. I know we're going to buy it. This is a great contract offer. We're gonna buy this. We went out and voted." As soon as the workers rejected the contract, "It wasn't thirty minutes later, David Eagle was on the TV, telling the news media just exactly how bad that contract was." Mullin concluded that the union leadership had made a deal with the company to recommend a contract benefiting Boeing. Union organizer Mike Burleigh gave credence to this idea even as he, too, exulted in the rank-and-file victory:

> The strike of '95 was a blow to Boeing because Boeing felt that we were very small people and that we should not be able to stand up to them like we did. They really was still rocking over that because they never thought that would ever happen. Right after the strike, I kind of took it upon myself to call one of the vice presidents of the company, who used to be our manager, and he came down and talked to us. And he said that he never thought that we would vote the second contract down. And you know, they never learn. And the people really will stand against them again.

Keith Thomas explained that he thought that Eagle behaved during the strike as if he were a "Boeing manager":

> David Eagle is a Boeing manager. In the second proposal [rejected by the rank and file in the 1995 strike], David Eagle went on television and read a letter on television down here that nothing was changed in medical benefits and that this was a good proposal, everything was fine, and this is a good contract and we should buy it. Well, it was an outrageous lie. He's been reelected twice since then, by the way. The contract was over, it doesn't make any difference that people rejected that contract, David Eagle did what he was supposed to do, he read that letter, he got rewarded for reading that letter by getting a paid union position which they had to create in the Quality through Training Program. So the president of our local is a Boeing manager.[2]

Thomas's hyperbolic description of Eagle's role brings into relief the ways that union officials increasingly play quasi-managerial roles, communicating management aims and participating in joint programs that blur the distinctions between union and management. Thomas himself took the training to work in the Quality through Training Program, but he turned down a position in its operation when it was offered to him. Again, the Administrative Caucus does not agree with the UDC that taking such a position makes one aligned with management at Boeing.

In my interviews both in Seattle and Wichita with Administrative Caucus representatives of Local 834 and District 751, it was my impression that most, if not all, are well-intentioned and committed people whose priorities are partially determined by institutional history and structure. They see working inside that structure, no matter how flawed, as the best way to get things done. The conser-

Figure 5. Keith Thomas speaking at the 1996 Conference of the International Association of Machinists and Aerospace Workers. Courtesy of Keith Thomas.

vative roles that such officials can play and have played come, for many, not so much from ill will, power trips, or even sympathy with the company, as they do from commitment to the running of the union, the bargaining process, and the interests of the workers as the officials define those interests. These leaders may not even realize that there is a pattern of conciliation and concession playing itself out over many decades in many unions or that they are part of the institutional machine that reproduces this too often doomed pattern.

Happy meetings with union officials were more characteristic of my visit in Seattle than in Wichita. Indeed, as I drove up once into the gravel parking lot of the little square Local 834 lodge in Wichita and pulled out my video camera, I witnessed union leaders escaping the building through the back door, getting into cars, and driving away. They may have simply had to leave on important business. Or because the Administrative Caucus was suspicious of Thomas and the other dissidents and saw me (rightly) as aligned with the project of union democracy, they may have been afraid of being represented in a negative light. Alternatively, they may simply have wanted to make completing my project, aligned with their internal opposition, more difficult. Whatever the reason, I am appreciative of the time they did eventually spend with me and for the access I had to the union hall and union members.

In this chapter, I will highlight some of the voices of union leadership and Administrative Caucus supporters and their description of their purpose and activities. Then I will describe some examples of what dissidents call "company union" behavior, drawing from the words of the activists. A central theme of the dissidents' arguments is that their leadership behaves in concert with management. One of the most significant arenas in which such behavior is evident, they argue, is in the promotion of joint quality and high performance programs like the High Performance Work Organization (HPWO) and the Quality through Training Program (QTTP).

The Boeing Company had completed its turn toward lean restructuring by the middle of the 1990s. Greenberg et al., in their longitudinal study of the effects of Boeing's organizational shifts on workers, are especially critical of the language and the reality of "teamwork." For executives, managers, and workers alike, the "team" concept (referring variously to elites, quality circles, global "partners," and the whole corporate culture) was what replaced the familialism of a gentler time. Greenberg et al. note that in 1998, CEO Harry Stonecipher told employees that they had to "quit behaving like a family and become more like a team. If you don't perform, you don't stay on the team."[3] Workers asked to participate on managerial quality teams reported that team autonomy and decision-making authority were low and that the rhetoric of teamwork did nothing to assuage the stress of perpetual job insecurity.

Historically, unions have offered a class-specific alternative to managerial "teamwork." However, like much of the rest of the labor movement, the union leadership in the IAMAW went along with joint programs like the HPWO and the QTTP. In such programs, union and management together attempted to bring the workforce in line with corporate goals. This trend toward collaboration fueled dissident agitation and may have generated the will on the part of the rank and file to reject a concessionary contract in 1995. The strike, in one worker's words, gave the rank and file the sense that "this thing"—the union, their future—was theirs.

Spokespeople for the IAMAW

I begin with union leaders because their voices largely represent the logic of cooperation identified by union activists. Even so, their stories exhibit impressive nuance toward the relationship between union and management. The IAMAW, like most industrial unions, has a bureaucratic structure involving elected positions of president, secretary, treasurer, and other officers; elected business representatives for districts and locals, who manage grievances and other everyday requests and problems on the floor; and stewards, who can be elected (as in Wichita) or appointed (as in IAMAW District 751 in the Puget Sound).

Caucuses inside the union's locals and districts run slates for these offices and propagandize for their candidates during union elections. Holders of these offices also hold a wide range of views and believe sincerely that they are representing union workers' interests.

In general, unions as institutions serve three purposes: First, they represent workers during contract negotiations and organize the logistics of a strike when it happens. Second, the union represents workers on the shop floor between contracts, using a system of stewards and business representatives to channel grievances to the company. Regular union meetings, generally sparsely attended, report on union activities and progress (and rarely are sites for all-out democratic deliberation of union activities). Finally, organizing new members into the union is a central goal of union leaders. Because Boeing in Seattle is a closed shop, organizing new employees into the union is automatic. In Wichita, however, where union membership is voluntary, it is unclear how much in the way of resources goes into organizing to increase the union's numbers. Mike Burleigh, a stout black man sporting a beard and mustache, was a paid organizer for Local 834 in Wichita. He described his duties to me:

> Well, what I do mainly is a lot of my work is meeting with new people. When Boeing was hiring a lot, I would meet with like thirty or twenty people at a time when they come in. We got an agreement that the organizer can meet the new people as they come in. So I go in and explain a lot of things to them and talk to them. And then they moved it to an auditorium where we was meeting a hundred at a time, and I talk to them, explain a lot of things that [we] had going on, talk about the strike, purpose of strikes and stuff like that. *And let them know that we're not here just for strikes. Ninety percent of our contracts are settled without a work stoppage, without a strike, so a lot of people think that's all we're about because that's all they see.* Then when I go out and I meet people. I work all shifts. I meet 'em, talk to 'em if they got a problem with the union, and I can understand people having a problem, and some of it is just perception, perceiving how things are, you know. But we have to let people know, too, that someone has to be a go-between between the company and themselves and if they don't have anything, they're in trouble. We're kind of, not lawyers, but kind of like a representative in legal matters of contracts and stuff like that, keep them on line with absenteeism, you know, and stuff like that, and help them understand what the contract states they can do and cannot do.

I have emphasized Burleigh's reassurance to prospects regarding strikes to highlight how union representatives see their role as servicing members rather than organizing them in a struggle against the company. A bit later in the conversation, Burleigh explained that new workers fear strikes, and he reassures them, "I'm not going to try to put you on strike. You get to vote if you're going on strike." Burleigh's comments contradict his observations later in our discussion that the strike is what teaches people what the union is about. In recruiting, he downplays the possibility of a strike and reinforces the image of the union as peaceable and cooperative negotiators with the company, seeking to avoid strikes through concessions. The major role of the union, in Burleigh's pitch to new workers, is as a legal and educational agent of the company that regulates what workers can and cannot do, effectively serving what sounds like a management role.

The main emphasis in union activities in both Wichita and the Puget Sound is on education. In Wichita, Garland "Bear" Moore, who was vice president of the local at the time of the interview, commented, "We have to teach people why this is happening. We have to make it their decision. It's their decision what to do, but they have to have all the facts, they have to know why it's important. They have to see what's going on."[4] He went on to discuss how many members do not automatically understand the extent to which the company subcontracts and off-loads jobs and therefore do not understand when it comes time to strike why solidarity is important.

In Seattle, education is such a priority that the district has an office and staff devoted to the tasks of member education as well as an archive of union documents. The education directors and librarians of District 751 of the IAMAW were, at the time of my research, Virginia Roberts and Sue Moyer. They spoke with me at length about the purposes of the union. Moyer and Roberts's office organizes education programs for stewards and, to a lesser extent, members at large on collective bargaining, rules for stewards, labor history, and "advanced" topics, for example, on sexual harassment and economics. Stewards in the IAMAW in District 751 are appointed, not elected, on the rationale that the union needs to control the way that the union is represented. (Similarly, while some unions elect negotiating committees, in the IAMAW the negotiating committee is appointed.)

There is a great deal of emphasis on steward training and discipline; stewards are expected to represent their workers to the union, but they also "need to be able to articulate what the union stands for." Stewards must enforce the contract (holding the company accountable and working out conflicts informally) on the shop floor and must support the union's political action committee (PAC). They are also charged with building union solidarity among "antiunion people." It is unclear whether dissenters inside the union are among those perceived as antiunion and in need of solidarity lessons.

Roberts described the overall role of stewards and other representatives in the union structure:

> Even though it sounds sort of not democratic, the structure that we have here, we have currently 37,000 members in the Puget Sound area, and the contract establishes the number of stewards that we can have who represents a specific area. So these people that you have to choose from as stewards are people who are really working in that specific part of the plant. And this is a closed shop, so we have to be careful about who represents the union in this process, because we can have entire jobs that are entirely in the union, and if they were to elect their own representative, that would actually very much be anarchy.
>
> But we have currently sixteen elected business representatives, and we have elected local lodge officers and district officers, district council elders, and some other kinds of things, so there are a lot of elected positions within the union. But the steward is viewed as someone who must . . . It's essential that that person understand what the labor movement, be an advocate for the union, and that sort of thing, and we can't trust that to a [inaudible], people who may not even understand their own union.

Stewards survey their members in advance of contract negotiations and relay developments—selectively—to their members as talks progress. Roberts and Moyer explained that in a workforce as large as Boeing's, it was impossible for everyone to be involved in or feel included in negotiations. Having meetings between negotiators and stewards is a mechanism in place to facilitate communication.

Everett New Crew activists Don Grinde and Tom Finnegan were skeptical. In a group conversation at Alfy's Pizza in Everett, Finnegan claimed that appointed shop stewards take away "the power of the rank and file on the shop floor to enable us to address the issues that we feel are important to us."[5] When I asked which people—senior or junior—usually were appointed, Finnegan replied, "Just their people," going on to explain that what that meant was workers who campaigned for the Administrative Caucus. Grinde pointed out that stewards were loyal to the Administrative Caucus because stewards have protected jobs during layoffs.

Roberts and Moyer explained that since being hired by the union in 1986, they perceived the organization to have become much more open and transparent, whereas before "stewards and active members were really afraid to show any sort of dissent from the mainstream leadership," according to Roberts. They marked the transition with the election of Bill Johnson as union president, replacing Tom Baker. Ironically, Johnson had nearly been beaten in an election by David Clay, whom the librarians regarded as a model steward, a knowledgeable worker, and an important resource in curriculum development—but also as strident and impractical.

I asked Roberts and Moyer what they thought about dissidents who challenged the appointment of stewards and other practices they perceived as undemocratic. While recognizing that "dissenters have legitimate issues," they said that they could have "more of a sense of humor" in delivering their criticisms. They also emphasized how dissenters were more critique than action. They felt that members of Machinists for Solidarity (MFS) and the UDC should work within the existing structure to make change. Roberts commented: "Now try being responsible. It's easy enough to stand up and criticize how the leadership is doing things, but trying being responsible every day for enforcing the agreement that you have, for answering to people's problems and questions on a daily basis, and meet all those commands, and then do that, and then decide, now how do you get in charge of this organization and steer it." At the end of our conversation, Moyer and Roberts expressed skepticism about dissenters inside unions, distinguishing between a moderate movement inside and the creation of a whole other system. Yet, Moyer acknowledged, "They have legitimate issues, there's absolutely no doubt about that." And they acknowledged that working within a secretive structure, never trying to get in trouble, leads to "less enlightened leadership" than the shot of idealism that reformers offer.

Both Roberts and Moyer supported the union PAC. Most unions have political action committees, funded independently from dues accounts, that organize and fund campaigns for political candidates who are perceived as being friendly to labor. However, these PACs also use dues funds for political work that is not supported by all of the members. As Roberts explained, "The district is very involved legislatively, by having a legislative liaison department, people from the local lodges who participate in the legislative community and do lobby, testify at legislation, and that sort of thing. So, you know, a certain portion of that is supported by dues dollars, but not individual contributions to campaigns." Generally, union representatives dismiss the dissidents' criticisms of the union as undemocratic. For example, Mike Burleigh, a paid organizer, told me that the union "does have" (an implicit response to the charge that it does *not* have) democracy:

> This union does have it. We, in my opinion, I believe we do a very good job of communicating with the people. At least I do. Anytime I talk to any of my members, I tell them to come to the meeting. You know. We could have all 8,000 people here at these meetings. We'd have to open up the doors to let them in. But a lot of times the people don't choose to come to the meetings. And that's point blank. We give out literature. I pass out literature by the tons,

different stuff. Some people say it might not be enough, but we do pass out a lot of literature. And all our members know where this meeting's at. If they don't, they should, because it's in our *Plain Dealer* [the Wichita labor newspaper] and our newspaper and all that kind of stuff. So they know where the meeting's at. But a lot of people choose not to come to the meeting because they think that's just for stewards, my steward can handle it, and stuff like that. But it's really hard to get people to come to meetings, it's just like church meetings.

Lack of rank-and-file involvement is a key issue in democratic unionism. Bringing new people into activism inside the union is extremely difficult whether you are sitting in a paid union position or the seat of a reformer or dissident. However, critics of internal union politics might observe that the union officials have less interest in bringing out thousands of people to meetings than rank-and-file organizations would and that an organization that people felt was "theirs" would draw more active participation.

Acting Like a Company Union?

I believe that the attitudes and alignments of members of the Administrative Caucus in the IAMAW at Boeing vary widely. On the one hand, some representatives of the official union defend the practice of appointing stewards (in Seattle) and endorse team programs with management (like HPWO, safety teams, and QTTP). Others are more ambivalent about these practices. In addition, while some representatives seem committed to determining and maintaining a rather conservative, concessionary course for the union, others are open to the reforms advocated by union democracy activists. There appeared to be a large amount of middle ground.

In Seattle, Stan Johnson occupied the latter location, telling me he thought it best to remain independent. Some activists, he thought, were "too extreme, that tend to come off so extremely negative, and yeah, people are going to put up barriers and they're going to fight because they see a fight coming at them."[6] He criticized the others for lumping all the union officials together and for taking complaints about the union to the media in ways that tar activists as troublemakers and damage the union's credibility in ways that seem antiunion. Unlike the others, he appreciates the Quality through Training Program as a resource for workers and sees a reason for appointing stewards in an enormous organization in which a mass election for stewards could become ugly and divisive on the floor. And he supports union meeting attendance as a prerequisite for running for office. His position is measured: "I've been on both sides. I've been on the opposition side, and now I've been on the incumbent side, so I've seen both, and I've changed my views. I don't see everything as evil." He said he thought it was easier to make change from the inside than from the outside, although he also relied on UDC activists to provide a radical flank that could pressure the union leadership in a healthy way. In a conversation among the Puget Sound activists in 1999, he recognized how opposition ideas have been implemented due to the pressure of activists who, having "gone up there like a faith-healing preacher," will never get credit for their efforts.

In Wichita, I had a conversation with another complex figure, Garland "Bear" Moore, who in 1998 was vice president of the local. He is a straightforward, no-nonsense speaker. "I try to let my actions speak for me rather than words," he said. "I firmly believe that you can teach somebody how to say the right things, but you can't teach somebody to get the job done." He was very proud of the workers for turning down the contract in 1995 (at which time he was not an officer in the union). He expressed a commitment to membership education about outsourcing, union busting, wages, and work conditions, and to a recruitment campaign among new hires: "They're a different breed of calf, you hand them a piece of paper and they read it and they want more, they want to read this stuff, they want to know what's going on." He was skeptical about politicians, citing an example of a Kansas politician who had promised to vote against the North American Free Trade Agreement (NAFTA), and then turned around and voted for it. A believer in the labor movement, he said he'd like to see everyone working "on the same side of the fence."

During this conversation, Moore hinted at intrigue in the ranks of union power. In 1995, responding to numerous complaints about lack of representation and lack of service on the part of union leaders, IAMAW officials from the southern district intervened in union business, taking over the District 70 office and taking control of the district from Dale Moore. Ron Eldridge was suspended as directing business representative. In 1998, an alternative slate ran candidates in a local election. They were defeated but later charged the Administrative Caucus with fraud, including instances of missing ballots, illegal absentee ballots, and other violations. Moore was not aligned with Thomas or the UDC but had been part of this alternative faction. "There have been two factions in this local for a number of years. It's pretty much like any other organization. You have an extreme side, this is my perception only. You have an extreme side and you have the norm, the people who have been there forever. And a group got together and made another faction, and for the most part they won the election with the new ticket and there are hard feelings on both sides." My impression was that by the "extreme side," he was referring to Thomas and the UDC.

He and his group attempted, in his view, to strike a middle ground. "I am not an extremist where I think we should bleed all over the newspapers. I think you should pick your battles. I don't think you should make every issue a battle. . . . I'm not a supporter of Keith's. Some of his ideas are not bad, but we two have chosen different directions in which to bend." He agreed with the reformers that things had not been done correctly or "by the book" in the union and that there was too much secrecy. He said he wanted to restore procedures that enabled the members to decide on issues affecting their fate. He ended the interview by stressing, repeatedly, "Labor people aren't bad. . . . Unions are not all bad." The exhortation not to "bleed all over the newspapers" bespeaks an awareness of the risks of public perception of division and corruption inside the union. Outsiders, including the company and the government, may use these issues as a pretext for weakening union power relative to the company.

Despite their professed commitment to the same ideals, even some members of the Administrative Caucus found themselves in opposition to Moore and his slate. UDC members and other reformers challenged the ways in which established union leadership devoted resources to external electoral politics. They charged the union with behaving as a company union when it comes to contract negotiations and joint programs. Especially, they objected to union leadership's concessionary stance in negotiations, failure to share crucial information with the rank and file, and lack of transparency about union decision-making processes.

In a conversation held in 1999, union negotiator Dick Schneider told me that the union negotiating team was not planning to push hard against off-loading work to other countries in the current contract. Surprised, I asked journalist Molly McMillin, who covered Boeing for the *Wichita Eagle,* whether she had heard about this strategy. She confirmed Schneider's remark: "I think they said that they're going to fight to keep jobs that are going to other U.S. companies. Their focus is going to be work that goes to other American companies. And it sounds as if the work that goes overseas, is going to, they say, have to be addressed by Congress and that the whole Airbus competition and fair-trade agreements and all that is the proper forum to try to do something real about that. They've been very open about that."[7] McMillin also reported that the company planned layoffs of more than 4,000 people in Wichita in the coming year despite a year of record-breaking productivity and profits. About upcoming contract negotiations in 1999, she said that there had been extensive conversation between the union and the company at high levels, so there "aren't going to be as many surprised, maybe they kind of already know where each other is coming from." She confirmed my impression, garnered from my conversation with negotiator Dick Schneider, that the relationship between union and company was cozier than it had been in past years. At the same time, as Moyer and Roberts explained, the parameters of international labor are shaped in trade legislation. "We have no industrial policy to protect us in that regard," Roberts said. "We need to be pushing for industrial policy as a labor movement."

Such a local retreat from the fight against the off-loading of jobs (and reliance on outside agency rather than the union's power to make demands on the company) is one thing that led the UDC and, to a lesser extent, the MFS to call the IAMAW a company union. Gary Washington expressed frustration with "people at the top" of union locals and districts. Like Thomas, Washington called attention to the ways in which union leaders seemed to attempt to represent both the workers, in the union, and management in the enforcement of quality of work programs. He commented, "I see that as playing both sides of the fence too much."

"The Membership's Getting the Joint": The Problem with HPWO and QTTP

Joint programs are one avenue through which Boeing can convince unions to accept concessions in exchange for increasing employee voice in training, quality regulation, and safety issues. Members of the UDC and other critics see this exchange as a sellout. Keith Thomas told me about the similarities between negotiations in 1989 and (at the time of the interview) upcoming contract talks in 1999:

> There was a lot of contention because of the 1989 strike. The company made a proposal that the union didn't bring to us. They said it was such a bad proposal and there were essentially no changes—the company had simply shuffled some numbers about benefits and pay packages—that they weren't going to bring it to us. There was a lot of dissension in the union in general over the fact that they didn't get to vote on that proposal.[8]
>
> It was in 1989 that they negotiated in the Health and Safety Institute and their Quality through Training Program, which of course resulted in more paid [union] reps. And they passed that as a gain of the 1989 contract.
>
> Well here you've got your rank-and-file member out there on the floor, who's supposed to believe his union leadership. It's just like right now they're telling us the same things they told us in 1989: Support your union leadership. We're supposed to do what they tell us. Now how in the world are we supposed to know that they've been told to lie to us and told to accept the contract, which was bad.

Here Thomas also noted that the QTTP was not necessarily good for workers even though it was presented to workers as a benefit of the contract.

On the other side of the issue, I met Seattle unionist Curtis Thorfinson, who was a "career guide developer" in the QTTP. Nearing retirement, his primary contract concern was about preserving pensions. He moved onto the QTTP sales site advisory board, ironically, because on the floor he was performing too many jobs that had been combined as a result of new work-flow organization. On the one hand, he defends workers on the floor who lack adequate training for their work. On the other, his primary job is to visit each work area and get an accounting of all of the knowledge, skills, and abilities one would need to perform those jobs. These skill sets become the basis of learning modules used in training and are posted on the Internet. The generalizability of skills allows people who have never done one kind of work to adapt quickly to it.

I shared my concern that documenting each job and sharing detailed skill sets with management might allow them to combine jobs and replace workers more easily, in addition to enabling members' career choices. Thorfinson said he once had held these concerns but saw the QTTP overall and his contributions as helpful to workers. He said he got reassurances from the union and the company that existing job descriptions, pay grade categories, and seniority systems would not be undermined by his work. His perspective: "Knowledge is great, bring it on, tell me more, I want to know."[9]

Thus, a number of union reformers felt that the training opportunities afforded by Boeing to workers both enabled layoffs and job combinations and presented the company as having workers' interests at heart. Gary Washington, however, embraced the training opportunities afforded him by Boeing, moving up in 2006 into a salaried supervisory position. (In 1998, he said that management was tempting because the union was no better. He called attention to how management tried to promote and train all the good stewards to get them off the shop floor.) At the same time, he was cynical about the new quality and performance programs: "It seems like they always come up with these new programs every three or four years and try to shove it down our throats, when really they need to come to us and ask us, 'How can we help you do your job better? What can we give you? Naw, but they want to spend two million dollars."

David Robertson, a longtime Boeing employee in Wichita, is a white man in his forties (at the time of the interview), a bit weathered and craggy. A longtime Boeing worker, he craved the sense of community among workers and the unity that binds people together through tough times. "If I know your family, your mother, your brothers, I'm going to be more apt to take care of and watch over you."[10] Raised on a farm, he looked to Boeing for the future of his daughters. He tells a long story about how, after his nose was broken during the strike (in the process of raising a tent), Sherri Hood, "a little bitty gal" (a District 70 delegate and women's committee leader) working security, looked after him. He joked with passersby that Sherri was "the lady that done this, please don't let her near me again, my God she'll kill me after that." Robertson had held numerous union offices, including that of Lodge 70 president, when I met him in 1998. He opposed the company's targeting of young people and retirees for lower wages and retirement pay and was angry about the two-tier wage system that remained even in the second contract rejected by members. He expressed some appreciation for Keith Thomas's point of view, saying, "Me and Keith fight a little bit on politics. But he's got the right to speak." Although energized by the rank-and-file decision, he represents a fairly mainstream union position. He told me why he appreciated the joint programs:

> Because I don't want to kill the goose that laid the golden egg. I want Boeing to make a profit. As long as they make a profit, I'm gonna keep a lifestyle for my children that I've got right now. That's what my father done for us. I feel like the Health and Safety Institute that I'm involved with, that the members vote on—four of us, two for first and two for second—the health and safety to me, if I can send somebody home that night that I've been able to help change a process that Boeing has that's unsafe, send them home will all five fingers to pick up their kid, or their grandchild, and also our QTTP they call it, which is Quality through Training, a lot of our members are using that and getting their different degrees, bachelor's, master's, you know, and these are people that are sheet metal workers and people look at them like, they don't know nothing but how to [buck?; unintelligible] a rivet. We've got a lot of members that are really using those programs, and that's getting them educated to where if they do phase out a job, they've got the education to move into something better, to keep that lifestyle for their kids.

Ironically, QTTP is a program that not only provides worker education but also enables layoffs as workers become more skilled in performing multiple jobs. Even at the turn of the twentieth century, author David Montgomery notes, workers immediately recognized the perils of "teaming up" with management. During the emergence of the first industrial unions, workers held knowledge specific to their trades and born of their experience that made them the experts in the workplace and indispensable to its operation. Organized workers, including those in the strong Machinists union, resisted Frederick Winslow Taylor's scientific management. Machinists in Worcester, Massachusetts, passed around Taylor's book *Principles of Scientific Management* to learn and strategize in response.

Executives attempted to reshape work relations to improve their efficiency and eliminate waste in the name of the greater good. Montgomery writes that Taylor and his coconspirators "had agreed that to harmonize the social order through soaring productivity also meant to diminish the worker's 'class-consciousness' by doing away with his 'class grievances' and 'in every way' making 'the individual working man more of an individual.'"[11] But attempts on the part of management to implement shop committees or team labor-management councils, and thus to dissolve workers' sense of collective belonging, met with resistance from unionists who argued that workers' power depended on their independent and antagonistic organizations.

HPWO and QTTP ask workers to become more productive in exchange for more employee voice in the production process; thus, they are part and parcel of a neoliberal paradigm in U.S. manufacturing. UDC member Madeleine Meuller called such programs "antiunion strategies. They pick your brain, and then you don't get paid for it. It's like [with the training] you can do this and you can do all these different jobs, and we don't have to pay you any more."[12] Likewise, Denise Harris commented, "If the company has programs that they want, to eventually lay people off, I don't think we ought to be involved in it. There's the Boeing Company and there's the union, and the union is to protect the people. We're not here to help them run their company. And I don't agree with us being too actively involved with them around their company because we have too much to lose by it."[13] The Machinists union at Boeing cooperated with the initiation of this organization, which, like Total Quality Management (TQM) and other similar programs, speed up the work process and enable the layoff of now unnecessary production workers (since other workers have taken on the work of one or two others). Mike Parker and Jane Slaughter argue that these programs provide the illusion of improvement in employees' work lives while increasingly enforcing the rate and quality of production. Members of the UDC and the MFS are vocal in their opposition to both the company and the union. With regard to outsourcing, off-loading, and layoffs, they call attention to profitability of the company that outsources, lays off tens of thousands of workers, reduces pensions and insurance benefits, and tolerates discrimination by race and gender.

I am reminded of reading an interview with workers during the UPS strike of 1997. A striker had been discussing management initiatives to streamline and harmonize the workplace. Asked what he thought about the language of "teams" becoming common as a way of co-opting union leaders by articulating their interests to those of management, the worker replied, "I don't need their f***ing team. I've got my team. It's called the Teamsters." Don Grinde wrote in a letter to me, "The company has implemented a new system for leads and the union has no say. They are called Team Leaders. The union made a grave tactical error. They forfeited any right in choosing these individuals. It is entirely up to management."[14]

Dissidents in the IAMAW at Boeing circulated massive numbers of handbills explaining the problems with management-labor joint committees, new models of lean production (also known as Toyotaization), and other team projects. An industry publication describes the imperative to "get lean": "These days it isn't enough for a company merely to cut costs. It needs to streamline processes while improving quality, becoming nimble while responding quickly to customer demand, and empowering employees while increasing profits. . . . At its root, Lean is about remaining competitive in a rapidly changing global marketplace."[15] Boeing undertook the implementation of Lean in the late 1990s, including a portable classroom called the "Lean Green Training Machine" to educate workers in lean manufacture and inculcate in them the "Lean spirit."

Rank and file machinists, however, doubt the promise of such programs to "empower workers." Starting in 1996, they engaged in concerted protest against streamlining shop-floor workers right into the garbage bin. In June 1996, the union organized a protest to let Boeing executives "know you didn't go on strike for 69 days to have your job eliminated."[16]

In response to such pressures, the UDC and the New Crew distributed educational materials from the University of Massachusetts Labor Extension Program warning that new processes and technologies "can eliminate the need for whole job classifications outright," "threaten seniority provision," demand "continuous change," enable contracting work out, and generally "undermine or even bypass contract protections."[17] "The common thread [in *kaizen*, Corrective Action Teams, employee involvement, steering committees, HPWO, etc.] is that management is sitting down with members of the bargaining unit to discuss changes in work processes. But these approaches generally leave the union in a weak position."

David Clay identified an additional problem with the joint programs: They bring some unionists into quasi-management positions that, in turn, render the union more aligned with management and less militant at the top:

> Well, what happens is, *jointness means that the union membership's getting the joint,* the people that are put in these positions, this goes along with General Motors and UAW, Ford, and the rest of them, the people that are, it's political appointments from the union to people out on the shop floor that could possibly be some kind of political rival or people that they can't fill them off just because they're not elected offices they can put them in, they can put them in these joint programs, and then it creates a pseudounion, pseudomanagement kind of position. They're kind of inept on nebulous position, and in these positions then, you're able to negotiate. It's like, there's negotiations going on,

> beyond the negotiations there's agreements being made good on the contract,
> you know, we have a couple of them here at Boeing that the whole populated
> sector from the union, they're nothing but political appointees.

Clay's impression has been that the union designates the workers who will take
part in team programs in order to give the union back-room influence with the
company.

Representing the union's position, Sue Moyer said that the HPWO and the
QTTP were beneficial to workers because the QTTP offered workers education that allowed workers to learn new skills. The union negotiated a provision
that allows each worker several thousand dollars each year for further education outside the company as well. However, the perspective of dissidents is that
these programs make layoffs profitable, enabling workers to perform—under
a great deal of stress and without attendant raises in pay—work that may have
been done before by three or four people. Further, the dissidents argue that the
programs align union workers with the interests of the company in an ideological effort to win worker goodwill and overcome the kind of antagonism that
could lead to a strike against outsourcing and layoffs. It is for these reasons that
authors Adrian Wilkinson and Hugh Willmott argue that workers and scholars
should resist quality evangelism to "make quality critical."[18] Workers may be
"responsive to initiatives that link their job security and prospects to changes in
work organization, including changes that intensify their work." However, such
efforts "are underpinned by structures of ownership and control that condition
the focus and limits of employee and 'involvement' within the employment relationship."[19] Likewise, Alan's Tuckman's history of TQM calls attention to the
ideological significance of a rhetoric that accepts the basic market relationship
while redefining "quality" in ways that benefit the employer.[20]

Even a few union officials have serious criticisms of the QTTP, HPWO, and
Joint Safety Team concepts. Denise Harris put it succinctly: "When you're part
of the Boeing team, then, when The Boeing Company's not doing so great, you're
more than likely wanting to help them out even more, and that's where all of
our concessions have come in the past." Mike Burleigh told me that he was also
suspicious of the team concept:

> They used to have this phrase, *empowerment,* we're gonna empower you to do
> this, and when I was on the shop floor they asked me to come to a meeting
> and talk about empowerment and introduced it, you know. And I was kind
> of one of the vocal stewards on the floor, so I wasn't saying anything in that
> meeting, and some of the managers say something's wrong. So he'd ask me
> after the meeting, what's wrong? I said you can't empower me to do something

and take it back the next day. And so if you empower me, I want to do it all. And so you start empowering people to worry about somebody else's paycheck and management need to manage, and management will always step in at the wrong time and take back the power. And that's part of that team concept. I don't have a problem with being on the team, but I want to know that the team is pulling for me, too. But it don't go both ways 90 percent of the time.

Critics of these programs feel not only that management still holds all the cards in team programs, but also that QTTP is a sham. For all that, the union still participates in the program. For example, Keith Thomas pointed out that Boeing historically had a reputation for superior quality, but with the advent of the new quality programs, quality control, ironically, has suffered:

Corporate America has redefined quality. A classic example: Boeing has a monopoly. There has been a lot of company loyalty. It used to be that the company took this job very seriously, about building the best airplanes. Now corporate America says you don't have to build something as well as it possibility can be built, just to pass. Anything over that is non-value-added cost. So there's actually less quality with these new quality programs. One manager said they're not about building airplanes; they're about adding value to stocks and company. Building airplanes is secondary to that. They can become slumlords and make their profits.

In this conversation, Thomas described a shift in the meaning of "quality" as a kind of doublespeak in which "quality" becomes a synonym for profits rather than for old-fashioned pride in the work.

Don Grinde, likewise, lamented the shift to lean production and the pressure for greater productivity from fewer workers. A member of the overhead crane crew in Everett—an incredibly important job since the cranes move all the parts of the plane around the biggest plant in the world in the process of constructing large aircraft—he made a DVD showing him and his crewmates at work. The video celebrated both the people and the work. He wrote to me: "The thought of us working our entire lives inside Boeing and then have absolutely nothing to show for it when we were done was unacceptable to me." The pride he feels is often at odds with the imperatives of the HPWO. Indeed, his same letter to me continues, "In terms of the union and The Boeing Company, it has only gotten much worse. Who really knows how much fight is left in people on the shop floor. The union is only a paper tiger to most members. The company is hell bent on a strategy almost surely to bring much hardship on our community."

Significantly, the letter also expresses grief on behalf of the company: "The sad thing is for me, Boeing has everything to pull it off! To really become a World

Class Company. They fail to capture the hearts and minds of the workers. Very few have real passion for life at Boeing. You see, the workers only want the company to be loyal to them and they will do the same for the company. When the workers do well and cut costs, the company reward them by offloading work. . . . The guys on the floor want jobs for our families and kids. We want a secure pension with decent medical. That about sums up what we need."

Grinde's conclusion is that worker loyalty comes from treating workers with respect. The HPWO and similar programs operate as a kind of shortcut; instead of offering workers the benefits they deserve, the company presents them with the illusion of voice. Union leaders participate in this illusion. Thomas explained that union people who help to oversee HPWO become compromised in a conflict of interest. "It's not in their interest to defend the rank and file. Union people involved with HPWO are Boeing managers. Putting union officials in these positions makes them managers, puts people working under them that they have to manage for the company."

Thomas summed up the dissident critique of the union's cooperative role with company management: "The company crisis is fabrication. Our labor unions, the leadership of them, the main disagreement they have with corporate America is how to manage our labor. They want their piece of the pie. They can keep going like this even though unionization levels are lower than in the 1930s. Why aren't they changing? They can continue to decline and keep their jobs. We lost a few million jobs in the workforce, but union management won't lose their jobs." Thomas's comment that union officials get to keep their jobs speaks to the analysis put forward by Paul Buhle: Union leadership becomes an entrenched class, separate from the rank and file, with different interests, including preserving their paid union jobs and credibility with the company in a historically conservative institutional environment.[21]

Summary

I have argued that the development of dissident organizations relies upon interpersonal bonds, an understanding of solidarity, and an antagonistic stance (to varying degrees) toward company and union. From this dissident stance, members of the UDC and the MFS in both Wichita and the Puget Sound mounted a steep critique of the official union's cooperative arrangements—including joint safety, team, and quality programs—and set out the goal of organizing and representing a fully educated and involved rank and file.

The realities of neoliberalism—manifest as rampant off-loading, offshoring, speedup, and layoffs—made these tasks profoundly difficult, as union leaders in this period assumed the necessity of concessions. However, the 1995 strike shook the union and the company and interrupted the steady implementation of neoliberal measures at Boeing. The 1995 strike demonstrated that when workers push from below, they can win gains from the company and hold the union, their fighting organization, accountable to the interests of the workers they represent.

As Keith Thomas put it in one of his email *Floormikes* reporting on the IA-MAW Aerospace Conference (1998):

INCREASE THE INVOLVEMENT OF UNION MEMBERS

To accomplish anything the people are going to have to get involved. Just waiting for life to happen can bring some real nasty surprises these days. For the most part it is the average union member who is missing from this conference. If the union is sincere about wanting to set up a dialog with the rank and file then they are going to have to quit attacking those who have a different approach than theirs.

The 1995 negotiations and subsequent strike against Boeing proved that the leadership is out of touch with the rank and file of the union.

Boeing is busily planning our futures. We should at least be as interested in our futures as the company is.

In the next chapter, I describe how the experience of the strike and how its aftershocks generated lessons for labor today.

5

The 1995 Strike and
the Rejection of the
Second Contract

During 1995, Boeing had eliminated nearly 35,000 union jobs, 26,000 of these in the Puget Sound area. Job security thus was central to the workers' demands as they entered contract negotiations, along with shorter contracts, wage increases, and improvements in safety, health, and benefits, even for laid-off workers.[1] The largest concerns for the workers were subcontracting and outsourcing. International Association of Machinists and Aerospace Workers (IAMAW) President George Kourpias gave voice to fighting words, accusing Boeing of "punching holes in America's future." The union members approved a strike authorization vote in September after the union brought the company's "last, best, and final offer" to them. The first time, the union recommended rejection of the offer, and it was voted down. The workers went on strike on September 13. In November, the company came forward with a second offer. Michael Cimini summarizes, "On November 19, a tentative agreement was reached between Boeing and the IAMAW. Although the IAMAW bargaining committee unanimously recommended acceptance of the pact, the rank and file soundly rejected it. Union members said that they were dissatisfied with the contract offer because it still called for increases in employee contributions towards health care and contained weak job security language."[2] The key point here is that the IAMAW bargaining committee attempted to sell the contract to the members. Many members felt that this recommendation was a sign of betrayal; the union had taken conservatism and compliance with company objectives too far. It was at the moment of the union endorsement of the second contract that the conditions for challenging a stale bureaucracy were born. In an unprecedented wave, the workers of the union slapped down the cautious recommendation of the leaders and voted to remain on strike. Worker accounts of this event are moving revelations of their sudden recognition of their own power.

This chapter explores three dimensions of the 1995 strike from the rank-and-file perspective: the lived experience of preparation for and enacting of the strike; the sense of ownership and pride at the rejection of a contract that, despite union endorsement of it, was unacceptable to the majority of Boeing workers; and the outcomes of the strike in terms of both the resulting contract and the significant place of this event in the long-term memory of union activists. I argue that the 1995 strike, and especially the rejection of not only the first but also the second contract offered by the company and supported by the union, filled rank-and-file workers with a sense of control over their destinies in a ruthless corporate climate. This victory over the neoliberal regime provides a lesson in what is necessary to the reinvigoration of unions today. The first necessary element is readiness to strike.

"We Must Be Prepared at All Times"

Sherri Hood, district delegate from Local 834 to District 70, described getting ready for a strike as preparing for battle: "My dad's a Teamster, so I grew up with the union. So I look at it as, when you go to battle, in the olden days, you always had your armor and your big old shield. And the best way I could say is that your armor is what you prepare yourself for as in to prepare for contracts, to get ready for a possible strike. Don't listen to what the company tells you. If you have an opinion, make sure you stand up and make your voice heard. And if you've got a question, ask until you get an answer. The union is your shield. They're your first defense." Nearly everyone I spoke with emphasized that workers can take advantage of this power only if they have prepared for a strike by having a side business or being ahead on house payments or having some savings set aside should a strike happen. Denise Harris, also a delegate to District 70 from Local 834 in Wichita, told me:

> Start a business, start doing something that you know is going to directly make you be able to do the one most important thing that you have to do as a member which is not for Boeing. Come to the machinists' union, come to your other members, have better communication going on between the stewards and the people who are under their stewardship, and gang up, come together. Because when the going gets tough, it's not after a month. Anybody who's worked for Boeing for very long should not be hurting very bad after a month on strike. The going gets tough later, when you really start getting down to the issues that matter. And you still say, "Now, I'm not going to accept that, I'm not ready for that yet, I'm sorry, I've got to go roof a house."

Figure 6. Panoramic view of workers on the Everett, Washington, tarmac during the 1995 strike. Photo by Don Grinde.

For a more militant union strategy to prove effective, rank-and-file agitators must mitigate the temptation to cross the picket line during a strike. Exhorting fellow workers to prepare in advance—and asking union representatives to do the same—sustains solidarity because workers who are not struggling financially have much less incentive to go back to work. In Wichita, Unionists for Democratic Change (UDC) member Gary Washington told a similar story. After 1989, he learned to save up and find outside work in preparation for strikes:

> There were some guys in our shop that wanted to go in [to the struck plant], but after a month I went to work with the construction labor union, and there was big turnaround in Texaco oil refinery, and they needed laborers. So I got a whole lot of people jobs because of that turnaround, there, up in El Darado, Kansas.
> They were ready to go back to work, and we were losing people by the week, too. Also, too, I've learned how to save money a lot better now, as then. In '95 I didn't even work a job. I was not ready to go back to work, too, when it was time to go back to work. Because I had worked so much overtime the

previous two years prepared for this. I mean, I even bought a house when we were on strike and sold my other house. I just wasn't ready to go back into the grindstone. Ten weeks was glorious weeks away from that.

Union representative Dave Robertson advised his co-workers to "sock away money" for a strike. "What scares me is a lot of our members that are basically living paycheck to paycheck and live off the overtime. I think we need someone in here to literally talk to our members about finances."

Workers' power during a strike depends on the ability to outwait the employer. Boeing workers are inherently powerful because they constitute a highly skilled and difficult-to-replace workforce. The longer they stay out, the more the strike cuts into the company's profits and pressures Boeing to come forward with a better deal. As Mike Burleigh told me, "We must be prepared at all times." He described in some detail the strategies workers could use to survive a strike: Shop together in bulk, pool resources, have a party—even pray. He saw himself as a resource to whom wavering workers could turn for help.

In Wichita, workers who were not well prepared were tempted to cross the picket line as "scabs." Sean Mullin expressed sympathy with one single mother who could not afford to stay on strike. But Mullin and many others also expressed disgust and frustration with scabs, noting that the "strike is our only weapon." The other group of workers most likely to scab, according to Mullin, was those employed in the quality and safety team programs. This tendency reinforced the UDC's criticism of these workers as having become "Boeing management." But despite these weaknesses and temptations, union workers at Boeing in 1995 were prepared to outwait the company—and the union leadership.

"You Can Stand for Something": The Experience of the Strike

The mood of the strike reflected this sense of agency. The workers with whom I spoke were active leaders of the strike effort. Gary Washington performed security duties. A rather reticent activist, Arlene Hoaglan worked in the kitchen rather than walking the line to confront scabs. Madeleine Meuller enjoyed the picket line, calling the camaraderie "fun," except, she noted matter-of-factly, "Every once in a while you've gotta watch out because someone will want to try and run over you and not stop." Keith Thomas and Kelly Vandegrift served as strike captains on the picket line; Kelly was vice president of the Local. In Wichita, about a third of Boeing workers did not belong to the union, so the risk of nonunion workers crossing the picket line was higher than in Seattle. Of course, in Seattle, the company could hire skilled workers from other companies and temporary work agencies, but replacing strikers there was more difficult.

Mike Burleigh explained his approach to several workers who had crossed the line in '89 and were likely to cross again: "I went to them personally, and I talked to them, not in a rough way, and I said please don't come in. If there's a time that you need food, you can come set your feet under my table. Those four that I had in '89 did not cross the line in '95. You have to work with people."

Mary Johnson agreed: "I found out that a lot of people going in were apologizing for having to go in. A lot of them weren't as mean. You know, I think it's the way you approach someone, you walk up, you're smiling, even in the dark. And 'scuse me, could you roll down your window please for a moment? And most of them did. If you're not so radical and hurtful, they listen. And I explained to them why I was out there and it could be you next." One man she spoke to actually turned around: "He turned around, and it was like 'Yaaaaay' [waving her arms to imitate the people on the line]. 'You know, who, whoo, whoo.' And I thought, who was that guy?"

This kind of interpersonal persuasion becomes even more crucial because legal forces at local, county, state, and federal levels restrict workers' rights to hold effective pickets. Striking workers often face injunctions against pickets and risk arrest for "offenses" such as blocking sidewalks, failure to disperse, and assault on scabs (who often provoke a confrontation themselves). In addition to a pattern of local injunctions passed against strikers, the Racketeer Influenced and Corrupt Organizations (RICO) Act passed in the 1960s and reinforced by Bill Clinton in the 1990s allows workers only small symbolic strikes and disallows the blocking of plant entrances (on the argument that they entail costs to the employer).[3]

Workers are often resigned to this state of affairs. Mullin told me, "Because the whole purpose of a picket line is not necessarily to stop these people from going in. It's to try and be able to have the opportunity to talk to them and explain to them: 'Hey. You're not helping yourself. Just because you're going in there and getting a paycheck every two weeks does not mean you're helping yourself.'" Because it is difficult to hold an effective picket that can shut down a plant, persuasion becomes crucial in the maintenance of solidarity. Sherri Hood explained how frustrating it was to work security when strikers wanted to confront scabs or when people she had walked the line with crossed: "I mean, I just wanted to, you know, sometimes you just want to grab them and shake them and explain to them, 'If you guys would just stay out and remain solid, we could end it a lot faster.' Working security like I said, we couldn't show [how] really mad and upset we were. We just had to maintain the peace so we didn't have people getting hauled off to jail and any violence real bad."

Vandegrift described holding the picket line: "We stopped every car. We came up with a line, and I was very proud to say that I was part of the spiel. Every morning it changed. We had the newspaper articles about [Boeing CEO Frank] Shrontz is going to die! He's got cancer! Prostate cancer! Anything, anything the paper reported, we'd come out there and quickly drum up a couple-minute spiel. You take 12,000 cars, you give them two minutes apiece, how long is that going to stop it up? A long time. And then you pull up to the thing and then you roll down your window, and I'm not gonna let you go until I talk to you."

I asked Vandegrift whether there was an injunction against holding a picket line that impedes progress into the plant. He said, "Well, yeah, there was an injunction against it. Who cares? I mean, an injunction was an injunction."

He had been proud to walk the line as an elected officer of the union, when other officers (specifically IAMAW President Kourpias) only appeared on the line when the media were present:

I'm sorry, I think less of a leader who shows up and spends five minutes on a picket line to appease the slobs in the street. You know, when you walk a line, and the media's there taking pictures of you, and you're there for maybe forty-five minutes. *And I know those wingtips are probably not the right shoes to picket in.* Well, they weren't there in the snowstorm when I couldn't see across the street from gate five to gate six. They weren't there on the morning when it was 28 degrees and the wind was blowing so hard you couldn't hardly stand up, you'd almost stand [leaning] at an angle. And we were there for four hours and five hours and six hours every day. *They [union leaders] forgot the meaning of the strike I guess. They put on a necktie and it cut off the oxygen to the brain and they forgot what it was.*

He added, "At the 1996 IAMAW convention, I stood up there in front of all of them and told the International president that he and all of his cohorts needed to take off their ties and come down to my picket line at one o'clock in the morning." These bitingly funny descriptions of union leaders in wingtips and neckties are synecdochical ways of framing a group out of touch with the members' reality of work and striking. The union leaders, having forgotten what "it"—the meaning of a strike—was, were unwilling to withstand the harsh conditions of a strike. Leaning against the bitter wind represents the situation of the rank and file in general, facing bitter resistance from the union and the company.

Madeleine Meuller also describes trying to persuade co-workers not to cross the line, one day at a time: "I tried all the time. A lot of times I'd say, 'Hey, couldn't you just not go, one more day?'" In Wichita, it was especially important to activists like Vandegrift to maintain an effective picket line because in a "right-to-work" (in his words, "the right to work for less, you stupid idiot") state, many more people cross the line than they would in Seattle, where every worker was a member of the union. The Wichita union leadership did not advocate challenging the injunction against plant blockades. With regard to the ability to stop strikebreakers from crossing into the plant, union organizer Mike Burleigh said that it was important to respect people's rights despite the occasional scuffle on the line. Thus the role of picketers is to win public support and to argue actively, often vociferously, with workers trying to cross the line to go into the plant to work. Mullin described what it was like on the line dealing with workers wanting to cross:

Well, the first day was pandemonium. Everybody and their mother was down there, just getting rowdy, getting stupid. But it didn't take but a week for people to really start thinning out. And after about two weeks, a pretty good percentage of those people who were out there that first day were driving their cars across the picket line.

[You say,] "I got a right to work," but you don't really understand. What you're doing today greatly affects what we're doing for you while you're in there. And people don't think about that. It's an all-for-me, it's a really selfish act to be a scab, I think. I think it's a terribly selfish act. Being a scab is not about unity. It's not about working together. The majority of the persons in the plant involved in the quality teams, and all of these little community outreach teams, and teams, teams, teams, the majority of them are scabs. [You say,] "Oh, teamwork, teamwork!" Well, you had the opportunity to get with a really big team and set yourself up to have better seniority rights, to have better health and safety issues, better education, which you left it up to basically 40 percent of us to do the work for you. And that was the feeling that a lot of people were going through. While they're out there walking in the cold and the wet, you know, and they're not going to the store or not going to the movie or not doing anything that resembled what they were doing before. You know, they had to watch their pennies because they had no idea when they were going back to work. Some people didn't care. They just acted like it was just another day, like a vacation, so they carried on, and pretty soon they were out of money and like, "Well, I gotta go back to work." And that was the mentality.

As did others, Mullin notes that it was the workers involved in company-union teams that were most likely to cross; he counterpoises the "big team" of the union during a fight-back to the illusory teams offered by management. It is remarkable how experience cuts through the everyday mystifications of the workplace. While the "team" ideology in large enterprises encourages worker cooperation with management objectives, a few days on strike dispels the illusion.

Gary Washington tired of confronting scabs in the 1989 strike, which was why he took security duty rather than picket duty in 1995: "I had a lot of hate and stuff for a lot of people when I came back in the '89 strike, and I didn't want to feel the same way this time. I know who the scabs were, I know every scab in my building to this day. But I didn't want to be up close and personal with them like I was last time."

After the strike, David Clay and Keith Thomas both described how difficult it was to go back to work on the line with those who had betrayed the union. Former scabs generally faced harassment and stigmatization after the strike, although, again, Clay and others expressed some sympathy for those in desperate need of work to feed children or get health care.

Among others, Mike Burleigh expressed regret that he could not spend as many hours on the picket line as he would have liked.

You're not on the picket line as much. You might be on the picket line for three or four hours or something like that. But in a case like mine I'm at the

local, I'm at the district, I'm going to get food, I'm helping lines, I'm talking
to people. We deliver checks out to people that can't come in because they're
hurt or it could be a number of things. We have a hotline, we're talking to
people, a lot of people are stressed out, and it's a constant thing. There's always
something to do. If you're not on the line, you can take coffee to people. But
the biggest thing is, people expect to see you there. It don't matter if they
come out for an hour, when they come they expect to see you. You know at
the time that I went over to the local and the district, I had 141 people that I
was steward over. So if my people come in throughout the day, they expect to
see me there. So, I'm a leader, and you have to be there. And that's the reason
why a lot of us put like fourteen to fifteen hours a day because you have to
be there to meet everyone that you're affiliated with and everyone that you
adopt. It's just one of them things.

Burleigh also captured the mood and determination of the workers who stood
fast for sixty-nine days. I had asked him what the most important moments for
him had been: "It was such a busy time, you know, when you're dealing with
fourteen-hour days. I think just some of the small moments when people would
come in and say, you know, 'I'm still standing.' I think some of the small moments where you find people and they say, 'I'm going through hard times, but
I'm still going to stick.' You know, that's some of the things that I find—people
bring their kids out and explain what we're all about."

When I asked Burleigh how he felt about the experience, he added: "It makes
me feel great. It gives me resolve. It tells me I'm doing something right, and after
the strike I have a lot of people come up and say, 'I did it. I did it.' And they feel
good about it, too. And they're a stronger member, too, because a lot of times
when I'm talking to them, the first thing they say is, 'Hey I made it through the
'95 strike, I can make it through anything.' And I think it really gives you an idea
that you can stand for something."

Burleigh's remarks—along with those of my other interviewees—reveal how
the strike itself gave workers a sense of their own power: a kind of influence that
depended on banding together and holding the line even during stress and hardship. But it was at the moment of the union endorsement of the second contract
that the conditions for challenging a stale bureaucracy were born.

"We Just Stuck That Finger Up There": The Rejection of the Second Contract

When the rank-and-file members of the IAMAW went up not only against Boeing
but also against the unaccountable leadership of the union itself, it was a mo-

ment of profound class-consciousness in which workers realized that they had the power to take their future in their own hands. The *Seattle Times* interviewed a two-generation Boeing family on the company's offer. "'No way I'm going to take it. . . . You got to stand up for what you believe it. If I don't, it doesn't pay any good to be in a union,' said Stan Eggers. The 1995 strike was his third in 27 years."[4]

Thomas's account of the rejection of the contract is worth quoting at length:

> I think the most important event, the portion of that strike that I'll remember for the rest of my life, it has to be the point where we turned down that second proposal. I think most union people understand it who've been on strike. You're not really tickled about being on strike. Obviously, you've lost income, you're looking at bills mounting up, you've got everything that people go through on a strike, especially when it gets to be a long-term strike.
>
> So when it was turned down, I was elated. I mean, I've just never been prouder of being a union member. I get tickled now. It was just an outstanding event, to think of just your rank and file, and the grassroots out there, had just had enough. They'd been lied to enough, they'd had enough from the company—and I think that the best gesture—they just set that ass down there, they stuck their finger up there, and they said I've just had enough. I'm turning it down. And everybody was telling them to take that [the contract].
>
> And when I say everybody, I'm talking about the International leadership, the district leadership, some of the local leadership even if they want to claim later that it was a mistake and they didn't really mean to claim that it was supporting it, the federal mediator, the company, the corporate media of course was selling this and the folks turned it down. I'm so happy because we turned it down. It was a terrible offer. And then of course the company was so convinced we were going to take it.
>
> I suppose the second happy event was that they sent us letters welcoming us back. So they really believed that union leadership did more than we have to recommend it, to present it. They'd obviously promised the company that we would accept that contract and did their level best to sell it. And it just didn't work. People out on the picket lines were waving their welcome back letters to the cameras and to the general public as folks would go by. And just how outstanding that was.

The images of workers metaphorically (and, in some cases, literally) giving their leaders "the finger" and waving the arrogant welcome back letters from the company on the picket line convey the sense of agency and defiance the rank and file felt at that moment.

Members of the UDC are quick to point out that while their agitation contributed to the rebellious climate around that contract, they would not claim credit for

Figure 7. Workers walk out of the Everett, Washington, plant during the 2008 strike. Photo by Don Grinde.

the rank-and-file victory. Thomas commented, "If anybody wants to know who I give credit for it, I give it to the rank and file out there. Will I say that we were part of that victory? Yes, we were part of that victory." One contribution the UDC made was to press the union to get copies of the proposed contract to workers in advance of the vote. Other workers, both members of the opposition caucuses and representatives of the Administrative Caucus, also expressed their elation at taking charge of that moment in their history. David Clay in Everett told me, "The shining moment in that strike was the membership took over the union. The membership realized we're the union. They have a say. We had lunchtime marches out to the twin towers, into factory. We disrupted delivery of 777s. We banged on pipes with tools and changed in the plants. We shook the walls. People got the idea that this thing was theirs. We shocked the union leadership." Clay was describing the rank-and-file-initiated protests, dubbed Operation Rolling Thunder, in which members marched across lots and through hangars and created havoc in the plants. Clay described these marches, which began before the actual strike, as what he called a "wobble," defined as an unauthorized brief walkout:

So in Everett, at lunchtime, we started out marching out to the twin towers where the bosses reside, and by the time we got there, we got sixty or eighty people the first day, and when we came into the factory, it was like streams coming into a river. When we went into the factory, these people just poured out of the jigs and down the main throughways and stuff and joined this parade, and it just got huge, and it was very interesting to see superintendents and general supervisors getting worked up. We were all singing songs and marching along. It was a scary thing, not that you don't know where this crowd was going, but we kept going out to the flight line, disrupted the first delivery of an AMA Triple 7—there were fourteen Japanese television crews out there—marched back to the factory, and got the rest of the people and marched out to the twin towers, you know, and shook the walls out there. It was incredible, the fact that we could do that, and that's where people started getting the idea that this thing was theirs, and I think we shocked the hell out of the union leadership, because they had no way of knowing that that would happen, and it was a spontaneous thing, and yet, when we went on strike, we voted for strike in '95, they weren't prepared.

IAMAW librarian Virginia Roberts was astonished at the level of involvement of the rank and file during 1995 contract negotiations:

I was working down in Auburn, and the stewards would call from the plant right before the noisemaking was about to take place, and we would put it on speakerphone over at the hall. It had to be deafening out there, because I couldn't hold the receiver to my ear. They were just pounding, pounding. And that level of participation gets the attention of the management, and it builds up enthusiasm on the part of the people. There were marches. They just spontaneously erupted all over the region; they would get up and leave their work and go out marching around the factory and stuff. I see that the stewards are the ones who do that sort of organizing and keep that level of enthusiasm up during negotiations and during the strike.

Jackie Boschok, the district recording secretary, remembers workers "shutting down the flight lane and marching through Everett," preventing new planes from taxiing out, shouting "Frank [Shrontz], you got yours, where's ours?" Boeing head Frank Shrontz reacted, "I guess I would have to say I, at least, underestimated the depth of the feeling" among the workers.[5]

In Wichita, the sense that "this thing was theirs" among the rank and file was similar. Gary Washington told me, "When we rejected the second contract, that was the most significant thing of the whole strike because we said no to our union leaders and we said no to Boeing, too. No, we're not going to settle just because we've been out for this many days right here and you think we're gonna come back in and buy this because this is what you think we can buy and live with. No, that's not it." Kelly Vandegrift exulted,

> We were on the picket line. I was on the picket line when the paper broke. The guys brought me the paper. And they said, 'Here Kelly, look at this, we did it! We turned down the second contract!' [Punches knee with fist to punctuate foregoing sentence] God what a thrill. You know, that starts blood flowing in me right now. It was thrilling because we not only told that company that we were right and that our members were strong, [pointing for emphasis] but we told our International that you don't push us around, you around, you don't run the union. We do. We are the union. You're just the people we pay to administrate things. They sold us down the drain, we knew it, we voted, and our brothers and sisters held together. What a thrill.

Contrary to the critique that they had sold members "down the drain," representatives of the International felt that they had not betrayed their members. Speaking from the point view of the union organization, Sue Moyer and Virginia Roberts explained why the negotiators recommended the second contract only with serious reservations. They told me that the union has to put an offer before the membership or the company will withdraw it. Sometimes the company can stipulate that the offer be recommended to the members or have it taken off the table; this is what happened with the second contract in 1995. Further, Moyer and Roberts argued that after nearly a month on strike, the members may have resented not being allowed to vote on an offer. As Thomas recalled in a passage already quoted, in 1989, the leadership rejected an offer without presenting it to the membership during the strike, and the members were outraged at the lack of information and inclusion in that decision. However, it is possible for the union to bring an offer and recommend rejection. Moyer and Roberts would agree with Thomas that the union's judgment was flawed at least in this one case. They thought that the negotiators were not sufficiently attuned to workers' concerns, especially over health care. Roberts commented:

> I don't know what it was. That [recommendation of the second contract] did damage a sense of trust in some of the rank-and-file workers there, but I didn't understand part of it, talking to you, that the company can make it so that the union reps have to say that they recommend the offer. But, of course, in '89 and '95 they could have said that the second offer wasn't something they could recommend, but then, of course, the membership might have been up in arms because they didn't get to see all the offers. I think all of that, it was bad judgment. I just think the negotiation committee did not put out enough

feelers, didn't even give us staff people a chance to say what we were hearing from the workers at all of the plants and what they were willing to fight for.

Other union representatives were also ambivalent. Mike Burleigh, who had been a steward during the strike, told me that he understood why the negotiators had brought the contract before the workers with a recommendation to accept. He said that he agreed with critics that the contract wasn't good, but he empathized with the negotiating team. "I agreed (hesitating here) [with the critics] that we hadn't got good language yet. And my problem is that I always tell people a lot of people look at the money issue and I look at the language and I didn't vote for the first one, I didn't vote for the second one, and I had very mixed feelings even about the last one we took. But it comes to a point where you say OK. We have another time to fight, too. You have to decide what you're going to do at that time, you know. And it pretty much was a decent contract. They had took out the off-loading in one way. And you just have to go. You've gotta go with what you got."

About the negotiators, Burleigh said, "I felt they done as well as they could with what they had. Because a lot of people do not understand when you're negotiating a contract. Everybody wants to know what's going on, and I'm under the impression that I don't need to know until you bring it to me. And when a lot of people start calling and what you getting for me and all this kind of stuff, it really confuses the matter, and then when they start giving reports to other people, . . . it really makes the negotiator's job pretty bad. So all in all I think they did pretty good."

Despite such sympathy for the negotiating team, both dissident organizers and most union representatives interviewed during 1998 expressed relief and happiness at the rejection of the second contract. However, Denise Harris said that even the third contract that was accepted by the workers still wasn't good enough: "We still took concessions, we still got beat back on our insurance. We didn't gain any more insurance, we're still doing co-pays, the deductible's higher, I have a health maintenance, an HMO, I had to start paying more on it, I had to start paying higher co-payments, my prescription card's gone up, I don't think we gained an awful lot as far as subcontracting, the language wasn't any stronger that they came up with, I felt like we just went out when the company felt it was good of them for us to go out, and we came back at a good time for the company."

On Harris's account, the workers should have stayed out even longer to win an even better contract. She explained that the Boeing workers, being highly skilled and difficult to replace, held the power to force the Boeing Company to give even more to the workers in the contract: "If you've got the best aircraft workers, which we should have at Boeing, if you have the best ones, if we shut them down, they are shut down. They can't go out and hire anybody else. And since the District 70 is over [organizes?] the other aircraft in town, we've got them wrapped up here."

Harris points out the actual power of unionized skilled workers to force a company's hand during a negotiation. Her disagreement with the approach of the negotiators in 1995 demonstrates, also, that the Administrative Caucus, of which she was a part, is not a monolith.

Like the dissidents, most union representatives regarded the 1995 strike as a real and positive turning point. Garland "Bear" Moore, who was vice president of Local 834 in 1997 (but who had not been a union officer during the strike), commented, "My most memorable night was the night that we had already been out for a while, and the contract that was brought back to us, that was basically unchanged, and these people turned it down by an overwhelming percentage. Right on the steps of this building, that was a memorable night for me. It's the first time it had ever been done here; it's the first time they had ever turned down a contract offer. And it was memorable in the fact that people are finally listening in a way that they'll stand up for what they want."

Moore also hailed the contract rejection as "a turning point in the way the company deals with its union. We were at a point to where it could buy contracts, and now I think that they've found out that that's not so." He explained that prior to 1995, Boeing management felt that they could offer one-time lump-sum bonuses to get workers to sign without consideration of the long-term consequences and that the willingness to strike in 1995 meant that workers were seeing through this strategy.

However, dissidents accuse these leaders of backtracking after the fact of rank-and-file rejection of the contract. "What happened after the strike was completely over is the union reps tried 'the devil made me do it' spin," Thomas said. He quoted a friend in Seattle who claimed that his directing business representative (DBR) said that the workers were "supposed to tell from his body language" that the union knew it was a bad contract that they wanted to see voted down in spite of the recommendation. Dissidents regarded the militant stances taken by union officials, including International President George Kourpias, in the media as shams. UDC member Sean Mullin expressed his feelings about the union representatives during this process: "It was like our leadership, when we went out to vote that second time, they had made some sort of agreement with the company where they would not make a recommendation on whether we bought it or did not buy it. And you couldn't get one of those guys on the podium to give their opinion on whether it was a good contract or not. We pay these guys to be our representatives and to go bargain and to come back and tell us what they think of the contract. Well, they made an agreement with the company to not give their opinion. Well, I'm sorry, but they don't work for the company. They work for my dollars. I pay their salary, and I don't go for that."

Mullin felt that the waffling of the union representatives, first recommending the contract, then offering no guidance, then condemning it only after the members had rejected it, suggested to the members of the UDC that the union was cooperating to some degree with Boeing.

At the very least, during the contract battles and strike, the representatives did not exert clear leadership, nor did they provide full information to the members. They recommended a contract that, at the end of the day, everyone knew gave away too much. The union members recognized these problems and took charge of the situation, challenging the company and the union both. Mullin summed it up when he said, "I think it was a victory for union members who wanted to send a message to their union and the company: 'Hey, we're not going to take your crap. We're not going to take you two getting in bed together and trying to sell us out, because we're not as stupid as you'd like to believe we are.'"

"Learning What the Strike Was About": Outcomes of the '95 Strike

By most accounts, the outcome of the 1995 strike was a tremendous victory for the union. Cimini reported that the terms of the new contract included a lump-sum bonus equal to 10 percent of a worker's base pay in 1995 and a similar 4.5 percent increase in 1996.[6] The contract included 3 percent wage increases in 1997 and 1998 and ongoing cost-of-living adjustments. The contract preserved employees' health benefits, provided without cost to the employee. In the crucial area of job security, Boeing also granted concessions, including mandatory meetings with the union to discuss planned subcontracting with ninety days' advance notice of job losses, a letter of understanding stating that no union worker could be laid off as a result of subcontracting, and a promise to retrain and reassign any worker adversely affected by subcontracting.

Workers felt that the company had been put on notice. Burleigh commented, "The strike of '95 was a blow to Boeing because Boeing felt that we were very small people and we should not be able to stand up to them like we did. And that's the transition that Boeing had to go through." No longer did workers feel that they were "very small people," and neither could Boeing afford any longer to take the workforce for granted.

Another indirect benefit of the strike was increased union awareness and solidarity. Mike Burleigh was impressed with the way in which the strike solidified union members and built a renewed sense of community:

> Then '95 came, and 95, like everybody said, was a turning point, because that was the time of really getting people to consent to off-loading and shipping your work out of the state and all this kind of stuff, and overseas, and the

Boeing company felt at that time that the people would take any contract, because everybody was scared of losing their jobs because they were laying off at that time, around in that time, too. But we held the line, and we voted their contracts down. So. And the biggest reason why is 'cause the people felt, hey, why vote this in when I would lose my job anyway. So, in turn, a lot of the people just held the line and says, hey, you need to go back and get us a better contract. So we did that, you know, we stayed out for sixty-nine days, and it really helped gel the union together, in my opinion, because a lot of people learned what a strike was about.

In addition to firming up the union, the contract offered tangible gains. Thus, the 1995 strike pointed the way forward for labor gains, not only at Boeing but also across U.S. industry. In the face of bureaucratic sluggishness on the part of the union and a relentless offensive on the part of the company, the rank and file stood up and used their collective strength to challenge both. The gains won could not have been realized under any other strategy.

The Association for Union Democracy (AUD) summarized the reform movement's importance in this victory in a published statement. This statement noted that the reform movement had successfully placed members in union elected office; Don Grinde and Keith Thomas had fought for and won the right of workers to see contract proposals three days in advance; they had organized rallies against proposals during the run-up to votes; and they had participated in campaigning for the "No" vote on the second contract. The AUD document concludes: "Five years of determined campaigning by the IAM insurgents, whose efforts continue, paid off for Boeing workers, and for the labor movement, which hails the victory."[7]

In the foregoing, I have recounted the stories that both official representatives of the IAMAW and the dissident members tell about the relationship between the company and the union. Spokespersons for the union express a sincere commitment to acting in members' interest. The UDC, New Crew, and Machinists for Solidarity (MFS), however, noted the extent to which the union collaborated with management in recommending a bad contract and, significantly, in supporting long-term partnership initiatives with management. Union democracy activists operate as an important check on official union common sense, calling attention to the conflicts of interest inherent in undemocratic practices of the union. The 1995 strike brought the clash of perspectives into sharp focus.

Summary

In this chapter, I have argued that the decision in November 1995 by Boeing workers to reject a bad contract recommended by their union leaders marked a watershed moment. At the height of neoliberal pressure, an industrial workforce brought one of the largest corporations in the world economy to heel. The workers' experience of solidarity during the strike and the resulting victory shaped their consciousness of themselves as people who could fight back in their own interests. They realized that they could make both the company and the union bend to their will. Their words—"you can stand for something"; "we *are* the union"; "we learned what the strike was about"; and "we're not going to take your crap"—reflect the sense of militant class-consciousness that arises from the shared participation in fighting back.

The UDC and MFS represented tiny minorities of workers in Seattle and Wichita in 1995. Yet these organizations arose from the same conditions that led to the strike: rank-and-file anger at the company and willingness to challenge the official union leadership. As did the Teamsters for a Democratic Union during the same time period, these organizations could have grown from their embryonic forms into sustained organizations that could carry forward the lessons and the spirit of 1995. It is in the absence of organization that such memories are lost. In 1999 and 2002, Boeing machinists accepted highly concessionary contracts in periods of corporate profitability. If the UDC and MFS had been sustained, their ability to attract numbers and reach workers with information about the contract—and about their own victorious history—might have influenced the morale and strategy of union leaders and members.

Instead, the UDC disbanded around the time of the strike. The MFS is still in existence, but its presence is less felt. In the interest of serving the labor movement as a whole in this era of seemingly invulnerable global capitalism, we must examine the reasons for the decline of the democratic union movement in the Machinists and, by extension, in the union movement more generally. The next chapter explores how the fundamental dilemma of fighting the union to use the union against the company generated a number of contradictions in the organizing strategies and tone of the UDC's and New Crew's campaigns. On the one hand, they believed the rank and file were potential everyday heroes whose moxie in 1995 had made everyone's lot better. All that was needed was more education and agitation. On the other hand, when organizing got tough, members explained the decision to disband in terms of the inability of caucus members to handle the level of intimidation they were facing. Burned out and tapped out financially, the core members of the UDC expressed the bleak idea that workers would from here on out be impossible to move again. It is the dilemma of representation: Democracy demands it, but once in place, its tasks distance the leader from those he or she represents.

6

"The Feeble Strength of One"

The fundamental condition for active members is their perception that there is hope for real change, and the belief that they,
not the leaders and staff, own the union. The obstacles are
some of the entrenched practices of the unions themselves. . . .
[M]ost union leaders hesitate before calling on the members
to do anything beyond confer their consent. . . . They do not
want to risk the emergence of new, potentially opposing forces
within the union. With some exceptions, rank and file and other
opposition groups have difficulty gaining equal access with the
leadership caucus to the union's newspaper and mailing lists,
and often are forced to make complaints to the Labor Department or to conduct lawsuits to bring the leadership to heel.
Even when there are good reasons to involve the rank and file,
leaders often say that the membership is "apathetic."

—Stanley Aronowitz[1]

In her influential essay "The Problem of Speaking for Others," Linda
Alcoff observes that standing up to, for, and with others poses a dilemma.[2] On
the one hand, if one chooses to speak for others—for example, to speak for the
rank and file as a leader of a union or of a dissident union caucus—one risks
irresponsibly substituting oneself for the people one is attempting to represent.
This stance also can entail elitism or paternalism: Thinking, "The workers can't
or won't speak for themselves; therefore, we who know better will challenge the
union," activists could assume that others want what they want.

On the other hand, however, there are perils in not speaking for others. Sometimes oppressed, isolated, and/or vulnerable people truly need someone more
secure in their situation and/or prominent in society—or maybe just foolhardy
enough—to give voice to their cause. Imagine if abolitionists had refused to
speak for the needs of the slaves or if radical labor leaders had not sounded the
call to organize. All movements require leadership, and leaders always run the
risk of standing in for the movement participants. Leaders who do so are subject

to criticism. For example, a number of civil rights and black liberation activists have criticized Martin Luther King Jr.—or, more important, the ways in which the legacy of King has been used by conservatives to warrant the erosion of civil rights reforms in a "color-blind" society—for representing the movement in one-sided, pacifist terms.[3] Malcolm X and the Black Panther leadership stand in public memory for the tradition of black militancy that was, in fact, much broader and more complicated. This inadequacy of representation is inherent in movements and therefore unavoidable by activists and leaders in the labor movement as well.

There is another problem at the core of leading a democracy group, namely, that the necessity of speaking with and for others for a better contract also positions the rank and file as antagonistic to the practices of the institutional union. From the dissidents' point of view, this dual agenda is necessary, since to get to the company they had to go through the union itself. Primarily, however, the rank and file is rightly interested in holding the line on their standard of living and may regard participating in a dissident or opposition caucus against the Administrative Caucus as a secondary or even self-undermining task. Thus, activists must maintain a balance between organizing and giving voice to rank-and-file demands (which may be more radical than those of the official union in bargaining) and doing the necessary work to clear space for the demands of the rank-and-file ideas inside the union itself.

The period after the 1995 strike was one during which management regrouped and the Boeing workforce settled in after their victory. To some extent, managerial and official union intimidation, along with the ongoing pressure on workers in the plants, can explain the difficulty that activists had in sustaining their reform organizations. However, in this chapter I describe how the activists themselves were caught up in the dilemmas of representation. Their commitment to democracy informed their critique from below of the discourse and practices of union leadership. Yet their taking on the tasks of leading a rank-and-file movement put them in a position to replicate, in form if not in goal, some of the habits they decried. In particular, focusing on getting elected to powerful union posts, making decisions on behalf of members of rank-and-file organizations, using top-down and double-edged legal tools to reform the official union, and decrying the passivity of the membership all contributed to the burnout and eventual retreat from dissident activity of many of the activists whose voices I chronicle here.

Cynthia Stohl and George Cheney describe how in employee struggles the pursuit of one goal (greater democracy) sometimes entails methods and secondary goals (like winning elections and exerting leadership) that undermine the first pursuit, putting actors into a paradoxical situation: "Lead democratically;

empower others."[4] Stohl and Cheney write, "Even staunchly democratic and egalitarian organizations can succumb to the temptation to oppress their members with restrictive notions of process when their larger intention is an open organization."[5] This logic certainly applies to the behavior of long-established unions; here I describe how the intersection of official union and dissident narratives puts the reformers in this uncomfortable position as well. Frustration with the difficulty of rallying large numbers of the rank and file can easily generate both pessimism and elitism, which in turn inform the choice of strategies and tactics on the part of reformers.

After 1995

During the agitation around the 1995 contract, workers throughout the plants were gaining militancy and a sense of confidence. They needed organizations and individuals to press for greater accountability on the part of elected union officials. The groundwork done by the Unionists for Democratic Change (UDC), the New Crew, and Machinists for Solidarity starting in 1990 enabled them to play a role in that process. Keith Thomas described the awakening of the rank and file around the 1995 contract. Given wrongheaded union leadership, he said, "We were going to have to figure out what to do on our own. Well, in 1995, the people did that. The person on the street may not even know anything about our caucus or the union leadership. But the average union member was able to read a contract that was being sold to him by the union leadership, by the company, and by the federal mediator and know that that contract was unacceptable. And I think that the fact that so many people could continue to stay out demonstrates the fact that the people really did realize that they'd been had."

In our early conversations (1998), Thomas expressed faith in the rank and file, placing any blame for union conservatism at the feet of the union leadership: "The fact that their leadership let them down really shows where the problem is, because the problem quite obviously wasn't what was in the hearts of the people. I am just so absolutely impressed with the heart that people showed in spite of everything that was thrown at them. Working people, I am moved by their courage." He and the other UDC leaders were also gratified by the work they had done. Thomas was especially proud of the UDC's member education handbills about letters of understanding (basically contract addenda imposed after the fact without bargaining) that made a number of promanagement concessions between contracts. "We were actually able to vote on those letters of understanding. The union leaders couldn't implement them. We were actually able to put enough political pressure that we were able to get our rank and file a vote on it down here."

Before 1995, the UDC was able to agitate around the implementation of the High Performance Work Organization, generating a lot of criticism toward a program that effectively entails "union officials managing workers for the company." The UDC and New Crew members (even after the organizations themselves disbanded) anticipated producing literature to educate members about the 1999 contract, especially in Seattle. In addition to job security, benefits, and pensions, a major issue in that contract became the company's plan to introduce irregular workweeks. Jerry Calhoun, Boeing's vice president for labor relations, supported a nontraditional workweek because "it really gets to our ability to increase productivity."[6] He and union negotiator Dick Schneider heralded the formation of "a foundation for new relationship"; Calhoun called the efforts of both sides to work together "so sweet."[7]

For activists in Wichita and the Puget Sound, the contract prospects did not look so sweet in 1999. The 1995 strike had been a real victory, but it could not stop the company from retaking the offensive as the decade came to a close. (As already noted, 2005 and 2008 saw workers once again on the move.) David Clay wondered whether the union would trade the flexible workweek for job security; he anticipated a strike. Although the UDC caucus had officially disbanded, several former members were still active. Sean Mullin told me that they had planned an informational picket to get an advance look at the contract. He said that they already had T-shirts made that read, "Contract '99: Get Ready for the Long One."

Similarly, Thomas told me, "We're going to come out there on the floor; we're going to try to work up a plan of action. We're gonna get the issues out there. Some of the issues people aren't gonna like, but our approach is going to be don't shoot the messenger; we're not the ones who tried to see you out." He continued, "The union has already started negotiations at the top, at the highest levels, completely out of any direction of the rank and file, completely out of the awareness of the person on the floor. And they're initiating actions that we never asked for. . . . I know that sounds a little silly for a group of a dozen or so of us saying we're going to accomplish all of those things, but I think the folks will look at what we've already accomplished. We pushed for an informed vote. We pushed for people knowing ahead of time what was in the contract. There's been votes taking place that I don't believe would have—like on those letters of understanding—if it hadn't been for our pressure."

However, during the latter part of the 1990s, workers became more quiescent and less confident as the company began to take back worker gains, including the most fundamental: job security. Activist groups like the UDC, had they been sustained, might have been a resource for greater agitation. As Thomas notes in the next chapter, one can hardly lay the responsibility for these setbacks at

the feet of union dissidents. And given that the decline of union reform organizations has been a nationwide trend within and across most unions since the
late 1990s, external economic and political offensives by the employers against
unions were factors in the decline beyond the reformers' control. However, some
of the dissidents' practices militated against the establishment of a sustained
movement caucus.

We cannot know for sure what might have happened otherwise, but if reformers had emphasized other strategies involving greater numbers of people at the
high point, perhaps they could have formed an organization strong enough to
hunker down in a routine of small-scale shop-floor recruitment and worker
education until the next explosion of worker dissatisfaction, when they would be
in a position once again—better organized and stronger as a result of prolonged
building—to amplify the voices of rank-and-file workers.

This argument may be idle speculation. However, an examination of the interviews and election materials of the UDC and New Crew in particular suggests that even until 1995, the organizations fostered habits of individual action,
minority decision making, and election efforts that foreclosed the possibility of
other collective, democratic, and rank-and-file work necessary to longer-term
organizational survival.

The Decision to Disband

There is really nothing like disbanding an organization to ensure that it will not
survive in the long term. The UDC in Wichita actually disbanded formally just
before the 1995 strike, having been active in the run-up to the strike deadline.
(In Seattle, the New Crew and Machinists for Solidarity both have sustained
small organizations.) Thomas explained that the escalation of threats against
UDC members—many of whom had not signed up for violence when they got
involved—informed their decision to disband that year:

> There had been a death threat, which by itself wasn't unusual. I've been get-
> ting death threats for a long time. But on this particular day, an older gentle-
> man down at the local told [UDC activist] Dave "Bones" Smith that what
> the UDC caucus needed was a good killing. About an hour later, there was a
> drive-by shooting in my neighborhood from the interstate. They fired at the
> houses through a break in the tree line. At the second break in the tree line,
> farther south on the interstate, they shot aiming back toward my house. My
> house wasn't hit, but the house next door was hit. Previously, someone faxed
> me a cartoon where I was all trussed up and supposedly had been shot. At

one point, people had been threatened in the union by a union member who had said that he had shot at some houses in the '89 strike. This person's also involved in our opposition, and I had [in my possession] signed statements from people about him making those threats.

We realized things were actually escalating to that next higher level. We had an AUD [Association for Union Democracy] pamphlet that talked about the various things to expect, and we were working through all the things that would happen. We could check off little boxes: OK, we've been called racists; OK, we've been Red-baited; OK, and we were just going through the line, and we got to the physical violence part. Don [Grinde], who's associated with our caucus, had already been punched out in Seattle by folks associated with the opposition. There had already been damage to cars, like paint scratched, breaking off things in your door lock, wood, packing dirt in there. Kelly [Vandegrift] had his brake lines cut, probably in '92. So then we had this shooting, and our feeling was that although we had expected a lot of this and had warned folks that extreme actions were possible, and where *folks would say well, that's OK, let's go, we felt well it has actually happened now, and we need to do something, have some kind of response to that, because we may have actually got people in a position where they found themselves in over their heads and actually fighting more than what they really wanted or intended to.* So we called a meeting, maybe fifteen to twenty people showed up. And we reached the decision at the meeting that we would disband the caucus down to the active members, which is essentially the cofounders and some of the folks who have been active and will stay active, about a dozen people, with just a couple of folks out in Seattle.[8]

I have emphasized Thomas's remarks regarding his decision that he had gotten others in "over their heads." He assumed that he knew "what they really wanted or intended." When asked whether he thought he was paranoid, Thomas replied, "Oh, God, yes. Paranoia can be real healthy. And it's certainly saved me in any number of circumstances. If you're going to be a reformist out there, you'd better develop a little paranoia if you haven't already got it. That's my advice to folks."

It is true that union reformers face serious backlash. The attacks on and intimidation of dissidents took a number of different forms in Wichita and Seattle. The Administrative Caucus actively harassed and maligned UDC members and the New Crew in Seattle. For example, Thomas noted that the Administrative Caucus would raise allegations about activists' sex lives and affairs. In addition, "They said that our organization was funded by drug sales." From harassing phone calls to death threats, the UDC and New Crew faced a number of frightening and demoralizing challenges. The Association for Union Democracy (AUD) recognizes the serious possibility of intimidation on the part of union or company officials against a reform campaign.

In response, the AUD recommends that reform organizations structure themselves democratically and allow for bottom-up voice and decision making. There is strength in numbers. Members of an organization have a right and an obligation to decide what risks they are willing to take for the cause. It is telling that Thomas remarks, "We may have actually got people in a position where they found themselves in over their heads." This formulation of the problem suggests that he and a few core active members saw themselves as shepherds to workers who were not as cognizant of the challenges ahead or prepared for the consequences of organizing. The discussion of disbanding is not an isolated expression of paternalism and pessimism about the ability and willingness of rank-and-file workers to become meaningful parts of the struggle. In a 2006 letter, Thomas wrote, "The rank and file has to accept a portion of the blame, the responsibility. We certainly provided them plenty of opportunity over the years here and in Washington to change things. At our very best we were unable to get more than ten percent involved. We lost to big screen television, sports, shopping, and apathy—the very things that make a coup possible."[9] This pessimism leads to the tendency for the dissidents to speak for the workers, assumed to be unwilling or unable to speak for themselves.

Speaking for the Workers

The AUD Web site lays out the following criteria for democratic union reform organizing: collective work, shared authority, willingness to confront management, spread of information, involvement and training of new activists, delegation of tasks, creativity, group-centered leadership, dialogue across difference, strategic thinking, and methodical action.[10] Not all of these practices are possible in all situations. As Thomas explains in the next chapter, it is difficult to share authority, delegate tasks, and involve new people who don't exist; democracy requires the activity of a layer of activists who may not come forward to participate.

Thomas and his fellow activists take scant pleasure in having predicted the company's ruthlessness. They express profound frustration that other workers had not responded to their previous efforts. In a 2002 letter, Thomas described an incident in which "a guy at work walked up to me and said, 'Well, you were right'" about getting laid off. "That's when I stayed outside the vote and telling people that with their vote they would pick the picket line or the unemployment line. And they did."[11] Thomas details the contract that year, when the sale of the Wichita plant to Onex was in the works; thousands were being laid off with little regard for seniority.

In 1998, Sean Mullin was prescient (given the sale of Boeing Wichita to Onex in 2005) when he remarked, "And I really wouldn't be surprised if Boeing just tomorrow sold the entire building that I work in to some little subsidiary of theirs. And said, well it no longer belongs to the Boeing Company so you all no longer work for the Boeing Company; now we're going to subcontract all the labor in here, on-site. So it's still going to be the same production, but if you want to work here, you have to go through this other company." These developments beg explanation. Who's to blame for the steep decline of union power? For the union dissidents, an apathetic and ignorant rank and file appears as a primary cause. At times, Thomas has been dismissive toward the mass of ordinary workers, some of whom, he argues, believe the lies of the Administrative Caucus in the same way they might take tabloid newspapers seriously: "There's always in all of us a certain element that wants to believe that kind of thing," he said. "People don't know enough about their leadership or the issues in union election campaigns."

Thomas's argument has some backing in the actual numbers of workers involved in reform efforts. Yet the organizers themselves cannot be let off the hook. In their assumptions that not very many ordinary workers would be involved, that most workers are fundamentally self-interested, and that a core group of dedicated activists could substitute itself for the rank and file, the UDC in some ways set itself up for failure. Attempting to stand in for masses of others also takes a personal toll on individuals and families. Personal burnout feeds pessimism and undermines energy for organizing efforts, thus fueling the conditions for further burnout as leaders continue to plow ahead with the entire burden of change on their backs.

The Personal Costs of Dissidence

All of the activists I interviewed described the intense drain on their personal finances, health, and family life required by dissident activity. For example, Shelley Thomas, Keith's wife, joked about Keith's singular dedication to union activism:

> You know, there are times I'd like to talk about my job and what's going on in my life if I can get his attention for five minutes, and then we're off on some other injustice against working people. [Laughs] But that's okay. I'm still useful for my computer skills.
>
> I had absolutely no idea what we were getting into, what it was going to mean in terms of our survival. I was glad I worked so we had some money coming in. We had been married just over a year, and we were planning to build a house, which obviously had to wait until the strike was over.

Figure 8. Don Grinde and Keith Thomas in Seattle, 2005. Courtesy of Keith Thomas.

How difficult is it to be married to such a single-minded radical? He's difficult, but he's worth it. [Aside to Keith: Aren't you glad to hear that, honey?] It's
hard not to feel neglected sometimes when he devotes so much of his energy
to the greater good than to my good or his own.[12]

At this point in the interview, Shelley joked that, for example, he did things like
invite researchers from Texas (referring to me) to come stay indefinitely at their
house. Her major concern was for his well-being: "It's hard on him sometimes.
He believes so strongly and so deeply, and when things go badly, it's just very
hard. And things often do go badly. But it is never boring."

Keith and Shelley have a solid marriage that has weathered the tribulations of
the movement. Likewise, Kelly Vandegrift and his wife, Debbie, who was actually
in lower-level management, worked out an understanding:

The '89 strike was really hard on us because we're both fiercely independent
people, we're very opinionized, and a lot of our opinions don't match, mix,
and never will. My wife, bless her heart, never asked me to cross a picket
line. . . . She was very proud of me and the bargaining unit for holding to
our principles. '95 was a lot easier for us. We both agreed that there were

principles and some subjects we couldn't touch on. And I was vice president of the union. In '95 we found it easier because we both knew our roles. And when we went to the strike line, I was a striker and vice president, and when she went to work, she was personnel manager, and when we came home; we're Debbie and Kelly Vandegrift.

Unfortunately, others among the activists saw their relationships and health crack under the strain of union activism.

Don Grinde's personal journal for the years 1991–1995 poignantly reveals the strain that the struggle in the union put on his relationships. Contract time in 1992 was particularly rough because Grinde and others among the New Crew went up against the District 751 union leadership in elections for leadership positions alongside agitating for a contract with fewer concessions than the union was willing to accept. Grinde and his family were subject to threatening phone calls and messages, as well as vilification by the union leadership. In addition, the Administrative Caucus had resorted to election misconduct to overcome opposition support. Kevin Maine, a union steward, wrote the International Association of Machinists and Aerospace Workers (IAMAW) international office describing the administration's busing of workers to the polls and the intimidation of voters at the polls themselves. At the time, Grinde was working nonstop on election campaigns. His son was getting into trouble at school, and his wife, Janice, was left dealing alone with household and family matters. She was often angry about the time he spent working and the disruption of their home life by union activities. Grinde wrote her a letter expressing his regret over this situation:

Hi, Dear,

I use the computer so much I thought I should put it to good use by telling you how much I love you! I'm sorry you have to work so much coupled with the fact that usually I'm home so little. I want you to know that I appreciate you and all the hard work you put into your job at work and as a mother and wife.

I really am looking forward to a time soon when we can spend some quality time together, becoming better friends. I would like very much just to sit next to you holding your hand softly watching T.V. I want you to know that I long for your affection.

If it wasn't for your Love and understanding I wouldn't be able to be involved with the union so much. The Union and the people mean a lot to me but the most important thing of all, is You and the Kids. I realize this more and more as each day passes, as another one goes by, one that I can't replace.

In a 2008 letter to me, Grinde lamented, "There isn't a day goes by that I see the pain. . . . I abandoned my family responsibilities to pursue union activities and threw my home life out of balance. My boys now in their late 20s are struggling still. Many tears have been shed for ignoring opportunities never to be regained."[13]

For women activists, the tension between family and union is that much more poignant. Arlene Hoagland, assigned third shift after she demanded an overdue promotion, said she wanted to be involved and to help Keith Thomas, because she trusted his motives: "It didn't seem like he had anything to gain from what he was talking about, and he had the information to back it up. But I was letting my support of the family down, because my husband would bring me dinner, and I just felt like, I don't know, I wasn't raised like my husband was supposed to bring my dinner. It was a little hard to take." She expressed empathy for other women who crossed the line: "When to be a mother, raising children, responsible for children with no other income, and you don't have the means to support your family any other way. I don't know that I wouldn't do the same thing if I were in their shoes. I think that's where men and women differ a whole lot. For our generation, you do what you gotta do as a woman to survive. But at the same time, a man, like my husband, he doesn't have to worry. He'll go out and find something, a second job. A woman on the other had, well, I've gotta find a job. The heck with the world. We're gonna raise our family." But when I asked her if she would be out again if they struck, she said, "Yeah, oh, yeah. That's our only weapon. If Congress don't take that away from us, we'll be doing OK."

Putting such a large burden on only a few backs was one factor in the groups' decline. Even with the dedication of a small core of activists, members of the dissident groups did not consistently recruit and train new layers of activists. The decision to disband reflected the assumption that members of the rank and file were unwilling or unable to fight in their own interests. Two other tendencies grew out of the same assumption: first, an overweening emphasis on seeking elected office inside the union (especially in Seattle) and second, the use of individual lawsuits based on the Labor-Management Reporting and Disclosure Act of 1959 (LMRDA) to pressure the union to uphold the rights of union members.

Electioneering for Reform

Dissidents and reformers in Wichita and the Puget Sound consistently ran slates of their members for elected union office. In this section, I recount some of the reasons for and criticisms of this emphasis. The themes in my analysis are that that elections are useful as opportunities to make propaganda, reformers seeking election pay a heavy price as the electoral work and personal relationships become intermingled, an exclusive emphasis on elections betrays pessimism about the capacity of the rank and file to fight in its own interests, and elections are an opportunity to perform the role of "loyal opposition" inside of the union. This last element is most important because the credibility of the activists depends on the recognition that they are not going to undermine the union itself.

At times, reformers' election bids were successful. For example, Kelly Vandegrift eventually became vice president of his local and established a strong leadership record in the union and the company. In 1998, he told me, "In the '89 strike I was executive board member. I was a trustee. I have been a delegate to the AFL-CIO Wichita, our central labor federation. I've been district delegate several times, and Grand Lodge delegate. I've been privileged to go to the IAMAW's school of leadership training I and II. I've been a safety committee member for two years, and now I ran again and I'm a safety committee member again. I was vice president of Local 834 during the 1995 strike, and I've held lots of other positions." In Wichita, neither Dave Smith nor Thomas won elections to officer posts,[14] but Vandegrift (whom Thomas called "Mr. Congeniality") got votes even during corrupt or irregular elections. Thomas commented on the Administrative Caucus's potential weakness: "They [leaders of the Administrative Caucus] still weren't able to stop us. And we would get within the top spot on a district-wide basis."

Thomas answered my charge that the UDC was consumed with internal politics and replicating the behavior of the Administrative Caucus. He agreed, in part, with other leftist activists who "bagged on us about being concerned primarily with getting elected. . . . But in the union, everything is politics." Rightly, Thomas and others stressed that elections give reformers a platform from which to "get people thinking about the issues." In contrast, on Thomas's description, Administrative Caucus candidates ran on reputation rather than on issues, thus raising an important distinction between two reasons (to win versus to propagandize) for and types of electioneering.

Sean Mullin ran for union local president in 1990 against David Eagle. Mullin got a third of the votes even without name recognition and used the election to reach out and spread the word about the new UDC caucus. For him, running candidates and agitating for reform go hand in hand: "It's the same 5 percent running the union. And that's just the way it is, because our membership refuses to exercise their responsibility and right to go vote. They say, 'Well, there's no candidates.' Well, UDC was formed just so we could field candidates, to give them the opportunity to have a fresh voice and a differing opinion of the way things are being done." Mullin gives voice to the contradiction inherent in representative politics: Workers refuse to exercise their democratic rights, but reformers can give them a reason to do so. Because class-consciousness is not a guaranteed or automatic result of working life, the intervention of groups like the

UDC is necessary to inform others about what it means to be in the union. Yet Mullin's language contains elitist overtones. The contract votes are opportunities for workers to become aware of "the fact that their leadership who is negotiating the contract, the [leaders] that they didn't vote for but allowed to be elected don't have the integrity that they really need to have to be negotiating for this many people." Against co-workers' arguments that individuals don't have any power, Mullin says that the 1995 experience "should have proven to you that your one vote does count because you got together and shot down that piece of shit that your leadership tried to sell you. We all put our one vote together, and we told them, we're not going to stand for this. That ought to prove to these people, don't think that you can't make a change, because you can."

In Everett in 1999, I spent some time with the New Crew, plus Tom Finnegan (who was aligned but never joined) and Stan Johnson (not to be confused with union president Bill Johnson), a member of the Administrative Caucus friendly with the New Crew leadership. Because the discussion involved a whole group— Finnegan, Johnson, Tom Jackson, Rick Herrmann, David Mascarenas, and Bill Sapiens—who got together in a pizza joint, the conversation rambled in microscopic detail (how much less was the pension, by how many votes was an election lost, how much money would Boeing save if they denied workers their ten-minute breaks, and so on) around various topics from the likely provisions of the coming contract (including the irregular workweek); interpersonal conflicts with union members; war stories of elections past and present; the merits of various kinds of beer; the problem of offsetting, off-loading, and outsourcing work; union practices like appointing stewards; the purpose of and prospects for my book; my politics; and their group's activity and plans. Herrmann marked the fact that we were able to get so many people together: "This whole movement is in everyone's blood. I mean, we invited fifteen or twenty people today, we're originals, and we just can't back away from it."[15] Again and again, the talk returned to the role of elections in the union reform movement.

Elections as Member Education

All of these longtime Boeing employees and union members emphasized the importance of membership education around contract issues. They were frustrated with members who did not believe them about the content of the coming contract. Having tried to explain Boeing's attempt to institute an irregular workweek (which Roy Moore, for example, thought was a smoke screen to distract people from the off-loading) and the likelihood of layoffs if workers were to accept the company's proposal, Herrmann offered a skeptical response: "They try to put me down as some kind of a wacko constantly" when "they can swing the outcome of this contract." At the same time, however, individual visionaries who take it upon themselves to harangue others into seeing the way forward may in fact be out of touch with the consciousness of those around them. Herrmann was understandably frustrated with his fellow workers. It is one thing to lead, but without others alongside, an activist becomes a vanguard of one. As with John Brown, there is a certain heroism in bearing up under ridicule and danger, and there is satisfaction in being right. But being right in itself carries little power.

As in Wichita, the activists in Seattle were daunted by personal attacks and the passivity of the membership. They wavered between recognizing the power and legitimate concerns of the rank and file and complaining about the "herd mentality" (in Finnegan's words) of the 37,000 workers around the Puget Sound. The campaign by established union representatives against New Crew agitators was brutal over a period of many years. In the 1990s, an election opponent named Zaratkiewicz circulated accusations that Grinde was antiunion and company oriented (an example, I suppose, of an Orwellian reversal of an accusation). Administrative Caucus supporters circulated rumors that he was racist and a Ku Klux Klan member, a wife beater, and a Communist. In reply, Grinde published a letter, signed by dozens of his supporters, telling the story of how he found out about the smear campaign in a conversation with a stranger who reviled him based on a flyer put out by the Administrative Caucus.

As the discussion went on, I realized just how important election campaigns were to the dissident group. Aside from contract seasons, elections offered opportunities for publicity, platform promotion, and rank-and-file education. Repeatedly, reformers ran for union office from the local to the district level. They won a few battles, but lost more. There were several election rules that, they argued, rigged every election in favor of the Administrative Caucus. For example, to run for district president, one would have to have served on the District Council. This rule eliminated any chance Grinde had to run for lodge president when he lost reelection for a seat on the District Council by twenty-three votes. In addition, block and compulsory voting causes independent caucuses to lose elections with multiple positions unless they have full slates (a candidate for every position, which militates against individuals running as independents).

In one 2004 email, Grinde wrote to "congratulate" Rick Herrmann after an official election loss: "Congratulations, RICK! You won a District 751 Local F Council Seat handily. . . . If it wasn't for block and compulsory voting! You took well over 50% of the VOTE! Way to go! I'm sorry our union runs elections with undemocratic, biased and simply unfair rules. The real sorry is not for your loss, but the loss of our members' freedom and American right to democracy which our fellow Americans are dying for it Iraq." In 2002, Tom Finnegan lost a run for Local C president, but the election was nullified after a Department of Labor investigation. It is very clear that the New Crew is not exaggerating in describing a concerted, decades-long fight against their winning any positions of influence in the union.

The UDC and New Crew groups did more than run for office, of course, but union elections were at the center of the New Crew's activity, so much so that there was little else to talk about. A visit to David Mascarenas's personal archive of New Crew materials revealed reams of flyers—exclusively about election campaigns. At Alfy's, I tried to shift the discussion repeatedly to talk about the group's plans for education and agitation in the plant, but most of the time one or the other activist would recount an election scandal or a personal conflict with someone in the Administrative Caucus. For example, I asked, "In 1995, what, concretely, did you guys do?" Grinde began to tell me that the UDC couldn't take credit for the uprising of the rank and file, but Mascarenas was carrying on a separate thread of conversation about the problems with union elections: "You see, they [Administrative Caucus] can get reelected by qualifying what is called block voting. . . . You must vote for all fifteen positions or they kick out your vote."[16] He also noted that many candidates were excluded from running because they had not attended a requisite number of union meetings, which eliminated the 98 percent of workers who did not attend meetings regularly from the pool of candidates.

Similarly, the conversation shifted very quickly from a discussion of "rabble-rousing" to how educational materials must be very accurate to avoid discrediting the reformists, to how close recent elections had been. Finnegan said, "Our votes have been so damn close. Some of us lost, some of us won." Grinde said, "I lost by twenty-three votes in the last district council election, which caused me to lose my bid for the presidency, and Rick lost his seat by twenty votes." Meanwhile, Rick Herrmann was still discussing how his interventions at local union meetings had been shut down, which was an opportunity to refocus the discussion on rank-and-file issues and education. Just as quickly, the discussion turned again, to gossip about former union officials like Tom Baker, who, although he was better, in their view, than the current administration, "went to jail for embezzlement, and the secretary . . . he let power go to his head. Well, he was a born liar." Later someone noted that in '92, Baker had been on his fourth wife, was dating a secretary, and nearly tripled her salary, at which point Finnegan quipped, "She made triple time for every time she—." There was a lot of talk about how much money union officials made (with Stan Johnson pointing out that it wasn't much more than an experienced shop-floor worker and others naming the kinds of cars union officials were seen driving) and the methods by which the Administrative Caucus conspired against reformers by digging up personal dirt and pitting individuals against one another.

The Political Is Personal

In this regard, 1992 was a very tough year for Don Grinde. The 1992 contract featured a number of givebacks on health care stipends and pay raises. In a TV interview, Grinde remarked that the contract would set the union and Boeing workers back thirty years. It was at this time that the UDC pushed in Wichita to have advance distribution of contract details. District 751 President Tom Baker took a neutral position on the contract, which was eventually accepted by membership vote.

At the same time, the New Crew/Rank and File caucus was running a slate of candidates during local and district elections. The elections themselves were corrupt. Grinde observed District 751 staff campaigning on the shop floor during work hours; Administrative Caucus officials called people to organize buses and vans (complete with Team 751 literature to take them to the polling places), they restricted other parking at the polling places, and they mishandled ballots. They also solicited absentee ballot votes from local retirement homes. On June 4, union leaders set up a fake "informational" picket (about which the locals, district, and Labor Council knew nothing) outside a restaurant frequented by Machinists and then ran the New Crew over the rails for crossing it.

Adding insult to injury, the Administrative Caucus circulated slanderous letters and flyers about the dissidents, while New Crew literature was systematically destroyed. Grinde received hundreds of harassing phone calls and hang-ups, one from lodge business representative candidate Don Branin. There were even threats against his wife. At union meetings and functions, Grinde was ignored or maligned. About one meeting on June 4, 1992, he wrote, "Pieces of flesh and blood were strewn all over the floor. Unfortunately that was me. Team 751 did a great job of character assassination. It took me about three days to overcome such a vicious attack on myself." Even though he also received numerous supportive calls and offers from others to get involved, so much pressure was placed on Grinde, who was told that the existing leadership would stop at nothing to defeat him, that he withdrew his candidacy for business representative. To add salt to the wound, the union fired Grinde and thirteen other dissenters from their appointed posts as shop stewards and threatened other stewards with the same fate if the stewards did not support Team 751 in the election. Grinde's materials provide extensive documentation of each of these offenses. In a letter to the Department of Labor,

AEROSPACE MACHINISTS INDUSTRIAL DISTRICT LODGE 751

AFL⋃CIO

THOMAS F. BAKER
District President

WILLIAM D. WALKAMA
District Sec'y-Treas.

9125 – 15TH PLACE SOUTH, SEATTLE, WASHINGTON 98108-5191

June 15, 1992

SEATTLE (206) 763-1300
RENTON (206) 235-3777
EVERETT (206) 355-8021
AUBURN (206) 833-5590
TACOMA (206) 627-0822
FAX LINE (206) 764-0303

DONALD GRINDE
15906 10TH AVE NW
ARLINGTON WA 98223

Dear Union Steward:

This is to advise you that we have notified the Boeing Company to relieve you of your duties as Union Steward in:

SHOP: T-6220   SHIFT 1st

LOCATION: Crane & Hooktenders, Bldgs. 40.21, 22, 23, 24, 30, 31, 32, 33

REASON FOR RELEASE: Administrative release

With many thanks for past service, I am

In solidarity,

Tom Baker

TOM BAKER
District President and
Directing Business Representative
District Lodge 751

opeiu8 afl:cio

Improving the Quality of Life through Collective Bargaining and Political Action.

Figure 9. Letter informing Don Grinde that he had been relieved of his duties as steward after his political challenge to the Administrative Caucus, 1992. Courtesy of Don Grinde.

Grinde wrote, "What good is it to belong to a union when you have to live in fear of the leadership who are supposed to guide and direct it?"

Grinde got caught up in exposing the corruption of the lodge president, Tom Baker, in winter 1991–1992. The corruption was closely connected to Baker's affair with his secretary, with whom he traveled at union expense. He gave her a raise from union funds so that her salary exceeded $78,000. The struggle against Baker was thus inseparable from the sides one took on the personal lives of the people involved, and at this time Grinde spoke frequently to Baker's wife, Diddy. Grinde quotes a District Council member named Diane Kezele, who said that $30,000 in union funds was unaccounted for because of Baker's expenses. "Tom told her that her concerns didn't need to get out on the shop floor." Kezele resigned. In conversation with other activists, Grinde had urged alternative candidates to steer clear of the affair/divorce scandal and focus on the missing funds. Baker wrote Diddy several threatening letters, claiming that he would no longer tolerate her trying to ruin his career. The tangled connections between personal life and union politics involved dozens of people with mixed loyalties and are impossible to separate out. Grinde was disappointed in news coverage of the dispute in the union, commenting, "My three points [about lack of democracy in the union] again are overlooked. The media is having a feeding frenzy about the apparent smut."

Grinde attempted to keep the emphasis of his work on the political shortcomings of the union even as he was drawn into these interpersonal scandals. During the events surrounding the 1992 election, Grinde cranked out letters to union leaders and the Department of Labor. He produced flyers for the New Crew's slate of candidates; gave numerous radio, newspaper, and television interviews; and spent hours on the phone each day. He was attacked by the district leadership for spreading information that would damage the credibility of the union in the media. By March, he was adding numbers of supporters to his mailing list. He received anonymous donations to his campaign. In his journal, he reported, "People are very supportive of me and the movement. Yet it is too early to say that I would run for the President's position because one must be elected to the District Council first." In May and June, members of the New Crew won offices in the locals. However, Team 751 had swept the district-level offices. Grinde filed charges against the union at the District Council and the International for election irregularities and called for a recount, but he was denied from speaking at the District Council.

Grinde Addresses the CEOs

Grinde felt obligated to struggle with the union and the company alongside—and, if necessary, on behalf of—other workers. Throughout the 1990s and into the 2000s, Grinde produced countless documents as the rhetorical face of the New Crew and its positions. Remarkable among these are letters he wrote to every CEO and other executives of the company. In 2002, he wrote to CEO Alan Mulally, negotiator Peter Calhoun, President Phil Condit, Harry Stonecipher, and others:

> You ask us to sacrifice while you line your pockets with millions of dollars off our backs. You act like, hey friend, can you spare a dime, while you sabotage your own work force. You speak daily with forked tongue and broken words.
>
> Boeing, your profits have doubled, your productivity has doubled, your off loads have doubled yet your [sic] not satisfied. You will never be satisfied. That is why we have unions, that is why we will fight back with every resource we have. That is why we will leave no one behind. That is why we will stand united for as long as it takes. . . . You will never rest as long as we have breath. . . .
>
> Terrorists come in many sizes shapes and colors. The terrorists I despise the most are the ones that come rapped [sic] in a flag with a smile on their face. The ones that scare me the most are the ones who are willing to sacrifice people for greed. The ones that scare me the most beg for billions and then in turn eliminate tens of thousands of workers needlessly.

This letter brilliantly connects the economic issues facing workers to a political critique of the priorities of the U.S. war on terrorism. Grinde expresses the basic class-consciousness necessary to effective union struggle: a strong sense of antagonism with the employer alongside a call to solidarity. He tells the executives, "The people who were on the fence are now coming to their senses and seeking solidarity. They see that as individuals they have no hope, no dream. With unity and solidarity they have not only those things but a vision as well. A vision of the future where each employee is treated with dignity and respect. A vision of a union that will stand with it's [sic] members. Union leaders with a vision who will lead at their own sacrifice." What is especially savvy about this letter is that it was an open letter not only sent to Boeing executives but also reproduced and circulated among workers. At the same time he challenged the company, he called out union leaders to stand with the members. Then he spoke directly to the rank and file: "People this is our chance to do something great for generations to come. Labor has always been about the future. Labor has always been about hope for tomorrow. . . . This is our mandate, this is our destiny. VOTE NO and REAFFIRM YOUR STRIKE SANCTION." This document addresses three audiences simultaneously with a mixture of threat and prophecy.

Others among his letters feature more humor. On the ascension of Harry Stonecipher to the position of Boeing CEO, Grinde wrote:

> Harry,
> Congratulations on your new assignment as company president and CEO. . . . It would be insincere of me if I said many of us were energized upon hearing the news. Most of us at the Everett factory were in a state of shock. . . . To be honest, your appointment felt like another new low in an already lengthy chronicle of bad news.

But Grinde went on to appeal to Boeing to honor its employees as a way of putting Boeing "back in 1st place in aerospace." He identifies the workers as important stakeholders in a plan "to focus and execute a plan that strengthens our relationship. We want to focus and execute a plan that is based on commitment, trust, and respect so that true human and material profit can be achieved." He went on to detail a seven-point plan that included both shop-floor voice and profit sharing.

This letter is interesting for the way it mimics the language of management: putting the company in first place, maintaining creativity and productivity, and focusing on plans to strengthen "relationships," "commitment," and "trust." Like Thomas and others among the reformers, Grinde is adept at calling attention to lip service and hypocrisy. He is aware that talk of transparency, mutuality, and shared benefits coming from management is shallow at best. In turning it back on them, he can get in details about an actual set of demands (again, circulated to union leaders and the rank and file) and let them know that he sees through the discourse of mutual respect and profit. He challenges them to take the high road, and rather than allowing the company to blame the union for divisiveness, he asks it to work in good faith or to "continue down the road of confrontation and distrust."

In another very funny letter addressed to Alan Mulally in 2002, Grinde refers to meeting the CEO in person at a recent town hall meeting with workers around the current contract negotiations. At that meeting, he had joked with Mulally about the executive's resemblance to Bill Clinton in being "a good communicator"—in other words a glad-hander and slick persuader. His remark, which sounds at first like a compliment, prompted long laughter and guffaws among the other workers present. Many members of the New Crew rose to speak during that meeting. In his follow-up letter, Grinde employs the tactic of sideways identification characteristic of the other letter: "Al," he writes, familiarly," It was a pleasure as always to meet you. In some ways we are the same in that we care deeply and have a passion toward our goals. I've always had a passion for the underdog, the little guy and the labor movement. . . . I cannot even imagine what your world looks like. . . . I wish to better understand The company logic so that I could be more effective in offering solutions that work for labor and the company." Again, he uses this platform of identification and openness to argue for job security, protection of pensions, and negotiations over off-loading. One implication of letters like this one is that Grinde does not trust the IAMAW bargaining committee to be so clear in its objectives in negotiating with the company. He feels that he must address company representatives himself. It is a poignant effort to represent the rank and file without the organization behind him.

Grinde and the New Crew adopted similar tactics in engaging union leadership. While Clay and the union leadership insisted on presenting a unified face of the union to the outside world, Grinde insisted repeatedly that unity is not unity if it depends on silencing all opposition. In a letter to IAMAW International President George Kourpias, Grinde and Tom Finnegan wrote: "If we are to have a strong union, then the rank and file must be allowed to participate in our microcosm of democracy without fear of reprisal and intimidation. The entrenched philosophy of the incumbent ticket (*the end justifies the means*) is strangling the life blood of our union."

These efforts met with some success. New Crew sympathizer Tom Finnegan won a seat on the District Council in 1992. Tom Baker was forced out of office (and given another high-paying job in the union) in 1993, replaced by Bill Johnson, who, according to the *Tacoma News Tribune*, "eliminated some of the Baker-era sins."[17] In another dispute, Local A was ordered to rerun its 1993 election by the Department of Labor for a violation of the Labor-Management Reporting and Disclosure Act (LMDRA). By the time the 1996 District Council election came around, the New Crew had renamed itself Rank and File. *Tacoma News Tribune* reporter Sean Griffin wrote, "The dissidents have strengthened. They're fielding full slates of candidates and are feeling buoyant by what they see as a swelling of support. . . . Rank and File has picked up a following and a certain level of sophistication."[18] However, in 1996 Grinde lost his District Council seat, by around twenty votes, to another reformer. In 1997, Bill Johnson barely beat his former supporter, David Clay, to win another term as president of the lodge.

Pessimism Prevails

Grinde and the rest of the Rank and File crew had been mired in an exhausting and complex election cycle against an incumbent group determined not to give ground. But at the 1999 group meeting with me, he consistently attempted to push the discussion back to what the group should be doing on the ground rather than analyzing elections past: "With a small group of dedicated people who believed in what they were trying to do, who'd share their message or concerns over the issues, whether it was something wrong with the union or wrong with the contract. We published flyers, we blanketed the factory with flyers and tried to make contacts as we could and develop an email list, a mailing list, and phone list, whatever it took, to try to build an organization." About the 1995 strike, he insisted that the UDC contributed to the rebellion of the rank and file by their involvement: "It helped prepare people to be active and helped them realize that they did have a voice and that there was something that they could do." He saw the role of the UDC subsequently as to educate the membership through handbills on issues like retirement, "and we can rekindle that solidarity, that fire in somebody's gut, if they realize, if we could show them how they're being wronged." Later, in the middle of a discussion about election campaigns, he interjected, "I think, really, it isn't absolutely necessary to be elected to effect change in the union. If you can build your caucus around core issues, educate your membership, like the retirement issue, we can really drive that home this time, because we have information that the membership doesn't know about. The union is presenting a contract to us like a car salesman would like to present a car to the first-time car buyer. They want him to buy the first car they fall in love with."

For the most part, however, the Everett crew replicated a more-or-less pessimistic and elitist tone about the rank and file. Grinde commented, "You know, when it's all said and done, a lot of the fingers still point back to each individual, every member. We blame everybody, we blame the union officers, we blame the company, but everybody wants to go home and drink beer or sit in front of the TV. . . . The members aren't demanding all that much." When I said that Dick Schneider said that he thought the members were ignorant and apathetic, Grinde said, "What else can they say? I agree with him 100 percent." From this perspective, it follows logically that the only way to change the union and get a better contract *for* the workers is from the top; hence, the emphasis on elections among the reformers. Mascarenas makes this clear: "I think that something's got to come from the top down instead of trying to force up, and the more everybody forces up, you just become bitter enemies, and the Boeing Company's sitting over there, enjoying it all."

The Vexations of the Loyal Opposition

Mascarenas has identified exactly the dilemma that is at the center of the dissidents' movement. When fighting the union becomes an end in itself *and* the activists see little way to fight the union except from its head, the company as the target of activism recedes from view. Johnson expressed this concern: If you revolt against the entire union leadership so as to impair a union's functioning (which, I would argue, is not a foregone conclusion), "Corporate America is going to steamroll over you." When a small group needles a powerful organization on behalf of workers whom they have not organized, they end up vilified and ineffective. One way—and I will suggest another later—to resolve this dilemma is, as Mascarenas advises, to join them rather than beat them.

The contradictions inherent in the position of "loyal opposition" come to the fore in the treatment of the New Crew. In 1992, a colleague of Grinde's wrote a letter supporting his right to dissent from the established practices of the union. Objecting to the abuse heaped upon Grinde, the author wrote:

> LOYAL OPPOSITION: Is this a contradiction in terms? . . . Without the concept of LOYAL OPPOSITION what position could our labor union maintain? What would be the necessity of a union if everyone saw things the same way? Would there be any need to grieve a company decision. Would we ever have the opportunity to walk a picket line in hope of a better contract if we agreed with everything the company did? . . . I believe the union movement is based on the premise that through disagreement and friendly dispute our lot can be *improved*. . . . This brings me to the thought of Mr. Grinde and his "*Reform Movement*." Must his need to express a differing point of view be squelched at all costs? Is there no room in our group for a voice of dissent? Has every political move made in our union by our union truly been for the good of the members? Is it not possible that greed and corruption may have come to our house? This possibility needs to be explored. The voice of dissent must not be squelched or lost in the roar of the crowd.

Citing the liberal principle of protecting the minority, the letter continues:

> Occasionally however the majority becomes obnoxious and/or self-serving by restricting themselves to a point of view that has not evolved to keep pace with the times. . . . [Their point of view is that] "We are the majority and the majority is always right, therefore whatever we do is right and any opposition to our view is, therefore 'WRONG.'" . . . I do hope that the present Leaders of our Union at both District and Local levels can find it in their hearts to allow for some LOYAL OPPOSITION and will not only welcome the *Reform Movement* but will encourage this activity as the healthy growing enabling thing it can be.

The letter concludes with a rumination that, if suppressed, a reform movement would become "divisive and unmanageable, even to the point of destruction of all we hold dear."

There are several important things to notice about this missive from a communication perspective. First, affirming the work of Kevin Real and Linda Putnam,[19] it works by arguing that the union is a form of "loyal opposition" to the company. Although this idea—that the union should be loyal to the company at all—might be questioned by the dissidents, it is rhetorically sophisticated in its positioning of the mainstream union leadership as a kind of loyal opposition so that they might identify with the perspective of such an opposition internal to the union. This move allows the writer to observe that the union might have become "obnoxious," greedy, corrupt, and unable to represent the good of the members. The author's analysis of the principle of the protection of the minority in a democracy is likewise smart insofar as it encourages union leaders to, if they are patriotic, understand their errors through the basic core values of American identity. The letter is an open letter, addressed primarily to reigning union leaders. It is a plea not only for tolerance but also for the welcoming of dissident voices in the process of making the union better. Implicitly, it is also a threat: We hope that the leaders of the union tolerate the reform movement—because otherwise the movement will become destructive of the union itself.

Such a welcome was not forthcoming. In Seattle, as in Wichita, facing constant calumny generated a sense of martyrdom among the activists. They saw themselves as a small group that "can show workers how they've been wronged." Grinde, for example, attempted to impress upon the group and especially upon Stan Johnson that reformers have good motives, and you can tell their motives from their willingness to sacrifice; he said he had "paid a terrific price" by putting union struggles ahead of his family. "But the point is that, whether you're a union rep or on the other side, on the rank-and-file side, if you're really involved, there's a huge sacrifice that our people are making." He wanted to know from Johnson:

> Why hasn't the union gotten to a point where they would sit down and talk with us and hear our criticisms, hear our suggestions, and try to work with us? Truly all we ever wanted wasn't a job, we wanted reform. We thought to reform was getting elected. We found that maybe that's not the case, maybe there's another route, maybe there's another avenue, and I think the union can see that we're sincere about what we're trying to do. We lost the elections and we're still there. Yeah, we've gotten discouraged from time to time, but we're still there and we're still offering good advice and suggestions and are willing to support them at the first opportunity. . . . Why won't they listen to us?

Beyond elections, Grinde implies, power would come with being heard by the leaders at the top of the union. Johnson replied: "Not all people are like you. You are truly interested in installing some reform and fairness. I don't think we ever want to just close our minds or our ears to opposing political views, because it's actually healthy." Johnson also was critical of activists who campaign on a reform program but really only want the official job and all of its perks (a point to which Mascarenas took offense). Grinde expressed skepticism that change can come from inside the system because "it is so gummed up that it can't. I think it wants to respond, but it doesn't know how." Throughout the whole meeting, Grinde was earnestly interested in how reformers could, rather than undoing the union, "create a union that we're all proud of and has meaning for us in our lives and that will protect working people."

In the run-up to the 1999 contract negotiations in Wichita, Keith Thomas also recognized the need for widespread agitation aside from internal union politics. He and the remaining UDC activists and their allies believed that the coming contract was going to be worse for the rank and file than the company's initial offers in 1995, that the Administrative Caucus was even more out of touch than it had been, and that the times were ripe for agitation. Thomas wrote (in a letter to activists), "The time is right to do something. People are starting to pay attention. A sense of immediacy is starting to develop on the shop floor as people become aware that the forces in place are starting to act upon issues that will affect their destinies." Recognizing that the remnants of the UDC and its allies were not going to be adequate to the task, Thomas recommended coalition building across caucus lines:

> I believe that collectively we can provide a stronger alternative voice with a greater chance of success to workers at Boeing. Individual caucuses will have little chance of success on a large scale although they can certainly have success for their respective spheres of influence. I think that the rank and file will be better served if we try and attain a victory for everyone.
>
> The UDC caucus will have very little impact or effect upon the Contract '99 negotiations.
>
> I believe that we should include as many outside groups or individuals that we can trust to a reasonable degree.
>
> We have quite the opportunity for a learning experience even if we lose. And, even if we lose we'll have the satisfaction of at least having tried to do the right thing by the rank and file. There will be a next time and other fights to apply the lessons that we learn.

Thomas urged concerted activism and propaganda efforts:

> We have the potential through the Internet to quickly reach thousands that we normally would not be able to reach. We can get them involved in what will be a highly visible labor struggle without the buffers and filters that the International Administrative Caucus has in place.

We need as many handbills as possible and a regular newsletter sent via email to as many as possible. Individuals can handle their own hard copy distribution in their respective areas.

Washington activist Dave Mascarenas had spearheaded the effort in 1989 to get workers the contract three days in advance of the vote—a reform that benefited workers during 1995 contract negotiations. Having foreknowledge of the proposal enabled workers to organize demonstrations and agitate around the contract.

In the end, these efforts proved insufficient to sustain the movement. However, I believe that dissident unionists could form lasting organizations with an emphasis on grassroots recruitment not only to election slates but also to the reform organization and its tasks. Such an organization can seek out broader solidarity with other reformers, especially if the various caucuses do not see themselves primarily as contenders for elected office. The propaganda and agitation efforts of dissident caucuses are the heart and soul of union democracy movements, the more so to the extent that they possess a long-term strategy that might not only create resistance to a contract but also build organizations involving greater numbers of activists.

In the United States, one is taught that elections are the best vehicles for change, and it is difficult to operate outside of this common sense: Elect new leaders to take a new course of action on behalf of the people. Not only does this idea affect the efforts of reform caucuses inside unions, it also prompts appeals to external leaders, like politicians, whose platforms contain pro-worker elements.

Such efforts may have merit, yet an emphasis on union and mainstream electoral politics is at odds with the reformers' critique that the Administrative Caucus wrongly politicizes the economic struggle in its support for politicians whose stance may be ambivalent toward workers or mixed with positions on which the rank and file would not agree. Then there is the problem that politicians don't necessarily return the favor. Clay described his disappointment in several Washington State politicians (Maria Cantwell, Dorothea Dix, Patty Murray, Brian Baird) for whom the influential IAMAW District 751 PAC had campaigned and raised money. When it came to supporting the rank and file in efforts to democratize the union, he said:

> They didn't have our back. We thought because we had worked for them in an official capacity and after I left that position and I knew these people and they know very well what's going on. We have a congressional investigation and record that says the union cheated and the whole thing should be overturned. The FBI and the whole nine yards. But when the IAMAW PAC is the eleventh largest in the U.S. and District 751 is the largest contributor,

and their stewards (600)—when you're a steward now under [Mark] Blondin they signed a paper that said they would—volunteer forty hours for political campaigns or lose their steward's badge. Not legal, but people who make the laws look the other way. We thought that when we went to them with our problems that they would listen. We abided by the process, went to committees, traveled to DC on our own time and money, and talked to politicians at the state and federal level, to no avail.

Political activity also runs the risk of displacing attention from shop-floor organizing, a real issue in Wichita's open shop, where union membership is voluntary and organizing a matter of active recruitment.

In a period of dampened rank-and-file activity, elections both inside and outside the union itself afford reformers some measure of agency. But this agency is a Catch-22: How does rank-and-file motivation arise? It cannot be entirely spontaneous. Rather, every union reform movement has required leaders and activists to enjoin the rank and file, to provide education and inspiration, as well as an organizational home to call their own.

The history of the Teamsters for a Democratic Union (TDU) is but one example of this process. In 1975, a small group of Teamsters, operating inside one of the most corrupt and undemocratic unions in U.S. history:

> drew up a list of contract demands and made plans to print and distribute a brochure to freight workers and organize meetings around the country. The group called itself Teamsters for a Decent Contract (TDC).
>
> TDC distributed thousands of flyers to freight Teamsters, organized meetings in dozens of cities, and held a demonstration in front of IBT [International Brotherhood of Teamsters] headquarters in Washington, D.C. They demanded that Teamster President Frank Fitzsimmons hold the line for a strong contract. The small group grew in numbers as freight workers responded to their message.
>
> The New York Times wrote that TDC was "creating a tremendous pressure on Mr. Fitzsimmons to bring home a contract that he can sell to the membership." Under this pressure, Fitzsimmons called the first national strike in the Teamsters' history. TDC pushed hard for an unlimited cost of living allowance clause and it was won.[20]

Through the 1980s and 1990s—which were bleak times for Teamsters, as they were for workers everywhere—they sustained their new organization, which became a deciding factor in both future contracts and union elections. It is notable that the TDU's main activity was centered on agitation around contracts, although winning the right to run and vote in union elections was also a priority.

A combination of strategies can rally the rank and file during periods of agitation; when activity is low, such an organization can sustain itself and train new leaders to carry the banner into the next fight.

The TDU was formed by a small group of militant workers, who then found themselves in the lead of other workers, who required information and confidence to join the struggle. Therefore, waiting for workers to rise up before involving them in reform efforts is folly, just as much as constant exhortations to involvement in periods of demoralization may also be fruitless. If one is attending nearly exclusively to political campaigns of one kind or another, one may miss signs of bottom-up anger and organizing opportunities as a small group of reformers pursue their individual goals.

In correspondence with me, Grinde described the problem of the electoral strategy: "Realize running for election may be the longest and hardest way to the solution. The minute you run for election every move you make is fair game and everyone judges your motives. You are suspect from that point forward. You lose the ability to make choices based on what is right, it also has to fit with getting elected. . . . Realize that just by pointing out a problem you become the persona of the problem." This is a key insight: The reformers became personae of the problems they pointed out. In a process of Orwellian attribution, the activists could appear in the minds of their adversaries as the corrupting and destructive influences that they found the established leadership to be.

Elections are not the only recourse for dissidents in times of downturn. Lawsuits against unions are attractive avenues for frustrated activists facing a concretized union bureaucracy. I turn now to a discussion of Thomas's successful use of the LMRDA to force the IAMAW to become more accountable to its members.

Arresting the Union

The Landrum-Griffin Labor-Management Reporting and Disclosure Act is a McCarthy-era law generated out of the distrust of unions and radicals in them. Dissidents have welcomed the provisions that give them the right to distribute oppositional literature and to seek democratization of elections and regular union business. In addition, the act affords reformers the investigative resources of the Department of Labor. An article favorable to the LMRDA concludes: "Industrial democracy presupposed union democracy because the union was the worker's voice in collective bargaining. This was the premise of Landrum-Griffin. Union democracy is the essential instrument of industrial democracy."[21]

Indeed, the Association for Union Democracy (AUD) strongly supports this legal strategy as one mechanism to force unions to become accountable to the rank and file. At the same time, the LMRDA was originally motivated by union busting and was strongly anti-Communist.[22] Under the cover of exposing "corruption" in industrial organizations, the federal government and employers could undermine the credibility of unions everywhere and insinuate themselves into union business. Business welcomed the act so as to weaken the power of unions (although they didn't want to see power in the hands of the rank and file, either). Doris McLaughlin and Anita Shoomaker reported in 1979 that it was unclear twenty years after the passage of the act whether it had had any democratizing effects in unions. While noting an increase in contested union elections, the authors attribute this activity not to the act but to economic and labor movement factors that prompted greater worker involvement.[23] Some aspects of the LMRDA have antidemocratic effects; for example, the requirement that insurgent candidates plan their campaigns up to eighteen months before the election (after attending a required number of union meetings).[24] There was concern that employers could use disgruntled employees by urging them to bring suit against their union; indeed the National Right to Work Legal Defense Foundation, an antiunion organization, has sponsored LMRDA-based suits by dissident members against their unions.[25]

The act empowers the Department of Labor (DOL) to investigate and intervene in union elections at will. The DOL's top policy makers are political appointees whose interventions may reflect their economic and political commitments.[26] Furthermore, the LMRDA requires unions to make full reports of their finances; these reports are public information available to employers and antiunion forces just as easily as to the government or anyone else.[27] On the one hand, holding union bureaucrats accountable for their spending is necessary. On the other, the question is, who is doing the holding? It may be a matter of the fox guarding the henhouse. In other words, union democracy does not happen from the top down or from the government to the individual plaintiff; to use the law in this way contradicts the spirit of union democracy. It may undermine it in reality, as well.

These efforts reveal the necessary tension between democracy and discipline: An entirely open union in not the most powerful one. Even so, I believe that union democracy can serve industrial democracy. The TDU used the power of the law to win the right to vote for union leaders in 1985. The TDU Web site explains how the members did not want the government to take over the corrupt union under the Clinton antiracketeering law (RICO), but once this happened, they used the opportunity to win voting rights:

> When the RICO suit was announced, TDU National Organizer Ken Paff wrote the U.S. Attorney General saying "there is only one 'reorganization' under

RICO that the government can effectively take: namely, to direct the IBT to hold rank-and-file elections." On March 13, 1989, the Justice Department reached an agreement with the IBT to settle the RICO suit. It established a court supervised Independent Review Board to clean out corruption. Most important, it provided for the direct election of Teamster officers. TDU's position against government trusteeship and for the right to vote had prevailed. The *Wall Street Journal* reported that "the terms of the settlement were greatly influenced by the concerns and platform of Teamsters for a Democratic Union."[28]

In this instance, a bottom-up movement of radicals in the Teamsters was able to use the law. Clearly, using what they had available to them, including the federal government, aided in their struggle. It is a different matter when such an effort does not involve an active, organized membership but rather is led from above on the basis of individual lawsuits. It is a difficult balancing act; neither horn of the dilemma between using the union and fighting the union is particularly comfortable. To the extent that the Administrative Caucus of established officials embraces business unionism, dissidents may make the union itself their main target, losing sight of the contract as the point of struggle and of the rank and file as the agents of change.

In 1999, Keith Thomas, with the assistance of the AUD, successfully mounted a civil legal case against the IAMAW. The suit contended that the IAMAW did not meet the requirements or inform workers of their rights as provided by the LMRDA in the form of a workers' bill of rights. Thomas explained:

> I wrote a letter to the union asking them to comply with the Labor–Management Reporting and Disclosure Act of 1959, as amended, that says they're supposed to inform union members of the provisions of the act. And it's about a one-sentence line in there, and really that's all it is. There's a section in this act that says that unions are supposed to tell their members about the provisions of the act.
>
> One of the most important provisions of the LMRDA as far as I'm concerned is the fact that it gave us a bill of rights as union members. It gave us those freedoms of speech that we value so highly, supposedly, in this society and that we prize. Because if they [IAMAW leadership] can't stifle your freedom of speech, they've got some serious problems.[29]

For Thomas, making such problems for the IAMAW is a good thing enabled by the LMRDA. In 1999, Thomas was gratified to win the lawsuit, which he called an outstanding victory: "Folks in unions don't know they have basic rights. They don't know that when they're told to sit down and shut up at a union meeting, they really do have a right to speak about any subject that they want. That right's protected by law, and not the union official."[30] The AUD recounts the rights afforded by this act to union members: equal rights in membership, voting, and running for elected union office; freedom of speech and assembly; protection from arbitrary dues increases without a vote of the membership; the right to sue the union; and protection of workers from improper discipline or punitive action on the part of the union. Further, the act requires unions to hold regular and open elections; to make copies of contracts for members' inspection before a contract vote; to adopt a constitution and bylaws specifying every aspect of union procedure; to keep open records of union finances, including pay of union officials (out of dues or by the employer, prohibiting conflict of interest in negotiations); to report regularly on the fiscal status of the organization; and to make all of these documents part of the public record available to anyone upon request.[31] Any labor organization in violation of these provisions may face legal sanction or be forced into trusteeship.

Thomas made a strong argument that the potential drawbacks of using the LMRDA were outweighed by the benefits:

> Prior to the LMRDA, labor unions could and would do anything to members that they wanted with their organization. There weren't any laws limiting what they could do internally. The construction trades were particularly brutal. (Still are.) Prior to 1959 when the LMRDA was passed, workers that were union members did not have freedom of speech, assembly, etc. It is the LMRDA that provides union members their bill of rights and defines their relationship with governing entities, just as our Constitution and Bill of Rights defines the relationship of citizens with the government. There is some limited carryover to the private sector through specific legislation.
>
> We needed our freedom of speech rights to deal with the company. Management was constantly throwing away our handbills. One of our guys watched the head of Boeing Wichita (Dryden at the time) direct people to remove our handbills. Union agents were also constantly throwing away as much of our stuff as they could lay their hands on.
>
> Union hacks were also telling people that our group and activities were illegal. We knew better. Companies are not supposed to get involved in union elections. So we simply started campaigning with our handbills and told company reps to keep their noses out of internal union business. It did put them back on their heels just a bit.
>
> It also demonstrated to the rank and file that we were legal (a bigger issue to them than us) and we had a government document that we could show them or that they could look up on their own.

We demonstrated that we were not afraid to take on the IAM and Boeing.

The court case also demonstrated that the IAM hacks were not the final authority in regards to our legal rights. They (Administrative Caucus) presented themselves as the final authority in determining LMRDA rights. They usually figured it out that we didn't have the right to exist or handbill or run for office or . . . well, you get the picture.

Other union reformists can use the groundwork laid by the lawsuit to assert their rights in dealing with their unions and companies. They fight the same battles.

People for the first time found out that they had rights.[32]

We ought not underestimate these achievements. Yet the original motivation in 1959 for the LMRDA was to curtail union power vis-à-vis the employer. The language of the act is strongly probusiness; section 2 (a) reads:

> The Congress finds that, in the public interest, it continues to be the responsibility of the Federal Government to protect employees' rights to organize, choose their own representatives, bargain collectively, and otherwise engage in concerted activities for their mutual aid or protection; that the relations between employers and labor organizations and the millions of workers they represent have a substantial impact on the commerce of the Nation; and that in order to accomplish the objective of a free flow of commerce it is essential that labor organizations, employers, and their officials adhere to the highest standards of responsibility and ethical conduct in administering the affairs of their organizations, particularly as they affect labor-management relations.[33]

This language suggests concern for the unionized worker, but to some extent that concern has served as a rationale for federal intervention—to the point of removing officers, voiding elections, and imposing trusteeship—into unions suspected of being corrupt, even when they were not. Furthermore, the public-records provisions make all union records, including financial records, available not only to members, but also to employers. Employer access to financial information could actually undermine workers' power during a conflict over a contract. For example, advance knowledge of the financial health and membership of a union allows employers to weigh their ability to wait out workers during a strike.

In addition, the original language of the act prohibited Communists (along with convicted felons) from holding elected union office. This provision was overturned in 1965 by the U.S. Supreme Court. Yet the LMRDA itself warranted decades of anti-Communism and suspicion of left-wing influence inside unions, a legacy that still weakens unions by the suspicion or exclusion of Socialist or Communist organizers from their ranks. As Robin Kelley, Sharon Smith, and a number of other labor scholars have noted, Socialist and Communist activists were instrumental in a number of the big labor victories of the 1930s and since.[34] The habits of shop-floor organizing and mobilizing the economic strength of workers were hallmarks of these organizations' efforts. New provisions in place in 2005 made even more work for unions to report the minutiae of their membership and finances, not just to union members, but also to the Department of Labor. They use the LMRDA to warrant doing away with card-check union ratification.[35]

Thus, while it is necessary to use all available means to democratize unions, one of the dangers of instruments like the LMRDA is that they open the union to federal and company scrutiny. There are other costs as well: Good activists may devote time and other resources to an individual, double-edged pursuit. Ultimately, this tactic makes the union, not the employer, the main target of reform-oriented activity, losing sight of what is powerful and necessary about unions: the marshaling of the collective power of workers.

It is absolutely true that the IAMAW and any number of other unions have been passive, needlessly conciliatory with business, and suspicious of shop-floor democracy—if not corrupt outright. In addition, we must recognize the effects on the rank and file of intensified outsourcing, off-loading, and lean production practices. Rank-and-file workers are less likely to rise up under such pressure. The Boeing Company has been a model offender in its ruthless amputation of the unionized workforce in Wichita, its layoffs of tens of thousands while demanding increasing productivity of workers who remain, and its detachment from the communities and lives of its employees. In this context, it is as or more important to arrest—stop, contain, and hold accountable—the company as it is to arrest the union organization.

Summary: For the Union Makes Us Strong?

The stories of Thomas, Grinde, and other leaders of the rank-and-file movement raise the possibility that the replication of the union's top-down methods was symptomatic of a broader neoliberal siege on workers in general. Pressures to perform under threat of layoff make for a cautious union. The dissidents' frustrations and pessimism are logical responses to the difficulty of maintaining a substantial base in the rank and file. At the same time, the enactment of the strategies of speaking for and speaking to, rather than speaking in tandem with, greater numbers of workers results from the paradoxical nature of representation. To be a critic is by definition to "get ahead" of the majority; it is an enormous organizational and rhetorical task to bring others alongside. Yet it is necessary to do so if one truly wants to lead a movement for greater democracy.

Lessons from these stories may inform the union democracy movement more broadly: Dissident organization can and must be sustained through difficult times so that when grievances spark renewed militancy, there can be effective organizational expression of that energy. It is contradictory to commit oneself to the rank and file while substituting the intense efforts of a few for those of a potentially broader collective. It was mistaken not to collect dues and keep the organization going even when it was under attack. Finally, it is necessary to train new layers of members to replace burned-out leaders and to sustain the organization independently of its founders through difficult times. Surely, unions as they exist today are not adequate vehicles for workers' agency in the new millennium, but it is wrong to reject the idea of the union: a type of organization that collectivizes workers at the point of production, where, standing up against globalization and its effects, workers still have direct power against employers.

Similarly to my argument, chroniclers of the 1994 Staley lockout Steven Ashby and C. J. Hawking criticize the international unions for relying on legislative and other top-down strategies; for them, these approaches represent the paternalism of business unionism.[36] These habits often stand in stark contradiction to the reformers' vision of change. For example, during my visit to the Puget Sound in 1999, David Mascarenas, a Boeing labor activist in the Everett plant, shared with me his extensive collection of photos and documents related to the Seattle general strike of 1919, which involved 350,000 people and shut down the city for nearly a week, demonstrating the power of labor solidarity. The strike was inspired by the Bolshevik revolution, and its leaders included many Reds and anarchists. The backlash against the strikers took clear aim at the radical influences on these events.[37] Mascarenas clearly drew inspiration from the 1919 strike. It represented a near-revolutionary moment, a glimpse of what workers' power might actually look like; yet it could not stand against a capitalist class bent on self-preservation protected by the forces of the state. Even so, it demonstrated the way forward for a labor movement that eventually would come into its own in the United States. This movement had its eye on the bosses and aimed at ending their systematic exploitation of working people.

It was a time before, before the extensive organization of unions and before institutional insinuation into the existing order of things, before the right to strike was even won legally and before the purge of radicals who were willing to break the law, before bureaucracies had formed to give shape to the pressure from below and before a new movement was needed again to reradicalize and reorient a labor movement antagonistic to the bosses and the fundamental exploitation of the capitalist system.

The Seattle strike popularized the labor anthem "Solidarity Forever," whose lyrics include the following words:

> When the Union's inspiration through the workers' blood shall run,
> There can be no power greater anywhere beneath the sun.
> Yet what force on earth is weaker than the feeble strength of one?
> But the Union makes us strong.

The force of one, or a few, is feeble when standing against a corporate behemoth like Boeing. Only a union organizes the collective common cause and common interest. Collective economic clout was, and could again be, a source of great power. How are we to remake old unions or invent new, inspiring ones that will make us strong against rather than aligned with business interests?

The undemocratic practices of entrenched union leaders and the harassment and obstructionism toward reformers are only partially responsible for the failures of union democracy movements. Also key is the lack of the kind of sustained organization that generates militant consciousness and confidence in the struggle. Perhaps it is necessary to harass and even dismantle existing unions, but to resign oneself to the tactics of the isolated few is to take the wrong lesson from the decline of U.S. unions. Feeble we are and feeble we will remain without an organized fight-back. Again, in the words of "Solidarity Forever," "Is there anything left to us but to organize and fight?"

7

Carrying the Memory of Agitation

A Dialogue between Keith Thomas and Dana Cloud

This exchange—referred to by both Keith Thomas and Dana Cloud as a "postmortem" on Unionists for Democratic Change (UDC)—was edited and compiled from two conversations: The first is a recorded interview between Dana Cloud and Keith Thomas in Wichita, Kansas, on July 17, 2001, the evening after a small demonstration at the union hall earlier that afternoon; the second source is a series of letters exchanged in summer 2006. I asked, Do you think you could have/should have done anything differently? Thomas replied, "Well, winning would have been nice."

Here Thomas complicates my arguments that mistakes and misdirected focus are to blame for the decline of the union democracy movement at Boeing.

DANA CLOUD: Why are there no more union activists in Wichita?

KEITH THOMAS: Well, you saw a good example of that at the union today. There weren't a whole lot of people there.

DC: That might be because there wasn't anything exciting or pressing on the docket. Just because things are quiet for a time doesn't mean the movement is over or that people are pessimistic or ignorant.

KT: When we were active, there was always something to talk about. There was always a lot of participation when we were active. But I think by the same token most of the people in our local were knowledgeable about stuff, saw the action we took time after time.

DC: You were part of galvanizing workers around issues that were already there. The opportunity was there, and the UDC filled a need. I think that need still exists.

KT: When I started as an activist, I'd be cussed all the way to the podium and all the way back. Just one obscenity after another, and that went on month after month. When we started this, I used to be the lightning rod, being the most vocal one. We figured they'd go after me and I'd just be the lightning rod and we'd have them wasting a lot of their

Figure 10. Keith Thomas leading an informational picket outside IAMAW Local 834 on July 14, 1999, in Wichita, Kansas. Photo by Dana L. Cloud.

ammunition on me and others would be able to get elected. I didn't always run for the top office, though some people like to make that claim. I ran for a variety of offices.

DC: What happened to Unionists for Democratic Change? Why did you disband the organization around the time of the strike?

KT: There were a lot of reasons for disbanding the caucus. The most important reason is that it just wasn't working. It was like we reached a point where we were just demonstrating how much of a beating we could take. No matter what we did, the leadership of the IAM [International Association of Machinists] was going to sell out the rank and file to serve Boeing, and there was no way that we could stop them. The people were quite willing for us to fight for them, but they quite simply weren't going to join in.

After the last contract before the layoffs started, I had a guy call me up in the plant and tell me how stupid I was for saying that it was a bad contract and provided no job protection in spite of the fact that the IAM hacks said that it did. He was laid off a few months later, as were a lot of others that voted to accept the contract. I would have rather been wrong.

The IAM's failures somehow made it more difficult to get people interested in doing something about the way things were turning against them. A lack of fresh bodies should be somewhere close to the top [of a list of reasons], followed by depleted resources. Since we had set up an EIN [Employer Identification Number], we felt that we should cover our legal bases by officially shutting the caucus down. I think that the personal toll in terms of health, marriages, finances, job (keeping it), etc. are also factors.

There is no reward system for reformists as defined by the general population. In spite of all the rhetoric, people really do things because it's the right thing to do. It's enough for some of us, but the reality is that ours is a rewards-for-actions-based culture. I'm still amazed at how little it takes to get people to toe the line.

Towards the last, the threats were certainly more intense, culminating in a drive-by shooting in our neighborhood after a death threat had been made earlier in the day. It was at that point that as a group people were finding themselves facing more violent circumstances than they had planned. In spite of assertions to the contrary, we did try to broaden our base and spread out. We expended a large portion of our limited resources reaching out on a local and national level. We also reached out on a personal level and interacted with reformists in other unions.

It always seems that there are those on the sidelines that could have done it better. It needs to be noted that it hasn't in fact happened. All across the country for the last few decades, tens of thousands of educated, dedicated, militant labor union reformists have attempted to bring about change in the labor movement. While there were some isolated success stories, overall, attempts at reform were unsuccessful. The same company union fucks that were running the labor movement into the ground are still doing it or have been replaced in kind. So, did *all* of us get it wrong? All the reformists in all the major unions all over the country? Is there perhaps another reason or other contributing factors besides all of us getting it wrong?

DC: What are those other contributing factors?

KT: I know that people, make that some people, are loath to assign any responsibility to the rank-and-file union member, but is that realistic, appropriate, or even remotely accurate? If we're willing to give accolades and credit to average people when they finally stand up for their rights and way of life, then I believe that it follows that all the times that they don't have to be acknowledged. Is that the fault of those who tried to organize them? I believe that the problem faced by the UDC and activist groups in general is deeper and more fundamental than apathy, though that is the word most often used by people, including myself, to explain the lack of interest or activism on the part of the general public.

A cultural shift has taken place. People started accepting contracts that for the most part left their wages and benefits intact but screwed over new hires. Same job, less pay. The new hires of yesterday remembered, and now they're screwing over retirees. Neither of the above actions was motivated by apathy. Self-interest and payback were and are the primary reasons behind what has been and is taking place.

The International Association of Machinists is now negotiating and recommending contracts that have no pension benefits for new hires. More importantly, unfortunately, people are accepting these contracts. Other forces besides apathy are in play here. (The IAM is also accepting and promoting piecework.)

The rank and file all across the board had the opportunity to bring about change. As a body, they chose not to get involved. It really wasn't for lack of education.

DC: I think maybe it *was* for lack of education. If people don't understand the history of concessions and how their actions today make their own lives better and those of generations to come, they need to be reeducated. We need to carry the concept of solidarity to the rank and file. I think people can be inspired, as I have been, by the history of struggle. Learning why the activists at Flint [Michigan] decided to sit down in spite of it being illegal, learning about how they organized: These are the kind of lessons that motivate people who aren't by nature self-interested or apathetic.

KT: But to use Boeing again as an example, we distributed literally millions of pieces of educational material in addition to being at the forefront of using the Internet for distributing information. Workers went out of their way to avoid being informed. If they had information, they couldn't use the excuse that they didn't know. I helped distribute the IAM material as well. What I found most often is that people valued what suited them personally, as in "I can live with this contract."

DC: You've missed my point a bit. I think people need education beyond the current contract to see the big picture.

KT: But what do you do when people expect less?

DC: You try to use history to raise their expectations.

KT: There are people working at Spirit [the company that replaced Boeing Wichita after the sale to Onex] today that are already willing to accept less, even after accepting across-the-board cuts when Boeing sold the Wichita commercial facilities to Onex. No amount of organizing has been able to combat that.

DC: I think there might be other factors—like economic change and the political climate—beyond people's short-term self-interest or apathy. I say short-term because actually it would be in people's interests in the most selfish sense to be part of sustained labor organization even through slow times. What do you think about that?

KT: [Don't we have to put] some responsibility on the people that are sitting on their hands? They aren't willing to invest their time, effort, or money to bring about a change. They are perfectly willing to watch someone else (others) take the beating. They may even encourage them to keep fighting! There's just so much of a beating that I'm willing or able to take, especially if the cause becomes either pointless or unwinnable. A good general knows when to stop, in victory or defeat. There were some victories, but the war was a lost cause. There will be tactical errors in most endeavors. We did reach out and train other people. They burned out. It isn't as if there are a lot of people out there willing to put in another forty-plus hours a week, give up their free time, spend their own money, and do all that with little chance of success and no reward unless risking losing your job is going to count as a benefit.

DC: Again, think about the long term. A few people can sustain a low level of effort over a period of time in order to be in place to recruit others when the climate becomes more agitational. Perhaps to *help* that climate become more agitational. To carry the memory of agitation to new folks. And the more people you involve, the less time and money any one person has to dedicate. Over the long term, there is a reward. I don't think people need direct, immediate, or personal rewards to be motivated to organize.

KT: The Administrative Caucus has a reward-based system firmly in place. So what you would see is all these activists kicking their brains in and putting themselves at risk, and their homes at risk, and their families at risk, because the stories are out there. Certainly people weren't ignorant of the kinds of things that were taking place. They were seeing all the kinds of abuse that we were putting up with at union meetings and would take those stories back to their shops. And for, in their opinion, nothing.

We also had people from locals where the pay and benefits weren't all that good. Same story. People still didn't want to get involved. Same reasons. We are lacking in the ability to give the general population humanity and the capacity to think in terms of what is good for others and not just for ourselves.

DC: We don't have to "give" people humanity. As I said earlier, labor organizing, democratic labor organizing is good for themselves; it's not altruistic. It's a long-term reward. Maybe if organizations offered education in labor history and strategy workers could recognize their long-term interests in making the unions work for the workers. Maybe then unions could be transformed and used by people in their own interests.

KT: In this country, on this planet, they aren't going to change. At best, the majority of unions are like banana republics. At worst, they're banana republic company unions like the IAM. In spite of terrible losses, the IAM has never stopped partnering with companies, including Boeing. They're helping companies eliminate jobs. Of course, they do get to put their cronies on the take (company payroll). They negotiate reductions in pay and benefits and help eliminate pensions.

If you look at the record of labor unions in our area, it isn't good. It has been one defeat after another. Not a glowing recommendation. When around 1,000 people lost their jobs in the Boeing to Onex sale, the union didn't do anything for them. Think those people will join again?

I understand that there is this idea of what a union could and should be just as there are a lot of ideal organizations that don't exist in any form other than a shadow of an ideal. The reality is that a major stumbling block to dealing with business in general and global corporations in a militant fashion is labor unions. The minority of militants that do take on business usually have to fight through their own unions first because labor union leadership runs interference for the companies.

DC: This is the main point of this book. But that doesn't mean that we should do away with the unions.

KT: When labor unions were more powerful, they abused their power to a greater degree against the rank-and-file militants. If you think labor unions can change, give it your own best shot. It will be five years before you can expect to see any results.

DC: Exactly. What's wrong with that?

KT: That is what we used for a yardstick as best we could figure out from our own observations of other reform groups. You can expect success at a localized level. After all, you'll be dealing with smart people. You will need to spend a shitload of your own money.

DC: What is your answer to my criticism that UDC contradicted itself by saying you were for the rank and file but not involving the rank and file?

KT: It certainly wasn't for lack of trying. Democracy just isn't as popular as it used to be. Not then. Not now. The message was certainly an accurate one. Should we blame the messengers or the recipients? Our message has certainly validated by what has happened. The IAM was unable to muster up token resistance here in Wichita. The great and powerful IAM District 751 of Washington State didn't even get involved. Boeing working with Onex busted the IAM here in Wichita for all practical purposes. The Spirit contract is absolutely company dominated. The rank and file of the great 751 wasn't interested enough in what was happening to their comrades in Kansas to do anything substantive. That's OK. Their turn in the barrel is coming up.

In their minds, since they're willing to work for less, everyone else should be as well. That's their rationalization for not being ready to stand up for themselves or anyone else.

A person can be passionately in love with someone who only wants to be friends. Should we blame the person with passion for being unable to make a friend fall in love?

DC: Nicely put. But unions are not individuals and they don't behave like individuals. I think some well-meaning people inside the union might be skeptical about the union bill of rights and the LMRDA [Labor-Management Reporting and Disclosure Act of 1959] because of their conservative provisions that actually undermine union power. Some of these provisions are pretty right wing. For example, there's the right not to belong to a union. You know that open-shop provisions undercut workers' power.

KT: These weren't on the bill of rights that I took right out of the IAM organizing material. I took the list right out of the IAM organizing material, and I repeated it word for word to the members. And these were rights that they were already telling people that they had; why wouldn't they pass it and put it in their constitution? What you find in their constitution is the suppression of freedom of speech. Which namely means that you can't say anything bad about a union official. The rights I was talking about had nothing to do with being antiunion. It was simply basic freedom of expression and assembly, freedom to run for office, access to records, rights that people had anyway. There was nothing in there that the IAM wasn't saying anyway. If you put it in the constitution, why would they object to that?

By filing and then following through with the lawsuit, I believe that we accomplished several things, some of which I've already covered in part.

We demonstrated that we were not afraid to take on the IAM and Boeing.

Many people for the first time found out that they had rights.

DC: How did you come to use the LMRDA?

KT: I worked with the Association for Union Democracy. The AUD operates under the premise that democracy makes unions stronger and therefore better able to stay in business. I'm sure that they have some kind of mission statement at their Web site. I think that you have a personal issue with using the government, including the legal system.

DC: I don't have a problem using the government in principle. The issue for me is that you undertook strategies by yourself (OK, with one or two other people) *on behalf* of others rather than empowering people to take action for themselves. I know you think that they won't do that, which led you to the legal strategy. The lawsuit is kind of the graveyard of social movements. Like the Democratic Party.

KT: Look. We were fighting the company, union, and the government. Why in the world would we want to make things even more difficult for ourselves by tying one hand behind our back and not use a tool available to us? We used the company and union rules to our advantage whenever possible. We didn't have to expend the group's resources since the lawsuit was filed by individuals.

DC: This is my point. The lawsuit is one kind of tool. Reformers need another kind of tool if reform is going to be real: the collective power of organized dissidents.

KT: If you live in this country, there are laws that work to your advantage. Should you not use them or step outside their protection? I suppose people could carry signs saying, "Mug me if you want. I won't use the legal system and press charges."

DC: I really do see your point. That's a pretty good argument.

DC: But the NLRB [National Labor Relations Board] and the LMRDA think it's a union member's right not to have to join a union in their workplace. You and I both know that closed shops enable labor to win more consistently. These laws may offer some advantages for union members, but laws are not the way to get the official union to reform. The goal of them is to undermine unions at all.

This issue speaks to the tension you raised between having to get through the union to the company. When you open the union to legal intervention, you risk undoing the union completely. I don't think the government is looking to help democratic unionists out.

KT: The rights I was talking about had nothing to do with being antiunion. It was simply basic freedom of expression and assembly, freedom to run for office, access to records, rights that people had anyway.

DC: As I said, we can think that it's about the union and its members, but the state is just too happy to get on board. Even if we don't reject the whole LMRDA. But it was a product of the Taft-Hartley era, and it was a follow-up to Taft-Hartley. The real issue is that the law had its origin in a right-wing, antiunion, Red-baiting moment. You can't just pick it up and use it any way you want; it has baggage.

KT: The bill of rights was not a right-wing-driven part of it. Open-shop provisions are not in the bill of rights part of the LMRDA. We can look it up. And actually most folks in this country don't know there's no such thing as a closed shop in the United States of America.

DC: But it seems to me that in its inception and in the way in gets used most of the time, the LMRDA perpetuates stereotypes about unions as corrupt and undemocratic and not representative, illegitimate organizations in bargaining. It's part of an ideological smear campaign.

KT: I know that most of the Socialists that I talk to got their knickers in a twist over the provisions of the LMRDA that are quite obviously antiunion. But then get your knickers in a twist about the entire Constitution. Did it stop the people in the civil rights movement that there was a racist document out there that said that I didn't even count as an entire human being? Now did they reject the entire Constitution or did they take the people to court? The women fighting for suffrage didn't say, gosh, the Constitution was created by a bunch of white, property-owning men to sustain their lifestyle. Black people weren't considered human beings, women didn't have the vote, we had child labor and indentured servants and any of other things, and by the way, we're slaughtering the indigenous population. They didn't say we reject that document so we're not going to fight it in the courts. That would have been stupid on their part to do that.

DC: That's an excellent point.

KT: So they used the sections of the Constitution and managed to get some changes. I could throw out the baby with the bathwater, say the whole LMRDA is corrupt, because there's this one section in there that talks about the Commies. But you have to go to the court cases to find that or to the notes at the end of the document for the amendments. But we fortunately in this particular document happen to have a bill of rights for working people and this is stuff that allows me freedom of speech, freedom of association, freedom to form a caucus in the union. We beat the IAM in a case charging that a dissident caucus constitutes dual unionism, which is illegal. That's the whole point of my court case. If you want to say there's a bad section in here let's not use any of it, then say that about the Constitution.

DC: Maybe it's not a good analogy; the right analogy would be if the parts of the Constitution that the movement wanted to enforce required all the social movement organizations to spill all the details of their operations and open themselves up to potentially damaging criticism. When we're looking internally to movement organizations, using laws against them rather than against the company, we might lose sight of the end goal. I'm just saying that some of the arguments that you have been making lately about unions being in bed with the capitalists could be interpreted as being antiunion. It plays into those same antiunion stereotypes.

KT: I guess there's a lot of things that I'm not. People could call me antisomething. But I am pro-worker. You can let someone else define you. Am I anti-labor leaders? They're the heads of banana republics. They have little dictatorships. They have these little quasi governments that they work for. But they're the worst thing you can have in the labor movement. The labor boss is not the rank and file. The people got all the heart in the world out there. The labor bosses are destroying the labor movement. They can't give up the reins, they can't give up the power. They are like CEOs. The union leaders are partners with Boeing. I'm not a partner with Boeing.

DC: Let's back up a bit. I think it's important to look to how the union was actually democratized for a brief and shining moment in 1995. It didn't have anything to do with constitutions and lawsuits. And it wasn't about one person doing all the work of democratizing the union, either, was it?

KT: What I did along with some other activists, and you can tell the activists by the people who are being outspoken and taking a position other than that being espoused by the Administrative Caucus. We didn't have the agenda of the Administrative Caucus because the company's profits weren't our concern. We had our own agenda. And then we simply started building very quickly from that core group. And what we called the guide members all had the same voice.

DC: Why didn't you build much beyond the initial core members? Doesn't it contradict the idea of rank-and-file power if just a few guys are in charge of everything?

KT: We didn't have the resources where we could have all-member meetings. We actually looked at the TDU [Teamsters for a Democratic Union] and their structure and found it a little too formal for our needs. It really wouldn't fit. And we knew that we couldn't get all those people there, so it was the guide members that actually handled the business. We had to make decisions about how to spend money. We had to have a secretary.

DC: The TDU was effective and lasting. So wasn't it pretty limiting for you guys not to have more members involved? What about the fact that you and only a few others put up most of the money and paid for everything that UDC did? Is it nobler for a few people to sacrifice everything?

KT: We'd have been better off if we'd had a budget. We were supplying the funding; the core group supplied the lion's share of the money. We probably spent more, Shelley [Thomas] and I, but I think that Kelly [Vandegrift] and Dave [Smith] and Doug [Stone]—all those guys—they all spent a bundle of money on this stuff, so nobody came out unscathed.

DC: You see, it seems to me that in terms of fund-raising and decision making, only a few people had control over the caucus that was allegedly about empowering the rank and file. I think this was a mistake. I don't think you would have had to deactivate the caucus if it had been able to breathe and grow and include more people instead of putting you few at risk and burning you out. What about the future generations? You left them with nowhere to go. You disbanded the caucus just as it was starting to grow.

KT: We couldn't find anybody to take that mantle of activism. Tactically, I think that it was a mistake to release people from their or any obligation to the UDC after the drive-by shooting. In one fell swoop, we cut the bottom out of the caucus. The people could have rallied and held with us, but they didn't. You could almost hear the sigh of relief from them.

DC: Did you give it a chance?

KT: Once again, I'm still there. Gary [Washington]'s still there. Kelly [Vandegrift]'s still there, Dave [Smith]'s still out there, Doug [Stone] is still out there. I damn sure will know an activist step forward when I see one. And I had a couple of instances where I thought somebody might be willing to do that and supplied them with some help, some information. But more often than not, people who call are looking for election help and don't want to be associated with me, and so I told the last person, "Well if you don't want to be associated with me, then don't." I said we did get elected, we did take the man on, we did win. We beat the company. We beat the IAM. We beat them in court, personally, with a couple of other guys that filed, but we also beat them at union meetings. We beat them on the shop floor. And we did accomplish a lot for the rank and file. We accomplished some good.

I still get the occasional person looking for advice. But my personal advice to them is don't get involved, because you don't have what it takes. To continue at this point would be to become the Adlai Stevenson of the reform caucus movement. And there is no caucus.

DC: It is very troubling to hear that you discourage new activists from getting involved. It seems a shame that going into the 2002 contract negotiations there will be no one representing the rank and file in the union.

KT: About the 2002 contract: There's not going to be anything happening. There isn't any way to put anything together. You can't build a reform movement in six months. We're not going to get that kind of organization together that quick. We'd have to go through all the same stuff again, and I'm simply not that healthwise up to that. Unfortunately, there isn't even anybody else that I could help make that happen.

DC: This is my point. You can't build a caucus overnight. You need to sustain it over time through good and bad times. You needed to keep the organization going. If you had, it would still be here.

KT: I don't think that simply saying we're continuing a group so that we can be ready when the time arises would have constituted success. That doesn't sound like a success strategy. It sounds like a survival strategy. Going underground isn't a victory.

DC: I didn't say anything about underground. There's nothing wrong with an organization surviving to fight another day. That is a kind of success. What about David Clay and his group Machinists for Solidarity?

KT: I think he's all about his own personal agenda. I'm not saying that he doesn't do good things. I'm not making all-encompassing statements to saying he doesn't accomplish something in his life.

DC: You make it sound so personal, when it is in fact a political thing to choose democracy over corruption and stagnation, to organize an independent group in the union. You went from being antiunion to being in the union. Clay went from Administrative Caucus to Machinists for Solidarity. I think Clay's doing that as much as you guys did, and he's still going. In 1999, UDC could have used that organization effectively in Seattle. In Seattle, the UDC wasn't as effective as Clay's group or as effective as you here in Wichita.

KT: Yes, I think that's true. They weren't as aggressive at organizing. They didn't have Gary. All it takes is one gifted person to make all the difference in the world.

DC: I know, but you and Gary and Kelly and Sean and Dave, each of you had some gifts, but it was also that you were not embittered so much at that point in time that you still had a lot of goodwill. And what I perceived among the Seattle folks, I have to tell you, was not so much goodwill.

KT: Yeah, I think that's probably true. They took stuff that we went through down here, was magnified. They went through more. I want to keep that in perspective. They had a lot more turned against them by the district and by the International than what we ran into down here. Not that we didn't run into our own opposition, but they ran into more serious opposition down there. Because they were stepping on a lot bigger toes out there.

DC: Did they have any success?

KT: Oh, yes. Alan Harwood filed a lawsuit about attendance rules, and they had some success with that.

DC: Again with the lawsuits.

KT: And the same kind of things, the handbilling. And Don [Grinde] was out there, and we were always proud of ourselves for being out there when the Administrative Caucus was telling everybody else to stay home. And we were still able to have some successful rallies. We were able to coordinate some rallies at the same time. We worked against, were actually successful in shooting down HPWO [High Performance Work Organization] the first time they tried it out there. And we supplied a lot of information to them out there.

DC: The Seattle UDC members were kind of obsessive about the elections. You all used the elections and tried to get elected, but it wasn't the only thing.

KT: Well, no, you run because you have to maintain some level of credibility. They always say, well all they ever do is complain but never try to run for anything. So why don't they try to change it? Well, it's kind of a scam because they're in charge of the ballot; they know they're gonna cheat, they know they're gonna pull off stuff that you can't monitor. But if you don't run, then you start validating that position. And if you've actually got some things you're going to want to accomplish between elections, then you have to buy some kind of validation.

DC: I think running for elections is a fairly limited way to get validation. I think it should be secondary to organizing the caucus on the shop floor and getting a movement from below started rather than trying to take the place of the people who are running it for themselves.

KT: But if you don't run to win, then you start to establish a reputation of always losing. And that's what they were facing out there, because they got hammered out there. Now where we might spend $5,000, have to come up with that to run for election, they'd have to come up with $20,000 to pay for handbills. We're talking fifty and sixty thousand people. And then you've got the Administrative Caucus. We've figured our loss in the plants on handbills was at least 50 percent. They were throwing them away as fast as we could, we were having to go back and handbill after them. We had to do one handbilling for them to throw away, and wait for them to pull that off a few times, and we'd go back and handbill again after them. Whatever it was.

DC: That's what I mean. It seems an ineffective use of resources to try to beat the Administrative Caucus at its own game instead of trying to get your own game going.

KT: We did things in between elections as well. And we used networks well. We could print a hundred handbills, and our network was so good, they'd think that we were papering the plants.

DC: The UDC is deactivated in Seattle, too, right?

KT: Yeah. I think Don at one point had kicked around the idea with some folks about stopping the rank-and-file movement. Not everybody wants to spend their retirement.

DC: That's true. Raising dues from a membership base could help. Clay said that his group's efforts—which included the routine production of 40,000 flyers—had enormous financial support from members and supporters. Organizations should really ask people for money.

KT: Yes.

DC: So why not collect dues?

KT: I don't believe that would have been any kind of guarantee for success. Our adversaries in the Administrative Caucus of the IAM would still have had deeper pockets.

DC: I never said it was a guarantee, just a necessary but insufficient kind of thing. Still, it would be good to have more resources rather than less, even if you'll never have the most.

KT: I remember one election where one of their opposition slates spent more money on one set of radio advertisements than we spent on the entire campaign. Charging dues would have brought/caused a different set of headaches. We would have had to delegate people to managing collection and tracking. What would we have done if people refused to pay? Had we acquired enough voluntary members, we probably would have revisited the issue of collecting dues.

DC: Any serious organization takes on these tasks of collecting and tracking dues. There are many ways of organizing finances that can allow people with hardship not to pay. You can make dues payment (except in hardship cases) the condition for getting to vote.

KT: Dues collection by the UDC would have added fuel to the fire in regards to their accusations of our engaging in what they called "dual unionism." [Author note: This is a more significant point in hindsight, since building an organization antagonistic to the union using members' resources could be regarded as a real threat to the union itself.]

DC: Do you regard unions as no longer relevant as potentially revitalized sites for workers' struggles for a better deal and a democratic voice? What are the alternatives that you see, and how will they give workers power and voice?

KT: Why not ask me something easy, like explain women?

Labor unions are just one part of the labor movement. The voice of labor unions is certainly not a reflection of the majority of their members. Politics provides a ready example of how unions are out of touch with rank-and-file people.

In the political area, the majority (over 90 percent) goes to Democrats. This certainly isn't representative of the membership by political party. When you stop and consider that labor unions suffered their biggest defeats under Democratic presidents and lost the most members under a Democratic-dominated Congress, it's funny that unions are so pro-Democrat. Make that sad.

I'm not sure who said it, but I think that it's accurate. At this point, labor unions simply want to manage workers for business. They're the straw bosses of old that never went away. They're raiding and merging, fighting over the already organized. They're a perversion and an aberration of the labor movement. With their billions in assets, they'll be able to flail and flounder for decades.

DC: So what are the alternatives?

KT: The alternatives, whatever they are, will all depend upon people believing that they can make a difference coupled with things being bad enough that they have to make a difference. The Internet will be useful in providing and disseminating information from all those lessons learned.

I expect and have predicted that a major economic event will occur within the next five years. And by major, I mean epic. Labor unions will jump into the breach on the side of business. [Author note: Thomas was quite prescient on this point.] They'll have to, because their economics are dependent upon the economics of business, thanks to their bloated bureaucracies and inflated salaries. They've become codependent.

Alternatives will be community- and Net-based (if there's enough accessible infrastructure) in the most likely scenarios. It really is going to be difficult to predict what will come out of the fog and chaos. It could be a whole lot worse.

DC: What would it take to democratize unions to meet these challenges?

KT: Labor union leaders would have to relinquish power in order to democratize their unions, and that isn't going to happen. They are in control. I think a final question that I ended up asking myself is could I in good conscience encourage people to join a union that would victimize them should they assert their rights?

DC: Do you think there are other ways to make workers' lives better beyond unions?

KT: I'm still active in the community. I'm on the library board. I served on the city council. While labor unions would have you believe I'm just this side of the Antichrist and right wing, left wing, there wasn't any kind of wing I wasn't called. But in my own community, I certainly was accepted, and my leadership abilities and knowledge. And that was a rewarding experience in Park City, Kansas.

DC: So if you had any advice beyond "don't even think about it" for budding democratic unionists today, what would it be? Do we still need activists? Do we still need caucuses?

KT: Yeah, you still need activists. But somebody's going to have to come up with a different approach.

DC: Are you pessimistic about the future of Boeing workers and/or unions?

KT: Finally! An easy one! If there's an endangered species list for factory workers, Boeing employees should be on it. There will continue to be Boeing workers in the category office help for a long time.

People told me that I was crazy when I said that Boeing would sell Boeing Wichita, too. I even posted a picture of a "4 Sale" sign in front of the admin building on the Internet. When reporters would call wanting to know where I got such an idea, I would refer them to the company Web site and tell them to read the mission statement.

I recently advised a friend who is younger to look for skill sets that aren't limited to aerospace, because in this country that will be a declining job market. That's advice that I would give anyone that is looking more than a decade down the road.

Most increases in employment will come from mergers and acquisitions of convenience. It reminds me of the time when royalty would marry off their progeny to solidify relationships with friends and/or enemies. Companies like Boeing set up businesses in areas to gain support from politicians, the citizens employed there, or to exchange work for plane purchases. It's a spider's web with captive workers trapped as bait all across the web.

Things don't look good for aerospace workers and Boeing employees.

DC: What about unions?

KT: Labor unions will continue as agents for companies for a long time. The billions in resources and infrastructure that unions have acquired over the years will be enough to keep union bosses flailing about like kids swinging at a piñata made of concrete for the foreseeable future.

In order to change, union bosses would have to give up power. That isn't going to happen. They run unions like they belonged to them, and they should have been running unions like they belonged to the rank and file.

Labor bosses spend the majority of the contract being all business-like and pushing cooperation and harmony in the work floor. People are paying x amount of dollars in union dues to have a union representative/priest act as an intermediary telling them to do what the boss says. On a personal level, that can be done a whole lot cheaper.

Unions have entered into unholy alliances with businesses and corporations. Add in government, and we have the new trinity. We have separation of church and state. We need to add to that separation of business and state.

DC: So, is there a place for the idea of the union, an organization that can stand up to business?

KT: Any organization that meets the definition of a union but isn't in collusion with business might be worth considering if their interest goes deeper than simply wanting to manage workers as assets for business. They will need to "walk the walk." That's something that labor unions no longer are capable of doing. They are corrupt at a fundamental level.

DC: So what's the alternative? What can work? As you know, I think you are right on some things but also think you are wrong to give up the idea of the union. I don't care if we called collective workers' organizations flowerpots so long as they might do the work of consolidating the clout that workers have in refusing to work. I know you think that's not going to happen. But what else can be done to defend workers and their standard of living? Where does our power lie now if not in collective organization?

KT: I don't know. I wish I did. I know what doesn't work. And I'm not involved enough now, but that doesn't mean somebody out there can't think of a new approach for this. And, yes, it'll be an activist. Will they be a democratic unionist? I really don't know.

But if they're taking on labor unions' leadership, then there really are a lot of nuts-and-bolts things that they can do. When you start thinking about long-term goals, whatever those goals may be, you're going to have to find kindred spirits that support those same goals that you have.

DC: If the time isn't right, now, it will be in the future.

KT: There's people still, I still get emails from people trying to start a union caucus there. Or they want to be a UDC chapter. But invariably, even though I took the Web site down, there are still folks saying, "I want the caucus. We want the UDC caucus." But generally

when you get those kind of calls, something just happened to somebody. There's an issue, but it's a flash in the pan. I've seen that before.
Boom, you have a little fire, maybe burns itself out, maybe doesn't,
but very quickly that goes away. Because any number of these people
could start a caucus. You don't need me to start a caucus. I don't care
what local you're in out there, and they say, "Well, shoot, those guys
aren't there, I guess we can't start one."

DC: You are making my argument for me. It takes more than one person or a few people. It takes a long-term, steady, organizing effort.
People are still hungry for democratic organization and voice inside
their unions. It would be better with you than without you, I have to
say. And I don't think the library board is a good substitute.

KT: Well, probably not. But it's not chicken feed. And it's certainly rewarding.

DC: But it doesn't take care of workers.

KT: My civic duty on the city council is a lot more rewarding. It's for the
workers of Park City. They know which side I'm on. I sent letters to
all of them.

DC: There's so much more you could do inside the labor movement.

KT: Not as I am now. I don't want my health to be affected. I don't know
that I had a personality that was set up for stress, anyway.

DC: But you do have one set up for leadership.

KT: Yes, I did, unfortunately. But I guess I could say at some point I
could go another four or five years and wreck my health entirely. I
just wasn't prepared to do that. I am fifty-three. If I started something else, I know I'd be at least fifty-eight or fifty-nine before it was
able to get something built that could start accomplishing things like
we had in the past. And I already know that we're gonna run into
the same things again. It's useless expenditure of that kind of energy.
There's no point in doing that.

DC: Here's what I think should happen, not that I want to put you in
charge of it, but that someone like you needs to step up and focus on
only not challenging the entrenched leaders in elections right away,
but just building support for ideas in the rank and file. And having
all-members meetings, with everyone involved, having a dues-based
organization, and building, building, building over the long term.

KT: Not interested here.

DC: I mean getting people involved educating themselves about contracts, High Performance Work Organization, the need for a demo-

cratic union that actually stands up for workers, talking to workers about all of this continuously, organizing over a period of years.

KT: We did.

DC: But I mean without diverting attention to elections.

KT: Can't be done. You can't. Unions are completely political. Period. Everything they do.

DC: But it's different on the shop floor among the rank and file.

KT: But you can't do one without being involved with the other. They won't let you. It won't happen.

DC: They won't let you talk to people on the shop floor unless you run for office?

KT: It's their union.

DC: They won't let you talk to people on the shop floor—

KT: I'm gonna get fired. We used to do this kind of stuff on our lunch breaks. We'd get as far as we could in the plant, go into a shop, talk for ten minutes, and make it back before the whistle blows. OK? It didn't work.

DC: What if you had that one person in each shop who could do that for you so you wouldn't have to do that yourselves?

KT: We didn't. We weren't able to. I have to say it, we just kept doing this stuff because we liked doing it. We couldn't find other people who were willing to do that kind of stuff because they're not interested in the message. You're talking about delivering a message. We tried to deliver that message. That message wasn't accepted any more than labor unions are able to sell their message about unions to the poor, or to the middle class for that matter. Labor unions aren't able to sell their message to people. It's not a message people are interested in. Now, is the message wrong, is it the person delivering the message, is it the person receiving the message? Is it the messenger? Shoot the messenger! Maybe the messenger is the problem. But you've still got a message out there. The message isn't selling. That's the problem in the plants.

DC: But I think people are attracted to ideas that are in their collective self-interest.

KT: You're not seeing it or you'd be running the country at this point.

DC: I have a very long-term perspective. We've got to exist long enough for it to happen. Organizations have to exist.

KT: I think we're starting to cover the same ground. Pay attention to some of the positive things. I met some great people like yourself who I really value in life. If we hadn't started the caucus, I wouldn't have gone to Decatur [to experience the War Zone struggles and meet those activists]. I wouldn't have met Gary, Kelly, Dave. I got to be involved in Detroit [newspaper strike]. Got to walk through a little bit of history. I've enjoyed these relationships. I found the Socialists to be some of the best labor movement people in the world.

DC: I'm grateful for having met you and studying the UDC. It makes me sad that you are so disillusioned about reforming unions.

KT: I'm not disillusioned. There was something that doesn't work. If I rule that out, people can save themselves some trouble. That's not disillusionment. For me, that's like if somebody's looking for a cure for cancer or something else, and there's a lot of people who have found that this pill doesn't work. Or for another disease, you find that this antibiotic doesn't work. Then they learned something. That's not disillusionment.

DC: But you don't give up on the idea of antibiotics.

KT: Well, no. But you look for a different antibiotic. That's exactly what I'm saying in all this. The reform party or caucus, that antibiotic isn't going to work. There's going to have to be some other kind of approach to be more effective. But I'm not disillusioned by it. I felt pretty good about it, actually.

DC: I still think there needs to be a caucus. I agree you get burned out and you can't do everything forever, you can't substitute yourself for the whole movement forever, but I hope a day comes when someone else will take that on.

One last thing:
In July 2006, Dana Cloud <dcloud@mail.utexas.edu> wrote:

Hi, Keith—
I was re-reading some of what you said when we first got started. I was wondering what you make of something you said back then, in 1998, I think. I wonder whether you still agree with what you had said. Here it is: Folks need to understand there is no good reason for not joining a labor union, so any reasons that I give, they're not excuses and they're not good reasons. I don't ever want to be on tape somewhere and somebody saying, Keith Thomas gave a real good reason for not getting in, because there isn't a good reason for not getting in. And I'm gonna say that I said the typical things, made the typical rationalizations that you can't make a difference, it doesn't make a difference, what happens, the leadership is terrible. I did the same things that people will

do with organized religion sometimes. There'll be some preacher out there who just commits some heinous acts and we will brand an entire religious group according to what this particular individual does. It can happen. And from the union leaders I'd seen, I wasn't very impressed.

DC: So what do you say now?

KT: If I went back to work at a place with a union, I would still join. (Hopeless isn't it?) And there's a body of work out there that we have laid in place that will assist those people. I left a real good trail. And five years from now, somebody says, wait a minute: Somebody's done this and somebody's been down that road and I know these guys are full of crap. Or gosh, I know somebody can win because I heard that guy tell that story one time. So there's people out there that do know. Our history isn't forgotten.

8

Communication and Clout

I have been a labor activist for twenty years. At the same time, I come to this project with an academic background in the field of communication studies, specifically in the areas of organizational communication and rhetorical theory and criticism, and I have aimed this work to address those academic audiences as well as the activist community. Activists and scholars alike are interested in the question of *how people come to a sense of their own agency*—the capacity to control and transform the conditions of one's life. Communication undoubtedly plays an enormous role in this process. The importance of communication is revealed by workers' narratives in making sense of their experiences at work; the sharing of stories shapes their attitudes and perspectives toward both employer and union. We may describe this process in terms of the rhetorical processes of consciousness-raising, identity framing, and the recruiting and motivation of activists.[1] Through what François Cooren calls the "organizing function of communication,"[2] Workers make meaning and build movements in various kinds of messages and relationships.

However, communication cannot make or transform the world of work without enlisting other kinds of power. Even in unions representing workers in communication fields,[3] economic clout is essential to winning wage and benefit increases, regular work hours, health care, pensions, and overtime pay. For example, a maquiladora worker cannot talk her way out of the sweatshop. Asking one's employer politely for an end to night work is unlikely to reset one's internal clock. But the stories we tell and the questions we ask are instrumental to the process of worker education, consciousness-raising, and mobilization. A movement of people who have recognized their common interests through conversation is in a position to wield the more direct power of refusing to work. Workers today, including those at Boeing, both exist in institutions and historical situations that constrain them *and* possess the capacity to create and act on consciousness of themselves as constituting a class with interests divergent from those of their employers.

As I have argued elsewhere, the communication field has largely neglected labor and workers' issues and consequently *overestimates* the accomplishments of communication in determining workplace relationships and experience. Communication studies privilege the role of talk in creating and sustaining social reality to the extent that material exploitation and antagonism between employers and employees recede into the background.[4] My work in this book is meant as something of a corrective to the absence of labor voices and organizations in the field's literature. Linking the stories that ordinary people tell to their experience of laboring in the capitalist workplace shows us that employers cannot completely colonize the common sense of U.S. workers, whose stories are the product of intersecting narratives that make sense of labor conflicts and conflicts internal to unions.

In its exploration of these narratives, this chapter first discusses the unique contributions of the present case study, unusual in its focus on labor unions as sites of activity and agency, to academic work on worker voice and democracy in workplace institutions. The gains won during contract struggles and strikes reveal how, ultimately, worker agency is a function of both communicative practice and economic clout. Second, I bring my past scholarship in rhetorical studies to bear on the union dissident activity at Boeing. This part of the chapter emphasizes the importance of a dialectical theory regarding the interaction of structure and agency. My argument is that the gaps and contradictions between lived experience of exploitation and the discourses that *justify or overlook* that exploitation are resources for critique and action. For both organizational communication and rhetorical studies, the present case forces the recognition that worker agency is a combination of communication and clout.

Three Avenues for Worker Voice

Organizational communication scholarship has extensively addressed the problem of structure and agency, or, in other words, how people get things done even in the context of powerful constraints. A number of influential scholars argue that communication provides a liberating context for workers and that managerial efforts to include their voices in joint decision-making processes allow workers to cocreate their workplace reality.[5] On the other hand, some scholars regard the corporate workplace as more or less a site of total top-down managerial control and efforts toward employee "voice" as disguises for discipline.[6] Of course, there are also positions in between these two because the entire matter of what counts as voice or participation will always remain contested, as democratic theory itself tells us.

My view is that each of these opposed positions has merit but that the degree of agency in a worker's self-expression depends upon its channel and, indeed, on who *controls* that channel. Most organizational communication studies assume a bi-level corporate structure, with management and employer on one end and the shop floor (or other work space, including "virtual" environments) on the other. Being brought into participation schemes from the top allows for a certain kind of voice, but not one that is faithful to the interests of the workers. Rank-and-file voice lacks focus and instrumental capacity without organizational expression. The union, in principle, is the intermediary organization that gives form to bottom-up worker voice. Yet, as we have seen, the channeling of worker voices via the union does not necessarily organize these voices in keeping with the interests of ordinary workers. Therefore, grassroots caucuses or dissident organizations such as Unionists for Democratic Change, the New Crew, and Machinists for Solidarity emerge as alternative channels for worker agency.

These three avenues for worker voice are in play at Boeing: company participation programs, union discourse and activity, and rank-and-file organization. As a number of organizational communication scholars argue, company participation programs more often than not align workers with the imperatives of management or ironically produce new forms of alienation.[7] Cynthia Stohl and George Cheney observe that workplace participation programs "often have the paradoxical effect of making the workers no longer think like workers."[8] Carole Pateman's classic work explains how most industrial sociologists conceive of "participation" not as actual worker control over management decisions but as a cover "used to persuade employees to accept decisions that have *already* been made by the management."[9] She stresses the point that we cannot conflate participation, much of which is "pseudoparticipation" enabling cooperation and efficiency, with democracy: Only participation in which workers have as much control over the conditions of and remuneration for labor as management, now rendered as equals, could be considered truly democratic participation.[10]

The union as intervening institution complicates and enables the negotiation of these interests. Unions, for better or worse, give shape to the terms on which workers' voices are heard. Communication scholarship in the areas of journalism and media studies,[11] rhetorical studies,[12] and organizational communication[13] has helped to account for how, even in the context of massive economic crisis, unionized workers discover and craft opportunities for resistance. Union structures have historically offered avenues for participation and voice from below; yet, under employer pressure, ideological narrowness, and the weight of bureaucracy, unions as sites of agency face organizational limitations not unlike those of management. Leaders of institutions that set out to challenge established power risk co-optation as they adopt the methods and working assumptions of powerful interests. As Paul Buhle documents, industrial unions are perfect examples of this problem.[14]

Rank-and-file organization is an alternative to the compromises of institutionally sanctioned avenues for voice. However, as I argued in chapter 6, efforts toward worker control reveal that even the best reformers face the dilemmas of organization and power. George Cheney's study of Basque worker cooperatives demonstrates how external economic and organizational pressures lead some initially radical efforts at bottom-up participation to bend toward the profit imperative and managerial interests.[15]

Such observations do not negate the possibility of bottom-up worker agency, which is contradictory and complex by virtue of its contextualization in multiple relations of power. Whereas Dennis Mumby emphasizes how the governing narratives of workplaces tend to circumscribe employee voice and legitimize status differentials, Stohl and Cheney recognize how organizing for democracy in the workplace generates complexity and contradiction.[16] Their insight is that workers seeking amplification of their voices often find themselves in acute tensions or even double binds.[17]

Two such binds are the necessity of *structure* in organizing *participation* and the requirements of *collectivization* in the pursuit of *individual* agency. These and other contradictions find expression in the words and actions of dissident unionists. To understand the process of negotiating these dilemmas, this book links the stories that ordinary people tell to their experience of laboring in the capitalist workplace. Neither employers nor media can completely colonize the *common sense* of U.S. workers, whose stories are the product of intersecting narratives that make sense of labor conflicts and conflicts internal to unions.

Kevin Real and Linda Putnam's work on union reform organizations is particularly salient on this point.[18] Reviewing dissident organizations in the Teamsters (Teamsters for a Democratic Union), United Auto Workers (New Directions), and United Mine Workers (Miners for Democracy), Real and Putnam note the following characteristics of union resistance communication:

> First, growing out of extended periods of abuse, these groups often engaged in subtle subversive tactics in addition to open campaigns. Second, they operated as outsiders who used socialist politics and employed militant rhetoric to

campaign against current union leaders. They held separate meetings, handed out leaflets at plant gates, published newsletters, petitioned to overthrow leaders, and distanced themselves from the union. A third pattern was to obtain substantial improvements in labor's general plight by securing legal protections, improving working conditions, and altering wage structures. Finally, oppositional groups of conventional unions employed so-called retrograde rhetoric as they aimed to return to the "good ole days," characterized by the democracy of social unionism. Their view of the past typically stemmed from perceiving union leaders as too willing to adopt management's initiatives.[19]

This study of the discourse of a group of reformers in a pilot's union concludes that "the themes that characterized the PDP [Pilots Defending the Profession, a reform caucus] campaign against the tentative agreement focused on defending the profession from damage to economic growth and viability, devaluing of pilots' image, threats to union solidarity, and endangering the union's viability."[20]

The stories and activities of union reformers at Boeing resemble those of dissident pilots, representing a repertoire of resources common to dissident groups: They employed tactics of subversion (for example, speaking critically in union meetings, agitating for walkouts, and picketing at the union hall), held meetings, leafleted, and picketed; they developed insider/outsider rhetoric in the depiction of union leaders as "Boeing managers" and constant expressions of antagonism against both the company and the union. They attempted and sometimes succeeded to oust union leaders and took legal action to secure workers' democratic rights as union members. They were militant, but not predominantly Socialist, in political orientation. Rather than simply distancing themselves from the union, the activists faced the dilemma of being for the union against the company while opposing entrenched union leadership. In other words, they, like the pilots, had to negotiate the difficult rhetorical position of "loyal opposition."

The presence of dissident organizers is a countervailing force against the confines of entrenched institutions. As Stanley Aronowitz puts it in his introduction to Paul Willis's *Learning to Labor,* "People cannot be filled with ideology as a container is filled with water. They reproduce themselves in antagonistic relation to the prevailing culture and ideological practices. Self-determination does not imply, however, that a new society is produced thereby; but it does mean that the future can never be as certain as the best laid plans of institutional authorities would have it."[21] In his analysis of male, white, working-class school culture, Willis himself explains that class-consciousness is crafted in and through individuals and groups, between external control and collective volition.[22] Labor is a particularly rich site for the manifestation of this dialectical process because it represents an active connection with the world, linking the embodied self to the world.[23] Workers possess the capacity to form intelligent oppositional culture in formal and informal settings. This work becomes the site for dismantling official myths and illusions.[24] As Willis observes, the oppositional culture of a class-conscious minority emerges out of interaction with prevailing ideologies and practices. During my experience with the reformers at Boeing, I witnessed this process in action.

Dialectical Agency and the Rhetoric of Class-Consciousness

Karl Marx wrote, "Men make their own history, but they do not make it as they please; they do not make it under self-selected circumstances, but under circumstances existing already, given and transmitted from the past."[25] This passage summarizes how elements of an existing oppressive situation can become resources against it in a dialectical process or, in other words, when contradictions in a given state of things motivate transformation in orientation and action. Communication can be the lever that pries open those contradictions to expose the nature of an alienating and exploitative system. Through communication, workers come to consciousness of their situation, assess the world around them, and plan and enact change in their own interests. The process is dialectical: Capitalism features a basic antagonism between contending classes and their interests. To wage an organized fight, workers must break with the dominant ideological discourses that rationalize exploitation and attempt to win worker identification with the interests of the employer. The capacity for such a break arises from the dialectical contradiction between the experience of and the mystifications of ideology. Marx understood this turning as the transition between a class simply existing *in itself* to one that struggles *for itself*. In itself, basic class existence poses only an objective situation and opportunity for radical rhetoric.[26] It takes rhetorical intervention to make meaning of that situation and to articulate a collective response to it.

Strikes at Boeing illustrate how workers exploit the contradictions in their experience to articulate a clear class antagonism. The dissidents' stories show how they gave expression to consciousness not only of their immediate needs but also of the longer-term, fundamental divide between worker and employer. Theirs is a rhetoric of broader class-consciousness. As I observed in an earlier chapter, rival union activists David Clay and Don Grinde came together to explain their grievances and motivation to strike. Grinde said, "We've been struggling for twelve years to get our pensions fixed, get them to union-scale standard that would provide a comfortable living for people so they wouldn't have to worry about how they're going to take care of their grandkids and family." Clay echoed Grinde's assessment, commenting also on workers' experience of continual mass layoffs and increasingly ruthless company behavior. "The recent layoffs cut 33,000 workers, but the workload didn't diminish. Some people are doing the work of three or four people. And we're working quite a bit of overtime. What we've seen is that we're getting squeezed. They want to get every drop out of us and not bringing back the number of people we need."

For Clay and Grinde, the accumulation of such experiences motivated explanation and action against the company's efforts to cut into workers' standard of living. Both activists understood the larger picture of how the company's drive to profits depends upon increasing pressure on workers. Grinde noted, "[Labor cost is] making up only 5 percent of the cost of an airplane. They act like we're the total cost of the company, when we're small part, yet we make the majority of the money for the Boeing Company. How is that fair? They don't talk about bonuses, stock options, and excessive salaries to CEOs. It's incredible. The new guy [new CEO James McNerney] gets $22 million in pensions, and he hasn't been here three months. And I've devoted a lifetime, we've all devoted lifetimes, to the company." In turn, this insight generates a commitment to union activism and broader class-consciousness: "We're not out here for the Machinists, we're out here for the working class, for everybody. We're fighting against divide and conquer. We're all in this together."

Three aspects of these unionists' discourse are crucial to an understanding of the dialectical relationships I have identified. First, the lived contradiction, over a period of decades, of intensifying exploitation alongside burgeoning corporate profits and executive compensation has clearly informed activists' consciousness of the nature of their situation. Second, the dialectical interplay of experience and ideas has led both workers to understand their place as part of a self-conscious class. Yet, as activists, they also know that not all workers are in the same place with regard to class-consciousness. They have taken on positions of leadership and organization in order to try to foster broader class-consciousness among divided groups of workers. They thus become communicative or rhetorical agents in the process of building a politicized general struggle out of a localized strike for narrower gains. All situations of conflict prime for the work of persuaders like these activists involve contradictions that leaders can exploit to raise the consciousness of co-workers and to agitate for the refusal of the employer's terms.

Summary

In this chapter, I have addressed how the stories of union dissidents at Boeing speak to the concerns of communication studies. Their accounts confirm the argument that worker voice on management terms is ridden with conflicts of interest. In addition, however, the Boeing workers' stories demonstrate that there is an alternative to managerial or official union frames of worker experience. For them, unions ought to "collectivize" and concentrate the economic power of workers in an antagonistic relationship to their bosses. The stories the reformers tell make good use of the contradictions between official stories and their lived experience in the decision to reject managerial compromise and embrace economic confrontation as the best source of agency in the struggle for workplace democracy. In the process, they truly make history.

The Beginnings and Ends
of Union Democracy

The union has to organize from within. The company
is running the show and the union with all the
full-time employees. It's not that they are evil; it's
that they have bought the union staff's loyalty. Who
wants to make waves when you have a cushy job?
That's where democracy could have a real impact at
Boeing by starting right on the shop floor!

—Don Grinde

Any organization that meets the definition of a
union but isn't in collusion with business might be
worth considering if their interest goes deeper
than simply wanting to manage workers as assets
for business. They will need to "walk the walk."

—Keith Thomas

The explosion of working-class anger that erupted in early 2011 in Wisconsin and elsewhere across the United States prompted observers to either
cheer the potential strength of labor or predict its demise. For example, Robert
Samuelson, writing in *Newsweek,* asked, "Is organized labor obsolete?"[1] Rather
than seeing the rallying of public workers as a sign of reemergence of the labor
movement, Samuelson concludes that what we are witnessing is its death knell.
The *Washington Post* asked, "Does labor matter anymore?"[2] Noting the importance of powerful unions in reducing income inequality, challenging the priorities of corporate America, and winning important social services, this article
concludes that unions should still matter. Likewise, *Guardian* columnist John
Logan wonders whether the U.S. labor movement is "over."[3] While he fears that
"these latest attacks will likely mark the start of another dark chapter in the history of American unions," he also heralds the new national debate about workers'

rights as an opportunity. He wonders whether the movement is "up to the job" of following through.

It has been my argument that unions' becoming "up to the job" requires the intensification of dissident efforts inside labor unions. Only organized pressure from below can make the lumbering labor bureaucracies move in the interests of the rank and file. If the years of the Congress of Industrial Organizations' (CIO's) emergence represented, in the words of Art Preis, labor's giant step, then perhaps the union democracy movement at the heart of this book represents another necessary but hesitant step forward for labor and allied social movements.[4] If those who are taking that step are to break into a run, labor activists must press their leadership to organize once again from the bottom up. Unionization rates and labor's strength are similar to the time before workers were organized across industry, race, gender, and nationality. We face a situation somewhat analogous to the beginning of the organizing drive that unionized General Motors (and in a context of deep economic crisis). Alongside agitating for greater union democracy, union dissidents are bringing fresh militancy to organizing workers from below.

The need for such effort is urgent. As noted earlier, union membership in the United States is at a historic low. The Bureau of Labor Statistics reports that in 2009, only 12.3 percent of U.S. workers belonged to unions. The real numbers are even more striking: The number of workers belonging to unions declined from the previous year by 771,000 to 15.3 million, "largely reflecting the overall drop in employment due to the recession."[5] These grim statistics need not portend the death of unions, however. Workers have come back from worse. Prior to the Great Depression, American Federation of Labor (AFL) workers were confined by the narrow craft-unionism of the union. It was illegal to strike. The memory of the Haymarket martyrs lingered in public consciousness, as did the effects of the repression of Communists and labor activists during the 1910s.

But during the Great Depression, workers rose up to defend themselves. There were growing pains as workers tested their power, and massive and innovative strikes like the Uprising of '34 went down to defeat. The state proved all too willing to crush strikes by force. Yet the workers—men and women, old and young, black and white, immigrant and native-born—pressed forward, break-ing injunctions and striking even when it was illegal to do so in order to win the right to strike. They invented new tactics like the sit-down and the flying squadron to adapt to the changing technological and organizational realities of capitalism. The period from 1936 to 1937 marked the most rapid union growth in U.S. history; in a single year, union membership leaped by 55 percent.[6] The 1937 autoworkers' victory was the capstone achievement of this movement. The CIO emerged in the mid-1930s as an expression of this new militancy. By 1939, 21 percent of U.S. workers were members of unions.[7] It was, in spite of everything arrayed against workers, a period of optimism for labor.

Even as early as 1936, though, legal scholars, politicians, and business owners noticed a potential wedge into labor's strength: the disgruntlement of some union members over what they regarded as the corrupt and undemocratic union leaders. In a remarkable 1936 *Yale Law Journal* article called "Disputes within Trade Unions," William Stafford argued that the government and the courts should intervene in such disputes so that dissenting union members would not be disciplined for exercising their rights. Already, he noticed, labor leaders were enjoying "lucrative salaries, social emoluments, government positions, property ownership, and, *above all,* power."[8]

Stafford notes the impatience with compromise of militant factions inside unions urging a more aggressive stance toward employers. He spends several pages describing unions in terms nearly identical to those of union dissidents today: Union leaders—without consulting their constituents—would sell short struggles that workers are prepared to continue to fight, ordering workers to stop striking at the first sign of any concession from the employer. They break the rules of union elections and harshly discipline their opposition, even when that opposition is very small. They resort to fraud, violence, and terror. They refuse public discussion of fundamental union principles and practices. Therefore, although the young National Labor Relations Board's (NLRB's) policy forbade government interference in union matters, union members are "compelled to resort to the courts."[9] The only remaining problem is that the courts are not empowered adequately or clearly to intervene on behalf of the dissenter. Stafford thus recommends nearly all of the pieces of the Labor-Management Reporting and Disclosure Act (LMRDA)—thirteen years before its enactment.

Stafford also observes that the CIO's embrace of rank-and-file militancy and involvement in union affairs were correctives to the craft orientation of the AFL. Yet, published on the eve of the Flint, Michigan, sit-down strike, his words mark a careful line. If not union democracy from the inside, in the form of new organizations that represent worker demands, then, perhaps, the state should step in. The argument was in place—and available to opportunistic appropriation against unions—just as workers were realizing the power of industrial organization.

These, then, are the two roads to union democracy: new mass organizations responsive to rank-and-file demands, or appeals to the powers that be, whose terms generally have favored employers over workers and the imperatives of capitalism. I have suggested that the present period—of rapid technological change and evolution of the nature of work, of increasingly complex workforce diversity, of massive social inequality, and of a labor movement in serious trouble—actually resembles the conditions in U.S. society prior to the rise of the CIO. In December 2008, 250 members of the United Electrical, Radio, and Machine Workers of America (UE) Local 110 occupied the Republic Windows and Doors factory, inspiring labor activists across the country—and even President Barack Obama. UE President Jim Sweeney commented that the occupation "summarizes where we are as a movement. We've come full circle. Seven percent of the workforce is unionized [in the private sector] and we're back to sit-down strikes like in Flint, Michigan."[10]

I do not deny that some features of the labor scene today are quite different from eras past. The practices of lean, just-in-time production mean that many workers operate in smaller, isolated groups, without the experience of shop-floor solidarity and the motivation of shared discontent. Even since neoliberalism went into crisis in 2007, employers like the Boeing Company can still muster the threat—and reality—of off-loading and offshoring work in order to win concessions from the union even in times of prosperity.

Indeed, the economic crisis that began in the United States in 2007 has made the present a make-or-break time for unions and workers. According to the Department of Labor, the U.S. unemployment rate is in double digits, the highest in twenty-five years.[11] There are more than 14 million unemployed workers in the United States today. Employers everywhere are looking to save their companies by asking workers to bear the brunt of the slowing economy. Recently the *New York Times* reported that union wages, "the wage that meant middle class," is nearly a thing of the past. "The $20 hourly wage, introduced on a huge scale in the middle of the last century, allowed masses of Americans with no more than a high school education to rise to the middle class. It was a marker of sorts. And it is on its way to extinction."[12] Layoffs, buyouts, givebacks, and the implementation of multitiered wage systems (in which one group of workers increasingly replaces those higher paid) have enabled the downward harmonization of global wages. Unfortunately, unions are to a large extent cooperating with these trends. The *New York Times'* Louis Uchitelle continues, "Tens of thousands of workers have accepted wage cuts pressed on them by embattled employers, cuts that in many cases pushed their wages below middle-class levels. . . . And as each new group acquiesces, the standard for what constitutes an acceptable wage comes down in America." As I have argued throughout this book, it is not so much workers who are accepting wage cuts as it is the leaders of their unions.

Such resignation need not be a foregone conclusion even during hard times. Belying common sense about the economic crisis, on September 6, 2008, Boeing workers went on strike. It turns out that they were acting not wildly but in a calculated manner responsive to opportunities presented by the economic situation at Boeing. Members of the International Association of Machinists and Aerospace Workers (IAMAW), representing about 28,000 workers in three cities, rejected Boeing's "last, best, and final offer" and voted (with an unprecedented 87 percent in favor) to strike Boeing plants for the second time in the decade. The union leadership's unilateral decision before the strike to call a forty-eight-hour truce with the company after the strike vote met with jeers and the waving of prostrike picket signs by members who objected to the hijacking of their decision.

The Boeing workers operated from a position of strength, for even in the context of looming major economic recession, Boeing was reaping record-level profits and facing a seven-year backlog of orders. A story on National Public Radio reported, "There's another reason the union wants to hold the line now. Over the past few years Boeing has posted huge profits and currently has a backlog of orders for commercial jets totaling $276 billion. From the union's perspective, the company has an obligation and the ability to reward its workers with job security."[13] In contrast to the rest of the industrial sector, Boeing was trying to *hire* workers even during the strike. A spokesperson for the company told a reporter that "They're at record production rates. They cannot hire enough people."[14] In

Figure 11. An Everett, Washington, rally during the 2008 strike. Photo by Don Grinde.

Figure 12. An Everett, Washington, rally during the 2008 strike. Photo by Don Grinde.

this situation, Boeing stood to lose millions of dollars while the workers were idle (and did lose $100 million per day);[15] postponed deliveries of the much-anticipated 787 superliner would have profound impacts not only on Boeing but on U.S. exports and the world economy. Indeed, the company lost $1.4 billion by the third week of the strike,[16] and its third-quarter profits were down 38 percent from the previous year as a result of the strike,[17] which paralyzed operations and alarmed suppliers, delaying deliveries after the strike by several months.[18]

The success of the strike—which won large raises and caused the company to back down from plans to slash retirement contributions and outsource production of the components of the 787—motivated Boeing to give more in bargaining with its engineers in the Society of Professional Engineering Employees in Aerospace (SPEEA) in December.[19] The Canadian *National Post* quoted a London stockbroker about the impact of the 2008 strike: "My big worry is that historically Boeing strikes tend to be protracted. . . . It is serious. This isn't just a dispute between the workforce and Boeing, but between the workforce and its own union."[20]

This dual dispute—between the rank and file and the company and between the rank and file and their union—is at the heart of this book. In her book *Subterranean Fire: A History of Working-Class Radicalism in the United States*, Sharon Smith notes that the divisions in American society between the wealthiest and the poorest have never been more sharply drawn, as rich corporations declare bankruptcy one after the other in order to warrant concessions from workers and to break their unions.[21] Many unions have cooperated with the carnage. Smith writes, "A return to class struggle is the only strategy that will shift the balance of class forces in the twenty-first century."[22] Stanley Aronowitz concurs: "The sufficient condition is the emergence of a Left within the labor movement that forces the issues, that opens wide a discussion in both major sections of Organized Labor."[23]

Michael Schiavone and Kim Moody share this vision of a Left with influence in the labor movement, arguing for what they call, respectively, "social justice unionism" or "social movement unionism."[24] Their vision of a revitalized union movement entails connecting the bread-and-butter struggles to struggles with, for, and alongside oppressed and hyperexploited groups in society. To the extent that successful and solidaristic rank-and-file struggles inside unions and against employers require breaking down barriers of racism, sexism, homophobia, and nationalism/opposition to immigrant labor, a union movement committed to fighting against these divisions is necessary for labor in the twenty-first century. In addition, many recent union struggles have been connected to social justice issues. For example, workers sitting in at Republic Windows and Doors welcomed an LGBTQ (lesbian, gay, bisexual, transgender, and queer) rights march that came to the factory in solidarity. The immigrant-rights' freedom rides and mass protest in November 2003 in Miami, Florida, against the Free Trade Agreement of the Americas (FTAA) show a willingness to fight back in an increasingly globalized economy. Immigrant-rights demonstrations across the nation in 2006 demanded both citizenship and labor rights. In 2008, longshore workers shut down West Coast ports in protest of the war in Iraq, demonstrating a commitment to both workers' rights and broader issues of social justice. In June 2010, dockworkers at the Port of Oakland, California, joined a thousand demonstrators in refusing to unload shipments from Israel in protest of that country's blockade against Palestine.

Of course, radicals in the labor movement must make struggles political as well as economic. Challenging oppression on the basis of race, gender, sexual orientation, nationality, or any other difference is crucial to rebuilding solidarity across groups, workplaces, and borders. At the same time, demanding broader social-movement activity from even the most militant unionists could pose a barrier to some dissident unionists who might break with the reformers' struggles over ideological disagreements. For instance, Don Grinde is well to the left of the Democratic Party when it comes to workers' rights. When it comes to the picket line, he is already as strong a supporter of women's rights in the workplace as anyone you will find. However, he is well to the right of the Republican Party when it comes to traditional "values issues," including abortion and gay rights. He is an excellent union activist, but he would likely balk at a broader social-justice unionism. Of course, it is crucial in his interests as a union activist to rethink his nationalist stance on immigration, since failures of solidarity with immigrant and international labor have a direct effect on the power of the rank and file in this country.

On this point, Julius J. Getman argues that broadening the union struggle both ideologically and tactically is necessary to the revitalization of labor. His account of the rise of UNITE HERE makes a case similar to my own: Workers need unions, but the leadership of organized labor is "blameworthy for losing sight of the need to organize and the need to maintain the spirit of a movement. They ignored warnings from within their own ranks and marginalized those who issued the warnings. They let the interests of the staff take precedence over the goals of the movement."[25] The history of UNITE HERE suggests to Getman some ways to rethink union organization, the practice of collective bargaining, and the reformation of the NLRB. The key component of powerful unions, he concludes, is "mobilizing existing membership for purposes of organizing."[26]

In his analysis of the complicity of many unions with business interests, Paul Buhle argues that working people themselves must choose whether the turn to a new, democratic, social-movement unionism will be realized.[27] He adds, "They will choose intelligently if they have the necessary information and, even more important, the opportunity to test democratic practices in their day-to-day lives. Challenging their employers, their government, and their economic rulers, that now heavily international class of corporate giants, will demand a challenge of labor institutions as well, but it can be done."[28] This book offers proof not only that challenging labor institutions *can* be done but also that it *has* been done.

Here I have recounted the stories of small groups of challengers dedicated to providing the rank and file with information and testing democratic practices. The narratives of activists like Keith Thomas and David Clay, like Sherri Hood and Sean Mullin, like Don Grinde and Kelly Vandegrift, like Arlene Hoagland and Gary Washington reveal the complexity of organizational storytelling and establish a reservoir of rhetorical resources, arguments that will continue to inform the consciousness and activities of unionized workers at Boeing in several ways.

Figure 13. (Left to right) Gary Bovey, David Clay, and Don Grinde, 2005. Courtesy of Don Grinde

First, their accounts are a record of trial, error, and success, so that future democratic unionists might heed some of the lessons of their experience. Second, these stories offer important and novel insights into the complexity of organizational storytelling. They have had to weave a trilevel chronicle in which their identity and purposes are constructed through a dual antagonism with the employer and the official union.

Third, in negotiating the position of the "loyal opposition," these dissidents are caught in a series of opportunities and binds. The opportunities include the possibility of helping to motivate independent action and thinking on the part of rank-and-file workers. In addition, there is an opportunity to found long-term organizations to carry the memory of particular struggles into the future. Activists are organizers not just of workers but also, potentially, of a radical and militant class-consciousness that organizes workers to take action in their own interests.

Finally, and most importantly, these workers create and lay claim to a peculiar kind of agency as activists independent of yet dependent upon the organizations that purport to give them voice. Their own stories reveal a critical consciousness born of desire for more control over their futures and frustration with the pace and conservatism of their union organizations; a political trajectory of moving into the ranks of power as a group of outsiders; defiance in the face of vilification and threat; and as navigation of the complex and dilemmatic role of having to use an institution and fight it at the same time.

Ultimately, this book has been an exploration of human agency in a context of constraint. The democratic reformers at Boeing are constrained by the exploitative relationship between employee and employer, given that The Boeing Company is an economic powerhouse whose interests lie in pressing workers for greater productivity at decreasing cost. The official leadership of the IAMAW also hampered the activities of reformers, impeded transparency and democratic practice, and sometimes stood in the way of workers asserting their right to a livable future.

This book introduced the activists and their organizations, agenda, and perspectives regarding the company and the IAMAW and its leadership. These activists rejected cooperation with management in the form of joint programs, criticized union leaders as operating as "Boeing managers," agitated for the restoration labor gains of previous generations, and called attention to how race, gender, and sexual orientation influence working experience. A key component of their objections against the union lies in the critique of joint safety and training programs, which, as David Clay wryly noted, gave members "the joint."

The turning point in the dissidents' narrative is the 1995 strike, when union workers rejected a contract put forward by the International for approval. The sixty-nine-day strike interrupted Boeing's shift to lean manufacturing and won major gains for workers. The 1995 strike, and especially the rejection of not only the first but also the second contract offered by the company and supported by the union, filled rank-and-file workers with a sense of control over their destinies in a ruthless corporate climate. In an unprecedented wave, the workers of the union slapped down the cautious recommendation of the leaders and voted to remain on strike. It was a moment of profound class-consciousness, in which workers realized that they had the power to take their future in their own hands. While the dissident unionists I interviewed were only a tiny minority of the workers who rose to reject the concessionary contract, their organizations expressed rank-and-file voice and had the opportunity to sustain such a voice organizationally.

However, the groups' ability to carry that movement forward came into conflict with several dilemmas inherent in the tasks of representation. Their commitment to democracy informed their critique from below of the discourse and practices of union leadership. Yet their taking on the tasks of leading a rank-and-file movement put them in a position to replicate, in form if not in goal, some of the habits they decried. In particular, focusing on getting elected to powerful union posts, making decisions on behalf of members of rank-and-file organizations, using top-down and double-edged legal tools to reform the official union, and decrying the passivity of the membership all contributed to the burnout and eventual retreat from dissident activity. Reliance on primarily antiunion legislation like the LMRDA was particularly problematic insofar as it displaced ordinary workers from the process of change.

Could the dissidents have formed an organization strong enough to hunker down in the longer term? It is possible that they could have sustained a routine of small-scale shop-floor recruitment and worker education until the next explosion of worker dissatisfaction. At that point, they would be in a position once again—better organized and stronger as a result of prolonged building— to amplify the voices of rank-and-file workers. These voices must primarily be directed at the company, and I have been critical of tactics that make the union, not the employer, the main target. Opening up these conclusions to question and challenge from Keith Thomas reveals the complexities of establishing and building long-term organization and the difficulty in avoiding the charge of antiunionism when putting pressure on union leaders through whatever means are available.

Leading a democratic movement entails paradoxical tasks. The union dissidents at Boeing faced a number of dilemmas associated with these tasks: how to motivate action in times of quiescence or how to defend the principle of mass participation even in isolation. It is paradoxical to demand so *much* democracy that the people whom reform is supposed to benefit are left behind the struggle. Such dilemmas of leadership in struggles for democracy are compounded by the difficulties of the stance of the loyal opposition. Social-movement organizations and frameworks, like unions and unionism, are like houses. When they are not protecting us from the elements, should we gut and remodel in the assessment that the basic structures are sound or raze them to the ground in rejection of their very foundations? For all of their shortcomings, unions have uniquely provided shelter for working people hunkered down against the employers' offensive. Demolishing them without first building an adequate replacement is foolhardy, and this book is written in the hope that they can become—under pressure—their own adequate replacements.

For the loyal opposition, the balance between pushing for reforms from below on the inside, on the one hand, and using external tools like the LMRDA to break in from the outside, on the other, is an unsteady one. Opening the IAMAW to Department of Labor and company scrutiny by legal means may damage the structure while giving workers greater voice; going to the media with complaints about union corruption and misconduct provides publicity useful in drawing the likeminded to your movement while feeding mainstream political and cultural hostility toward unions. One possible resolution to these dilemmas is to refrain from outpacing one's constituents in the struggle; instead, activists should draw in sustained, even if limited, support during lean times to enable the growth of mass support in the moment of crisis. In this way, the dissident who was once regarded as a berserk traitor becomes an effective internal leader whose voice, in concert with those of many others, asserts control of an emerging legitimately powerful institution: the democratic union.

As of the time of this writing, there are important signs that worker militancy and efforts toward democratic unionism are on the rise, most notably among them the massive wave of resistance to Wisconsin Governor Scott Walker's 2011 attempt to slash wages and benefits and gut the union rights of public sector workers.[29] Although not every story has a happy ending,[30] reformers in unions are becoming visible and powerful.[31] Such waves of organizing, efforts toward democratic reform, and militant action are causes for hope, at Boeing[32] and across the U.S. labor movement.[33] Labor may yet return full circle to its origins: a time of possibility when people are re-learning the lessons of the CIO and gaining confidence and experience. At such a moment, we will face a new need for labor activists inside unions to bend those organizations to the will of the rank and file, to carry forward the memories of what activists past have done badly and done well, to impart the history of victories and defeats, and to rally ordinary people to create, join, and use their unions.

As class-consciousness in the United States grows in the wake of deep economic crisis, the making and remaking of democratic organizations that represent workers are urgent tasks. But the success of union organizing and the outcome of labor action depend largely on the presence and strength of union activists who can apply pressure to both union and company at key moments of opportunity. Keith Thomas, other members of Unionists for Democratic Change, the Rank and File crew, and all the other activists out there who want to fight their union to use their union in the larger struggles that are certainly ahead face these tasks today. It is their role—exceedingly burdensome and little sung—to provide workers with the information they need, create sites for the democratic practice they crave, and carry forward the memory of prior struggles well into the new millennium.

Notes

Preface

1. Lee Sustar, "A Bailout for the Auto Industry?" *Socialistworker.org,* November 10, 2008, http://socialistworker.org/print/2008/11//10/bailout-for-auto (accessed December 4, 2008).

2. Greg Shotwell, "In Defense of Autoworkers," *Socialistworker.org,* December 4, 2008, http://socialistworker.org/print/2008/12/04/in-defense-of-autoworkers (accessed December 4, 2008).

3. Nick Bunkley and Mary M. Chapman, "On Strike at G.M., Resolute but Anxious about the Future," *New York Times,* September 25, 2007, C1.

4. Profitability has returned to U.S. automakers, inspiring UAW President Richard Trumka to proclaim in a Detroit speech, "Today, more than ever, we need to feel the passion of the labor movement"; Louis Aquilar and Bryce G. Hoffmann, "Unions: Restore Concessions," *Detroit News,* June 15, 2010. http://www.gminsidenews.com/forums/f12/unions-restore-concessions-92791/ (accessed June 12, 2011).

5. Gerard Hauser, *Vernacular Voices* (Columbia: University of South Carolina Press, 1999); see also Kent Ono and John M. Sloop, "The Critique of Vernacular Discourse," *Communication Monographs* 62 (1995): 19–47.

6. See Kevin Real and Linda L. Putnam, "Ironies in the Discursive Struggle of Pilots Defending the Profession," *Management Communication Quarterly* 19 (2005): 91–119; Linda L. Putnam and Tricia S. Jones, "Reciprocity in Negotiations: An Analysis of Bargaining Interactions," *Communication Monographs* 49 (1982): 171–91.

Introduction: "To Get to Boeing, We First Had to Take on the Union"

1. Lawrence Mishel and Matthew Walters, "How Unions Help All Workers," *Economic Policy Institute,* August 26, 2003, http://www.epi.org/publications/entry/briefingpapers_bp143/ (accessed June 8, 2010).

2. Bureau of Labor Statistics, "Union Members Summary," *United States Department of Labor,* http://www.bls.gov/news.release/union2.nr0.htm (accessed May 21, 2009); Bureau of Labor Statistics, "Median Weekly Earnings for Full-Time Wage and Salary Workers," *United States Department of Labor,* http://www.bls.gov/cps/tables.htm#weekearn (accessed May 21, 2009).

3. Pew Research Center for the People and the Press, "Favorability Ratings of Labor Unions Fall Sharply," February 23, 2010, http://people-press.org/report/591/ (accessed June 16, 2010); Karlyn Bowman, "Labor Union Blues," *Forbes.com,* March 8, 2010, http://www.forbes.com/2010/03/05/unions-labor-polls-opinions-columnists-karlyn -bowman.html (accessed June 16, 2010).

4. Brian Wilkinson, "Consumer Debt Continues to Increase," *Sierra Star,* July 16, 2009, Lexis/Nexis database (accessed June 12, 2011).

5. Heidi Shierholz, "Job Losses Ballooned in the Last Quarter of 2008," *Economic Policy Institute,* January 9, 2009, http://www.epi.org/publications/entry/job_losses_ ballooned_in_final_quarter_of_2008/ (accessed August 1, 2010). See also Bureau of Labor Statistics, "Labor Force Statistics from the Current Population," *United States Department of Labor,* http://www.bls.gov/cps/ (accessed September 5, 2010).

6. Julius J. Getman, *Restoring the Power of Unions: It Takes a Movement* (New Haven, Conn.: Yale University Press, 2010), 325.

7. Walter Fisher, *Human Communication as Narration* (Columbia: University of South Carolina Press, 1987).

8. Michael Cimini, "Labor-Management Bargaining in 1995," *Monthly Labor Review* 119 (1996), http://www.bls.gov/opub/mlr/1996/01/art3full.pdf (accessed March 19, 2011).

9. Ibid.

10. Interview with the author, April 12, 1998.

11. While there are many sources chronicling official union history and even more telling the story of the American workplace from the standpoint of owners and managers, there are not as many documentary records of the ideas and activities of rank-and-file activists. There are a number of excellent oral histories; see Alice Lynd and Staughton Lynd, *Rank and File: Personal Histories by Working Class Organizers* (Boston: ILR Press, 1973); Jacquelyn Dowd-Hall, Christopher B. Daly, Lu Ann Jones, and Robert Korstad, *Like a Family: The Making of a Southern Mill World* (Chapel Hill: University of North Carolina Press, 2000); Julius Getman, *Betrayal of Local 14* (Ithaca, N.Y.: Cornell University Press, 1998); Brian Kelley, *Race, Class, and Power in the Alabama Coalfields, 1908–21* (Urbana: University of Illinois Press, 2001); Rick Halpern and Roger Horowitz, *Meatpackers: An Oral History* (New York: Monthly Review Press, 1999); Dan Georgakas and Marvin Surkin, *Detroit: I Do Mind Dying* (Cambridge, Mass.: South End Press, 1998); Philip A. Korth, *The Minneapolis Teamsters Strike of 1934* (East Lansing: Michigan State University Press, 1995); Farrell Dobbs, *Teamster Rebellion* (New York: Pathfinder Press, 1972); and Philip A. Korth and Margaret R. Beegle, *I Remember Like Today: The Auto-Lite Strike of 1934* (East Lansing: Michigan State University Press, 1988). While UDC and New Crew mem-

bers make up the bulk of my interview data, I also interviewed one community-labor activist in Wichita, several "Administrative Caucus" (elected union officials) machinists in Wichita and Seattle, and two Boeing corporation spokespeople. In addition to the interviews, I have collected media coverage of the 1989 and 1995 strikes and of the 1999 contract negotiations for background context. In addition to IAMAW archive materials, members of the UDC have generously given me materials from their archives constituting a sample of election campaign materials and other agitation-related leaflets, buttons, and documents. Don Grinde's collection, for example, contains hundreds of phone messages, emails, letters and other documents, and his four-year-long personal journal.

12. Linda Alcoff, "The Problem of Speaking for Others," *Cultural Critique* 92 (Winter 1991): 5–32.

Chapter 1. Business Unionism and Rank-and-File Unionism at the Turn of the Millennium

1. Brian Wilkinson, "Consumer Debt Continues to Increase," *Sierra Star,* July 16, 2009, Lexis/Nexis database (accessed June 12, 2011).

2. Heidi Shierholz, "Job Losses Ballooned in the Last Quarter of 2008," *Economic Policy Institute,* January 9, 2009, http://www.epi.org/publications/entry/job_losses_ballooned_in_final_quarter_of_2008/ (accessed August 1, 2010).

3. Bureau of Labor Statistics, "Labor Force Statistics from the Current Population Survey" *United States Department of Labor,* http://www.bls.gov/CPS/ (accessed March 21, 2009); Heidi Shierholz, "True Unemployment May Be Close to Ten Percent," *Economic Policy Institute,* February 12, 2009, http://www.epi.org/analysis_and_opinion/entry/true_unemployment_may_be_near_10_percent/ (accessed August 1, 2010).

4. *Commonwealth Fund 2008 Annual Report,* http://www.commonwealthfund.org/usr_doc/site_docs/annualreports/2008/index.html (accessed August 4, 2010).

5. Bureau of Labor Statistics, "Productivity and Costs: Preliminary Fourth Quarter and Annual Averages for 2007," *United States Department of Labor,* http://www.bls.gov/lpc/ (accessed March 21, 2009).

6. On the problems with labor's emphasis on EFCA, see Julius J. Getman, *Restoring the Power of Unions: It Takes a Movement* (New Haven, Conn.: Yale University Press, 2010), 131–38. Getman argues that instead of pushing for the extremely unpopular secret ballot, labor should have called for ending the right of employers to replace strikers permanently, a move that would strengthen workers mightily.

7. Lee Sustar, "The Labor Movement: State of Emergency, Signs of Renewal" *International Socialist Review* 34 (March–April 2004), http://www.isreview.org/issues/34/stateofemergency.shtml (accessed August 1, 2010).

8. For that breadth, I refer readers to the ten-volume series, Philip S. Foner, *History of the Labor Movement in the United States* (New York: International, 1994); Jeremy Brecher, *Strike!* (Cambridge, Mass.: South End, 1997); Melvyn Dubofsky and Foster Rhea Dulles, *Labor in America: A History* (Wheeling, Ill.: Harlan Davidson, 2004);

John H. Hinshaw and Paul LeBlanc, eds., *U.S. Labor in the 20th Century: Studies in Working-Class Struggles and Insurgency* (Chicago: Humanity Books, 2000); and Sharon Smith, *Subterranean Fire: A History of Working-Class Radicalism in the United States* (Chicago: Haymarket 2007).

9. Smith, *Subterranean Fire,* 37.

10. David Montgomery, *The Fall of the House of Labor* (Cambridge: Cambridge University Press, 1987).

11. Philip A. Korth, *The Minneapolis Teamsters Strike of 1934* (East Lansing: Michigan State University Press, 1995), 184.

12. Ibid., 195.

13. Steve Early, *The Civil Wars in U.S. Labor: Birth of a New Workers' Movement* (Chicago: Haymarket, 2011), 1.

14. Genora Dollinger, *Striking Flint,* http://www.marxists.org/history/etol/newspape/amersocialist/genora.htm (accessed March 15, 2011).

15. Ibid.

16. Sidney Fine, *Sit-Down: The General-Motors Strike of 1936–1937* (Ann Arbor: University of Michigan Press, 1969), 338.

17. Art Preis, *Labor's Giant Step: The First Twenty Years of the CIO: 1936–55* (New York: Pathfinder Press, 1964), 236.

18. Brecher, *Strike!* 246.

19. Preis, *Labor's Giant Step,* 403.

20. Sasha Reuther, "How the UAW Can Get Back Its Horsepower," *Time,* June 14, 2010, http://www.time.com/time/printout/0,8816,1996401,00.html (accessed June 16, 2010).

21. Preis, *Labor's Giant Step,* 3.

22. Robert H. Zieger, *The CIO: 1935–1955* (Chapel Hill: University of North Carolina Press, 1995).

23. Ibid., 255.

24. Ibid., 376.

25. See Brian Kelley, *Race, Class, and Power in the Alabama Coalfields, 1908–21* (Urbana: University of Illinois Press, 2001); Robin D. G. Kelley, *Hammer and Hoe: Alabama Communists during the Great Depression* (Chapel Hill: University of North Carolina Press, 1990).

26. Zieger, *The CIO.*

27. Ibid., 304.

28. Ibid., 374.

29. Ibid.

30. See Smith, *Subterranean Fire,* 39–46; Kelley, *Race, Class, and Power in the Alabama Coalfields;* and Kelley, *Hammer and Hoe.*

31. Nelson Lichtenstein, *Labor's War at Home* (Cambridge: Cambridge University Press, 2002).

32. Brecher, *Strike!,* 249.

33. Paul Buhle, *Taking Care of Business: Samuel Gompers, George Meany, Lane Kirkland, and the Tragedy of American Labor* (New York: Monthly Review Press, 1999); Michael Schiavone, *Unions in Crisis: The Future of Organized Labor in America* (Westport, Conn.: Praeger, 2008), 15–17.

34. For an analysis focusing on corruption (versus emphasis on the structural location of union leaders as aligned with business) in the labor movement, see Robert Fitch, *Solidarity for Sale* (New York: Public Affairs, 2006).

35. Early, *The Civil Wars in U.S. Labor*, 24, 144. Election rules were such that independent candidates faced the impossibility of getting elected. Like many of the democratic unionists I interviewed for this book, Early found himself on the receiving end of harassment on the part of unions he criticized. SEIU International President Andy Stern criticized Early for mounting a "full time campaign against SEIU"; Early, *The Civil Wars in U.S. Labor*, 21. See also Fitch, *Solidarity for Sale*, 290–314.

36. Nelson Lichtenstein, *State of the Union* (Princeton, N.J.: Princeton University Press, 2002), front matter.

37. Early, *The Civil Wars in U.S. Labor*, 40. Early notes, however, that in the UFW, power was increasingly concentrated in César Chávez's hands.

38. American Postal Workers Union, "Great Postal Strike of 1970: From Collective Begging to Collective Bargaining," http://www.apwu.org/about/history-1970_strike .pdf (accessed March 22, 2011).

39. Early, *The Civil Wars in U.S. Labor*.

40. Dan Georgakas and Marvin Surkin, *Detroit: I Do Mind Dying* (Cambridge, Mass.: South End Press, 1998).

41. Ibid., 24.

42. Ibid., 25.

43. Ibid.

44. Ibid., 28.

45. Ibid., 29.

46. Stewart Bird, Rene Lichtman, and Peter Gessner, dirs., *Finally Got the News* (Icarus Films, 2003).

47. Brecher, *Strike!* 314

48. For a well-supported case about the consequence of the pairing of labor and the Democrats, see Mike Davis, *Prisoners of the American Dream* (New York: Norton, 2000); see also Lance Selfa, *The Democrats: A Critical History* (Chicago: Haymarket, 2008), 28–38. Early documents the consequences of labor investment ($85 million from the SEIU alone) in the Barack Obama presidential campaign in 2008 and the SEIU's conceding to President Obama's insurance-company-driven 2010 health care reform bill and sacrifice of the Employee Free Choice Act; Early, *The Civil Wars in U.S. Labor*, 257.

49. Brecher, *Strike!*, 315.

50. Buhle, *Taking Care of Business*, 17.

51. Ibid., 15.

52. Ibid., 92–93.

53. Ibid., 136.

54. Ibid., 197.

55. Ibid.

56. Peter Rachleff, *Hard-Pressed in the Heartland: The Hormel Strike and the Future of the Labor Movement* (Boston: South End Press, 1993), 81.

57. Ibid., 82. In 2010, the P-9 strike reached its twenty-five-year anniversary. Rachleff's analysis of P-9 is that the conflict was the product of the end of implied social contract between labor and capital, a contract that ended when Reagan fired the air traffic controllers in 1981. Nesbitt quotes Rachleff to the effect that "the strike signified a shift in the kind of economy in the U.S. toward a stronger government, more privatizations and deregulation. 'There is a lot of beating-up on unions. . . . The strike stands on the front end of that'"; see Kurt Nesbitt, "P-9 Strike Reaches 25-Year Anniversary," *Austin (Minn.) Post-Bulletin,* August 14, 2010.

58. Julius Getman, "The National Labor Relations Act: What Went Wrong? Can We Fix It?" *Boston College Law Review* 45 (2003): 125–46; Julius Getman, *Betrayal of Local 14* (Ithaca, N.Y.: Cornell University Press, 1998).

59. *Work-to-rule* refers to a strategy by which long-experienced workers conduct their labor strictly according to job description and training manuals. The process severely undermines productivity while the workers break no agreement with their employer.

60. Steven K. Ashby and C. J. Hawking, *Staley: The Fight for a New American Labor Movement* (Urbana: University of Illinois Press, 2009).

61. Ibid., 229; emphasis in the original.

62. Dana L. Cloud, "Fighting Words: Labor and the Limits of Communication at Staley, 1993–1996," *Management Communication Quarterly* 18 (2005): 509–42.

63. See also Deepa Kumar, *Out of the Box* (Urbana: University of Illinois Press, 2008), 182. For a contrasting point of view, see Getman, "The National Labor Relations Act: What Went Wrong?"; and Getman, *Betrayal of Local 14.* See also Kate Bronfenbrenner, Sheldon Friedman, Richard W. Hurd, Ronald Seeber, and Rudolph A. Oswald, eds., *Organizing to Win: New Research on Union Strategies* (Ithaca, N.Y.: Cornell University Press, 1998); Jarol B. Manheim, *Labor Pains: Corporate Campaigns in the Healthcare Industry* (St. Michaels, Md.: Tred Avon Institute Press, 2003); and Schiavone, *Unions in Crisis.*

64. For an account of the debate over the Corporate Campaign Strategy, see Ashby and Hawking, *Staley,* 37–39, 112–23, 223.

65. Getman, "The National Labor Relations Act: What Went Wrong?"; Getman, *Betrayal of Local 14.*

66. Buhle, *Taking Care of Business.*

67. Early argues that Sweeney's administration modeled the restructuring of labor unions from the top rather than out of rank-and-file initiative. The SEIU was behind a number of labor conflicts in the 2000s, including with UNITE-HERE and

the United Health Workers. Today the regime of Andy Stern "abhors rank-and-file initiative, shop floor militancy, and democratic decision making by workers themselves"; Early, *The Civil Wars in U.S. Labor*, 15.

68. Deepa Kumar, "Mass, Class, and Democracy: The Struggle over Newspaper Representation of the UPS Strike," *Critical Studies in Media Communication* 18 (2001): 285–302; Deepa Kumar, *Outside the Box: Corporate Media, Globalization, and the UPS Strike* (Urbana: University of Illinois Press, 2008).

69. Lee Sustar, "Sparks of Resistance in the Labor Movement?" *Socialistworker.org*, December 10, 2009, http://socialistworker.org/2009/12/10/sparks-of-labor-resistance (accessed July 8, 2010).

Chapter 2. Not a Smooth Flight for Boeing and the Union

1. Robert J. Serling, *Legend and Legacy: The Story of Boeing and Its People* (New York: St. Martin's Press, 1992).

2. Ibid., 383.

3. For example, Winpisinger coauthored books published on the union democracy press's *Labor Notes*. In this sense, he might be regarded as a paradoxical "democratic bureaucrat"; see Jane Slaughter and William Winpisinger, *Concessions and How to Beat Them* (Detroit: Labor Education and Research, 1983); William W. Winpisinger, *Reclaiming Our Future: An Agenda for American Labor* (Boulder, Colo.: Westview, 1989).

4. Serling, *Legend and Legacy*, 392.

5. Ibid., 274.

6. The Teamsters at Boeing were the union of choice for management throughout the company's history; see Serling, *Legend and Legacy*, 381.

7. In addition to the Puget Sound and Wichita, Boeing has had plants in St. Louis, Irving, Tex., Portland, Ore., and other cities.

8. Dana L. Cloud, "Fighting Words: Labor and the Limits of Communication at Staley, 1993–1996," *Management Communication Quarterly* 18 (2005): 509–42.

9. Serling, *Legend and Legacy*, 399; see also David Turim, "Timeline of Change at Boeing," *The Seattle Times*, November 1, 2009, http://seattletimes.nwsource.com/cgi-bin/PrintStory.pl?document_id=0177698&zsection_id=2003750727&slug=boeingtimeline01&date=20091101 (accessed July 8, 2010).

10. Deepa Kumar, *Outside the Box: Corporate Media, Globalization, and the UPS Strike* (Urbana: University of Illinois Press, 2007), 19–20.

11. Edward S. Greenberg, Leon Grunberg, Sarah Moore, and Patricia B. Sikora, *Turbulence: Boeing and the State of American Workers and Managers*, Kindle ed. (New Haven: Yale University Press).

12. Ibid., Kindle location 625.

13. Ibid., Kindle location 402.

14. Ibid., Kindle location 444.

15. Ibid., Kindle location 519. Greenberg et al. conclude that the company cannot

escape the economic pressures that led its leaders to make these changes, and unions cannot resist the impact of globalization (entailing offsets of work on parts). Because they regard these issues as structural and therefore not amenable to transformation in the labor-management bargaining process, they recommend a number of social-democratic public welfare measures on the part of the capitalist state that can protect workers from the worst effects of job insecurity, layoffs, and alienation.

16. Serling, *Legend and Legacy,* 435.

17. Ibid., 436–37.

18. Mike Parker and Jane Slaughter, *Choosing Sides: Unions and the Team Concept* (Boston: South End Press, 1998).

19. Serling, *Legend and Legacy,* 458. Keith Thomas reports that total quality programs resulted in a lowering of quality. "We had a reputation of building the best planes that we could. That was non-value-added cost. Thanks to quality programs and statistical process control, the emphasis became building parts just good enough to pass"; personal correspondence with the author, March 17, 2011.

20. John Olienyck and Robert J. Carbaugh, "Boeing Versus Airbus: It's Getting Ugly," *Business Week,* September 20, 2004, http://www.businessweek.com/magazine/content/04_38/b3900083_mz054.htm (accessed March 19, 2011).

21. J. R. Wilson, "Anatomy of a Merger," *Interavia Business and Technology,* June 1997, 44–47.

22. Bruce A. Smith and Sumiko Oshima, "Boeing Taps Japan for Technology Work," *Aviation Week and Space Technology,* February 4, 2002, 45.

23. "Crash Landing," *Economist,* January 30, 1993, 29.

24. "Banking on a Big Bird," *Economist,* March 12, 1994, 73–74.

25. See Jeffrey Garten, "Labor Peace Is in the Air at Boeing," *Business Week,* May 10, 1999, 22; Woodruff Imberman, "Why Engineers Strike—The Boeing Story," *Business Horizons,* November/December 2001, 6–16.

26. Olienyck and Carbaugh, "Boeing Versus Airbus."

27. Peter Harvison, "How the Year of the Tiger Bit Boeing," *Interavia Business and Technology,* Jan. 1, 1999, 28.

28. Dana L. Cloud, "The Null Persona: Racialized Rhetorics of Silence in the Uprising of '34," *Rhetoric and Public Affairs* 2 (1999): 177–209.

29. Jerry Useem, "Boeing vs. Boeing," *Fortune,* October 2, 2000, http://money.cnn.com/magazines/fortune/fortune_archive/2000/10/02/288426/index.htm (accessed March 19, 2011).

30. Ibid.

31. Jonathan Turton, "Architect for Change," *Corporate Finance,* January 2000, 22–25.

32. S. H. Verhovek, "Boeing, Jolting Seattle, Will Move Headquarters," *New York Times,* March 21, 2001, A3.

33. D. Barboza, "Chicago, Offering Big Incentives, Will Be Boeing's New Home," *New York Times,* May 11, 2001, C1.

34. Verhovek, "Boeing, Jolting Seattle, Will Move Headquarters."

35. Imberman, "Why Engineers Strike."

36. Greenberg et al., *Turbulence,* Kindle location 1187.

37. Stanley Holmes, Carol Matlack, Michael Arndt, and Wendy Zellner, "Boeing Attempts a U-Turn at High Speed," *Business Week,* April 16, 2001, http://www.businessweek.com/magazine/content/01_16/b3728103.htm (accessed July 15, 2009).

38. Paul Nyhan, "Boeing Machinists Prepared to Strike," *Seattle Post-Intelligencer,* July 22, 1999.

39. Ibid.

40. Ibid.

41. Bruce A. Smith and Sumiko Oshima, "Boeing Taps Japan for Technology Work," *Aviation Week and Space Technology,* February 4, 2002, 45.

42. Stanley Holmes, "Boeing's High-Speed Flight," *Business Week,* August 12, 2002, 74–76.

43. David Jensen, "Outlook 2003: Perseverance and Change," *Avionics Magazine,* January 1, 2003, http://www.aviationtoday.com/av/categories/military/Outlook-2003-Perseverance-and-Change_661.html (accessed August 4, 2010).

44. "Boeing Company 2008 Annual Report," *Envisionreports.com,* http://www.envisionreports.com/ba/2009/12ja09001m/index.html (accessed July 27, 2010).

45. K. Schultz, "Layoff Roundup," *The Daily Deal,* September 17, 2001.

46. Peter Kilborn, "Slump in Plane Travel Grounds Wichita," *New York Times,* April 16, 2003, A14.

47. Boeing Company, "Boeing Reports Fourth-Quarter and Full-Year 2003 Results," http://www.boeing.com/news/releases/2004/q1/nr_040129a.pdf (accessed February 2, 2011).

48. K. M. Song, "CEO of Boeing Commercial Airplanes Faces the Firing Line on Talk Radio," *Seattle Times,* 2001.

49. M. J. Fieldstein, "Lean and Mean," *St. Louis Post Dispatch,* April 16, 2004, C1.

50. David Greising, "Onex to Bring Contract Fight Directly to Works," *Chicago Tribune,* May 27, 2005, http://www.chicagotribune.com/business/chi-0505270147may27,0,5435769.story (accessed August 4, 2010).

51. Dominic Gates, "Boeing Admits No Guilt in Scandal," *Seattle Times,* May 16, 2006, http://community.seattletimes.nwsource.com/archive/?date=20060516&slug=boeing16 (accessed August 1, 2010).

52. Holmes et al., "Boeing Attempts a U-Turn at High Speed."

53. Reuters, "Boeing Says to Lay Off 25 Percent of Wichita Workforce," April 17, 2006.

54. Boeing Company, "The Boeing Company 2005 Annual Report," http://www.boeing.com/companyoffices/financial/finreports/annual/05annualreport/05AR_links.pdf (accessed August 11, 2010).

55. Robert G. Rodden, *The Fighting Machinists: A Century of Struggle* (Washington, DC: Kelly Press, 1984), 10; for some IAMAW history at Boeing, see Liesel Miller

Orenic, *On the Ground: Labor Struggle in the American Airline Industry* (Urbana: University of Illinois Press, 2009), 76.

56. Rodden, *The Fighting Machinists,* 18.

57. Ibid., 21.

58. Ibid., 31.

59. Ibid., 41

60. Ibid., 45.

61. David Montgomery, *The Fall of the House of Labor* (Cambridge: Cambridge University Press, 1987), 277.

62. Rodden writes approvingly of the IAM's conservatism; Rodden, *The Fighting Machinists,* 107–11.

63. Ibid., 100.

64. Ibid., 129.

65. Ibid., 157.

66. George Lipsitz, *Rainbow at Midnight: Labor and Culture in the 1940s* (Urbana: University of Illinois Press, 1994), 157.

67. Rodden, *The Fighting Machinists,* 199.

68. Ibid., 216.

69. Ibid., 224–45.

70. Ibid., 253.

71. Ibid., 269.

72. Michael Barone, "George McGovern on the Unions," *U.S. News and World Report,* http://www.usnews.com/blogs/barone/2006/5/22/george-mcgovern-on-the-unions.htm (accessed May 22, 2006); George McGovern, "My Party Should Respect Secret Union Ballots," *Wall Street Journal,* August 8, 2008, A13.

73. Rodden, *The Fighting Machinists,* 293.

74. John McCann, *Blood in the Water: A History of District Lodge 757 of the International Association of Machinists and Aerospace Workers* (Seattle: IAMAW Lodge 751, 1989).

75. Winpisinger, *Reclaiming Our Future, 25.*

76. Ibid.

77. Ibid., 184.

78. Interview with the author, July 10, 1999.

79. McCann, *Blood in the Water.*

80. Ibid., 34.

81. Ibid., 59, 77.

82. Ibid., 83.

83. Rodden, *The Fighting Machinists,* 40.

84. McCann, *Blood in the Water,* 103–15.

85. Ibid., 131.

86. Ibid., 236–69.

87. "Can a Deal This Big Ever Fly?," *US News and World Report*, November 27, 1995, 16.

88. Michael Cimini, "Labor-Management Bargaining in 1995," *Monthly Labor Review* 119 (January/February 1996). 25.

89. Ronald Henkoff and Maura Griffin, "Boeing's Big Problem," *Fortune*, January 12, 1998, 96.

90. Boeing Company, "The Boeing Company 2008 Annual Report," *Envisionreports.com*, http://www.envisionreports.com/ba/2009/12ja09001m/index.html (accessed July 27, 2010); "Boeing Company Filings," *United States Securities and Exchange Commission*, http://www.sec.gov/Archives/edgar/data/711513/000119312510024415/d10k.htm (accessed July 27, 2010).

91. Henkoff and Griffin, "Boeing's Big Problem."

92. Ibid.

93. Stanley Holmes, "Boeing Meets with Machinists Union," *Seattle Times*, June 12, 1998.

94. Jeff Cole, "Unions Say Boeing's Job Cuts Pander to Wall Street," *Seattle Times*, December 2, 1998, Lexis/Nexis database (accessed June 12, 2011).

95. Nyhan, "Boeing Machinists Prepared to Strike."

96. Stanley Holmes, "Boeing Contract Talks 1999—Machinists Vote to Authorize Strike," *Seattle Times*, July 22, 1999, http://community.seattletimes.nwsource.com/archive/?date=19990722&slug=2973156 (accessed August 1, 2010).

97. Stanley Holmes, "Machinists Union Seeks Seat on Boeing Board of Directors," *Seattle Times*, August 24, 1999.

98. Aaron Bernstein, "Boeing's Unions Are Worried about Job Security—the CEO's," *Business Week*, July 5, 1999, http://www.businessweek.com/archives/1999/b3636061.arc.htm (accessed August 4, 2010).

99. Martha Modeen, "Machinists OK Strike Authority," *Herald-Net*, July 22, 1999.

100. Paul Richfield, "Seattle Stung by Boeing Cuts," *Air Transport Intelligence*, December 2, 1998.

101. Stanley Holmes, "Boeing Agrees to Limit Subcontracts, Setting Hopeful Tone for Union Talks," *Seattle Times*, May 12, 1999, http://community.seattletimes.nwsource.com/archive/?date=19990513&slug=2960476 (accessed August 1, 2010).

102. Stanley Holmes, "Boeing Meets with Machinists Union," *Seattle Times*, June 12, 1998.

103. Stanley Holmes, "Within Striking Distance at Boeing," *Business Week*, August 22, 2002, http://www.businessweek.com/bwdaily/dnflash/aug2002/nf20020822_3193.htm (accessed March 19, 2011).

104. Stanley Holmes, "Why Boeing May Welcome a Walkout," *Business Week*, September 9, 2002, 56.

105. Stanley Holmes, "Boeing's Big Win: It's Still Too Soon to Crow," *Business Week*, September 30, 2002, 38.

106. Stanley Holmes, "Boeing: Putting Out the Labor Fires," *Business Week*, December 29, 2003, 43.

107. In July 2010, Buffenbarger pushed and won an unprecedented ten-year contract for workers at Spirit in Wichita, arguing that the long contract would "help the company survive and grow in order to protect the members"; see Molly McMillin, "Labor Experts Say 10-Year Spirit Contract Unusual," *Kansascity.com*, July 6, 2010, http://www.kansascity.com/2010/07/06/v-print/2065790/labor-experts-say-10-year-spirit.html (accessed July 8, 2010).

108. Slaughter and Winpisinger, *Concessions and How to Beat Them*, 55.

109. The Machinists voted on what was to have been the company's final offer. However, in a divisive, unusual, and confusing move, union leaders decided not to count that first election and reopened talks in conjunction with federal mediation. Dissidents, who organized against the next proposal, felt that the union was stalling to get a face-saving offer from the company that would forestall a strike. The final offer garnered only two-fifths of the membership vote but was saved by the undemocratic IAMAW rule that only a two-thirds majority could authorize a strike, while Boeing CEO Alan Mulally stated that a walkout would hurt the company. In the aftermath, IAMAW District 751 President Mark Blondin sided publicly with the company, saying, "We have to fight *for* Boeing, *with* Boeing, to keep Boeing jobs here"; see Dominic Gates, "Machinists Chief in Boeing's Corner: Union Splits from Labor," *Seattle Times*, June 13, 2003, http://community.seattletimes.nwsource.com/archive/ ?date=20030613&slug=blondin13 (accessed August 2, 2010). IAMAW International President Buffenbarger claimed that Boeing had wanted a strike. "We knew it was not the time to strike," he told the *Seattle Times* (Gates, "Machinists Chief in Boeing's Corner"). In the Seattle legislature in 2003, Blondin and his lieutenant Linda Lanham promoted Boeing's agenda. Contract critics and laid-off unionists felt betrayed; meanwhile, the IAMAW negotiator claimed that Boeing "wanted a strike." But David Clay, whose accounts I feature in this book, said that the company's threats and appeals to workers helped persuade them not to strike. "The company was completely on message, while the union was in disarray. . . . The company kept saying, 'Times are tough. This isn't going to be good for our customers,' and all that talk affected some workers" (quoted in Steven Greenhouse, "Boeing Strike Vote Fails; Company Offer Is in Effect," *New York Times*, September 15, 2002).

110. J. Lynn Luns and Kris Maher, "Boeing Strike May Emerge as Test of Mettle," *Wall Street Journal*, September 6, 2005, A2. The rank-and-file activists of the UDC opposed this contract. "My vote is a 'No' vote," UDC member Don Grinde commented. "The company keeps trying to buy us off with bogus bonus money. This is not the contract that we should have at this crucial time. There's no commitment on job security. There's still potential for thousands of more jobs to be lost."

111. Quoted in Darin Hoop and Lee Sustar, "Tentative Agreement with IAM Contains Few Gains," *Socialist Worker*, September 30, 2005, 11.

112. Interview with the author, April 14, 1998.

113. Slaughter and Winpisinger, *Concessions and How to Beat Them.*
114. Ibid., 55–81.

Chapter 3. Enter the Dissidents

1. Interview with the author, April 12, 1998.
2. Interview with the author, April 12, 1998. Unless otherwise noted, all other quotations from Sean Mullin throughout this book are from this interview.
3. Ironically, David Clay moved into the ranks of management in June 2009 but left management in 2010, claiming continuing loyalties with the rank and file.
4. Interview with the author, July 14, 1999.
5. Interview with the author, April 12, 1998.
6. Thomas is referring to two labor tragedies, the 1911 fire at the Triangle Shirtwaist factory in New York City, in which 147 locked-in women died, and the fire at a North Carolina chicken-processing plant that killed twenty-five people; see Leon Stein, *The Triangle Fire* (Ithaca, N.Y.: Cornell University Press, 2001); Robert Smothers, "25 Die, Many Reported Trapped, as Blaze Engulfs Carolina Plant," *New York Times,* September 4, 1991, A1.
7. Interview with the author, April 12, 1998.
8. Interview with the author, April 12, 1998. Unless otherwise noted, all quotations by Kelly Vandegrift throughout this book are from this source.
9. Dana L. Cloud, *Control and Consolation in American Culture and Politics: Rhetorics of Therapy* (Thousand Oaks, Calif.: Sage, 1998); Robert Whitaker, *Mad in America: Bad Science, Bad Medicine, and the Enduring Mistreatment of the Mentally Ill* (New York: Perseus, 2002); Jonathan M. Metzi, *The Protest Psychosis: How Schizophrenia Became a Black Disease* (Boston: Beacon, 2010).
10. Interview with the author, April 12, 1998.
11. Interview with the author, July 26, 1999. Unless otherwise noted, all quotations by Don Grinde throughout this book are from this source.
12. Interview with the author, July 27, 1999. Unless otherwise noted, all quotations from David Clay throughout this book are from this source.
13. Interviews conducted concurrently with the author, July 27, 1999. Unless otherwise noted, all quotations by Sue Moyer and Virginia Roberts throughout this book are from this source.
14. Joel Geier, "More Than a Recession: An Economic Model Unravels," *International Socialist Review,* no. 58 (March–April 2008), http://www.isreview.org/issues/58/feat-economy.shtml (accessed August 13, 2010).
15. David Harvey, *A Brief History of Neoliberalism* (Oxford: Oxford University Press, 2005), 3.
16. David Harvey, *The New Imperialism* (Oxford: Oxford University Press, 2005), 63.
17. Boeing Company, "The Boeing Company 2008 Annual Report," *Envisionreports.*

com, http://www.envisionreports.com/ba/2009/12ja09001m/index.html (accessed July 27, 2010); "Boeing Company Filings," *United States Securities and Exchange Commission,* http://www.sec.gov/Archives/edgar/data/711513/000119312510024415/d10k .htm (accessed July 27, 2010).

18. Interview with the author, July 25, 1999.

19. Interview with the author, July 27, 1999. Unless otherwise noted, all quotations and information attributed to Roy Moore throughout this book are from this source.

20. Interview with the author, April 12, 1998. Unless otherwise noted, all quotations and information attributed to Sean Mullin throughout this book are from this source.

21. Interview with the author, July 20, 1999. For a discussion of the mental and physical toll of layoff cycles on Boeing employees, see Edward S. Greenberg, Leon Grunberg, Sarah Moore, and Patricia B. Sikora, *Turbulence: Boeing and the State of American Workers and Managers,* Kindle ed. (New Haven: Yale University Press).

22. Interview with the author, April 14, 1998. Unless otherwise noted, all quotations and information attributed to Mike Burleigh throughout this book are from this source.

23. Interview with the author, April 14, 1998. Unless otherwise noted, all quotations and information attributed to Mary Johnson throughout this book are from this source.

24. Draper Alan Draper, *Conflict of Interests: Organized Labor and the Civil Rights Movement in the South, 1954–1968* (Ithaca, N.Y.: Cornell University Press, 1994).

25. Mary Triece, "Appealing to the 'Intelligent Worker': Rhetorical Reconstitution and the Influence of Firsthand Experience in the Rhetoric of Leonora O'Reilly," *Rhetoric Society Quarterly* 33 (2003): 5–24; Mary Triece, *On the Picket Line: Strategies of Working Class Women* (Urbana: University of Illinois Press, 2007); Ruth Milkman, *Gender at Work: The Dynamics of Job Segregation during World War 2* (Urbana: University of Illinois Press, 1987); Ruth Milkman, *Women, Work, and Protest: A Century of US Women's Labor History* (London: Routledge, 1985); Dorothy Sue Cobble, *The Sex of Class: Women Transforming American Labor* (Ithaca, N.Y.: Cornell University Press, 2007).

26. Rick Halpern and Roger Horowitz, *Meatpackers: An Oral History* (New York: Monthly Review Press, 1999).

27. Genora Dollinger, *Striking First* (Chicago: L. J. Page, 1996); Brian Kelley, *Race, Class, and Power in the Alabama Coalfields, 1908–21* (Urbana: University of Illinois Press, 2001); Robin D. G. Kelley, *Hammer and Hoe: Alabama Communists during the Great Depression* (Chapel Hill: University of North Carolina Press, 1990).

28. Interview with the author, July 27 1999. Unless otherwise noted, all quotations and information attributed to Jackie Boschok throughout this book are from this source.

29. Interview with the author, July 27, 1999. Unless otherwise noted, all quotations and information attributed to Sherri Hood throughout this book are from this source.

30. Triece, "Appealing to the 'Intelligent Worker'"; Triece, *On the Picket Line;* Milkman, *Gender at Work;* Milkman, *Women, Work, and Protest;* and Cobble, *The Sex of Class.*

31. Interview with the author, April 14, 1998. Unless otherwise noted, all quotations and information attributed to Denise Harris throughout this book are from this source.

32. Interview with the author, April 12, 1998. Unless otherwise noted, all quotations and information attributed to Arlene Hoaglan throughout this book are from this source.

33. Interview with the author, April 12, 1998. Unless otherwise noted, all quotations and information attributed to Gary Washington throughout this book are from this source.

34. For an exception, see Kitty Krupat and Patrick McCreery, eds., *Out at Work: Building a Gay-Labor Alliance* (Minneapolis: University of Minnesota Press, 2000). This topic receives attention in a number of works on the "new" diverse labor movement; see Gregory Mantsios, *A New Labor Movement for a New Century* (New York: Monthly Review Press, 1998).

35. Interview with the author, July 28 1999. Unless otherwise noted, all quotations and information attributed to "Joe" throughout this book are from this source.

36. Krupat and McCreery, *Out at Work.*

Chapter 4. The Problem with "Jointness"

1. Steve Early, *The Civil Wars in U.S. Labor: Birth of a New Workers' Movement* (Chicago: Haymarket, 2011), 51, 58; Paul Buhle, *Taking Care of Business: Samuel Gompers, George Meany, Lane Kirkland, and the Tragedy of American Labor* (New York: Monthly Review Press, 1999).

2. Interview with the author, April 14, 1998.

3. Edward S. Greenberg, Leon Grunberg, Sarah Moore, and Patricia B. Sikora, *Turbulence: Boeing and the State of American Workers and Managers,* Kindle ed. (New Haven: Yale University Press), Kindle location 1126.

4. Interview with the author, April 14, 1998. Unless otherwise noted, all quotations attributed to Garland "Bear" Moore throughout this book are from this source.

5. Interview with the author, July 26, 1999. Unless otherwise noted, all quotations attributed to Tom Finnegan throughout this book are from this source.

6. Interview with the author, July 26, 1999. Unless otherwise noted, all quotations attributed to Stan Johnson throughout this book are from this source.

7. Interview with the author, July 10, 1999. Unless otherwise noted, all quotations attributed to Molly McMillin throughout this book are from this source.

8. Interview with the author, July 14, 1999.

9. Interview with the author, July 27, 1999. Unless otherwise noted, all quotations attributed to Curtis Thorfinson throughout this book are from this source.

10. Interview with the author, April 14, 1998. Unless otherwise noted, all quotations attributed to David Robertson throughout this book are from this source.

11. David Montgomery, *The Fall of the House of Labor* (Cambridge: Cambridge University Press, 1987).

12. Interview with the author, April 12, 1998. Unless otherwise noted, all quotations and information attributed to Madeleine Meuller throughout this book are from this source.

13. Interview with the author, April 14, 1998. Unless otherwise noted, all quotations and information attributed to Denise Harris throughout this book are from this source.

14. Don Grinde, letter to Dana L. Cloud, August 1, 1999.

15. Maureen Jenkins, "Getting Lean," *Boeing Frontiers* 1, no. 4 (August 2002), http://www.boeing.com/news/frontiers/archive/2002/august/cover.html (accessed March 19, 2011).

16. Byron Acohido, "Machinists Protest Boeing's Plans—Workers Fear Job Losses from Firm's Efficiency Drive," *Seattle Times,* June 13, 1996, http://community.seattletimes.nwsource.com/archive/?date=19960613&slug=2334425 (accessed August 1, 2010).

17. Labor Extension Program, "Treat It as Continuous Bargaining: Dealing with the Changing Workplace," University of Massachusetts, 2006.

18. Adrian Wilkinson and Hugh Willmott, eds., *Making Quality Critical: New Perspectives on Organizational Change* (London: International Thomson Business Press, 1994).

19. Ibid., 14.

20. Alan Tuckman, "Ideology, Quality, and TQM," in Wilkinson and Willmott, *Making Quality Critical,* 33–53.

21. Buhle, *Taking Care of Business.*

Chapter 5. The 1995 Strike and the Rejection of the Second Contract

1. See Edward S. Greenberg, Leon Grunberg, Sarah Moore, and Patricia B. Sikora, *Turbulence: Boeing and the State of American Workers and Managers,* Kindle ed. (New Haven: Yale University Press), Kindle locations 1384, 1414. They observe that workers at Boeing had been accustomed to routine layoff cycles during which they could reasonably expect to be hired back on. In the 1990s, this pattern shifted with the transition to lean production so that layoffs were increasingly permanent.

2. Michael Cimini, "Labor-Management Bargaining in 1995," *Monthly Labor Review* 119 (1996), http://www.bls.gov/opub/mlr/1996/01/art3full.pdf (accessed March 19, 2011).

3. Employers use the RICO Act, upheld by the U.S. Supreme Court since the 1960s and reinforced by President Bill Clinton in 1994, ostensibly to prevent antiabortion

clinic pickets and to label picket lines as part of a conspiracy engaged in extortion. Based on this law, employers win injunctions limiting numbers of picketers or forcing them to move to sidewalks away from plant entrances; see "Civil Rights . . . Even at Work," *Labor Party Press,* http://lpa.igc.org/lpv44/lpp44_civrghts_main2.html (last accessed August 14, 2010). In addition to the RICO provisions, judicial favoring of employers during collective bargaining and strikes has reduced the viability of large-scale plant closings. Julius Getman writes, "Today, courts are more likely to see collective bargaining as an interference with the benevolent working of the market, and, thus, inconsistent with economic efficiency most likely to be achieved by un-encumbered management decision making. This change in theory is well illustrated by the Supreme Court's 1981 decision in *First National Maintenance Corp. v. NLRB* removing the issue of plant closings from the bargaining table, and by subsequent decisions removing other areas involving capital investment from the bargaining requirement." Getman summarizes the situation for strike pickets today: "Since the NLRA's [1935 National Labor Relations Act's] passage, the legal protection of the strike weapon has been significantly reduced. At the moment, the right to strike is so constrained by legal and practical barriers that strikes are rarely used and even more rarely used effectively. Strikers and unions employing the strike face panoply of official sanctions that, taken together, make the right to strike a costly and risky endeavor. In addition to their legal right to hire permanent replacements, employers can often bring lawsuits against unions that, one way or another, run afoul of the many legal proscriptions on the strike. The range of penalties that might be imposed on strikers and unions by employers, courts, and government has been broad, and the penalties imposed often costly. Martial law, criminal indictments, fines, and military action have responded to major strikes. Strikes and picketing have been enjoined. Strikers have been fired, and unions have been fined and held liable for damages. Union leaders have been arrested, jailed, and convicted of crimes for encouraging violence, sometimes with very little evidence of personal misconduct. The combination of RICO, a newly expanded view of the Hobbs Act, and a greater willingness to find that union officials encouraged or participated in violence, all combine to increase the vulnerability of unions and union leaders to criminal and civil penalties for acts of strike misconduct"; Julius Getman, "The National Labor Relations Act: What Went Wrong? Can We Fix It?," *Boston College Law Review* 45 (2003): 136.

4. Flor Angela Davila, "The Boeing Strike—Machinists' Resolve Runs in the Family," *Seattle Times,* October 13, 1995, http://community.seattletimes.nwsource.com/archive/?date=19951013&slug=2146662 (accessed August 17, 2010).

5. Jim McMahan, "Machinists Victors in Strike against Boeing," *Workers World,* December 28, 1995, http://www.hartford-hwp.com/archives/45b/052.html (accessed August 17, 2010).

6. Cimini, "Labor-Management Bargaining in 1995."

7. Mark Hunnibell "Boeing Strike: A Lesson in Union Democracy," *Association for Union Democracy,* Pilots Issues Page, URL unknown (accessed December 9, 1996).

Chapter 6. "The Feeble Strength of One"

1. Stanley Aronowitz, *From the Ashes of the Old: American Labor and America's Future* (New York: Houghton-Mifflin, 1998), 221.

2. Linda Alcoff, "The Problem of Speaking for Others," *Cultural Critique* 92 (Winter 1991): 5–32.

3. See Laurie Green, *Battling the Plantation Mentality: Memphis and the Black Freedom Struggle* (Chapel Hill: University of North Carolina Press, 2007).

4. Cynthia Stohl and George Cheney, "Participatory Processes/Paradoxical Practices: Communication and the Dilemmas of Organizational Democracy," *Management Communication Quarterly* 14 (2001): 349–406.

5. Ibid., 363.

6. Stanley Holmes, "Boeing Meets with Machinists Union," *Seattle Times,* June 12, 1998.

7. Ibid.

8. Interview with the author, July 10, 1999.

9. Keith Thomas, letter to Dana L. Cloud, June 10, 2006.

10. Association for Union Democracy, "Checklist of Basic Principles of Democratic Organizing," http://www.uniondemocracy.org/Legal/handouts.htm#checklist (accessed August 4, 2010).

11. Keith Thomas, letter to Dana L. Cloud, July 17, 2006.

12. Interview with the author, April 14, 1998. Unless otherwise noted, all quotations attributed to Shelley Thomas throughout this book are from this source.

13. Don Grinde, letter to Dana L. Cloud, July 1, 2008.

14. Thomas did win elections for steward, safety committee, or delegate to the Kansas AFL-CIO, District 70, Grand Lodge Convention.

15. Interview with the author, July 26, 1999. Unless otherwise noted, all quotations attributed to Rick Herrmann throughout this book are from this source.

16. Interview with the author, July 26, 1999. Unless otherwise noted, all quotations attributed to David Mascarenas throughout this book are from this source.

17. Sean Griffin, "Confident Machinists Go to Polls: Mood Is Upbeat, but Tactics Are Getting Ugly," *Tacoma (Wash.) News Tribune,* October 2, 1996, B10.

18. Ibid.

19. Kevin Real and Linda L. Putnam, "Ironies in the Discursive Struggle of Pilots Defending the Profession," *Management Communication Quarterly* 19 (2005): 91–119.

20. Teamsters for a Democratic Union, "How the Reform Movement Has Changed the Teamsters Union," http://www.tdu.org/node/754 (accessed August 17, 2010).

21. Clyde Summers, "From Industrial Democracy to Union Democracy," *Journal of Labor Research* 21 (2000): 3–14.

22. See Doris B. McLaughlin and Anita L. W. Shoomaker, *The Landrum-Griffin Act and Union Democracy* (Ann Arbor: University of Michigan Press, 1979); and Herman Benson, *Rebels, Reformers, and Racketeers: How Insurgents Transformed the Labor Movement* (Brooklyn: Association for Union Democracy, 2005).

23. McLaughlin and Shoomaker, *The Landrum-Griffin Act and Union Democracy*, 11.

24. Ibid., 30.

25. Ibid., 103.

26. McLaughlin and Shoomaker cite incidents of antiunion intervention during the Richard Nixon administration in ibid., 172.

27. Ibid., 162.

28. Teamsters for a Democratic Union, "How the Reform Movement Has Changed the Teamsters Union."

29. Interview with the author, July 10, 1999.

30. Ibid.

31. Office of Labor-Management Standards, "Labor-Management Reporting and Disclosure Act of 1959, As Amended," *U.S. Department of Labor*, http://www.dol.gov/olms/regs/statutes/lmrda-act.htm (accessed February 8, 2011).

32. Interview with the author, July 10, 1999.

33. Office of Labor-Management Standards, "Labor-Management Reporting and Disclosure Act of 1959."

34. Robin D. G. Kelley, *Hammer and Hoe: The Alabama Communists during the Great Depression* (Chapel Hill: University of North Carolina Press, 1990); Sharon Smith, *Subterranean Fire: A History of Working-Class Radicalism in the United States* (Chicago: Haymarket, 2007).

35. The National Labor Relations Act is similarly double-edged. It allows for mediation and recognizes unions' right to bargain, but it gives the company and government a wedge or opportunity to get in the way of organizing. The whole process of certification elections is rigged against unions. These laws give employees the right to decertify their union, which sounds good on paper. What it means in practice is that organizing is more difficult.

36. Steven K. Ashby and C. J. Hawking, *Staley: The Fight for a New American Labor Movement* (Urbana: University of Illinois Press, 2009).

37. Pacific Northwest Labor and Civil Rights History Projects, "Seattle General Strike Project," 1999, *University of Washington*, http://depts.washington.edu/labhist/strike/ (accessed August 2, 2010).

Chapter 8. Communication and Clout

1. Working in a feminist context, Karlyn Kohrs Campbell describes consciousness-raising as a form of discursive practice that "links recovery, recuperation, and the development of theory" about "dynamics of suppression"; Karlyn Kohrs Campbell, "Consciousness-Raising: Linking Theory, Criticism, and Practice," *Rhetoric Society Quarterly* 32 (2002): 45–64. On identity framing, see Dana L. Cloud, "Foiling the Intellectuals: Gender, Identity Framing, and the Rhetoric of the Kill in Conservative Hate Mail," *Communication and Cultural Critique* 2 (2009): 457–79; S. A. Hunt,

R. Benford, and D. A. Snow, "Identity Fields: Framing Processes and the Social Construction of Movement Identities," in *New Social Movements*, eds. E. Laraña, H. Johnston, and J. R. Gusfield (Philadelphia: Temple University Press, 1994), 185–208.

2. François Cooren, *The Organizing Property of Communication* (Amsterdam: John Benjamins, 2000). Cooren argues brilliantly that social organizations are emergent and structured like narratives. Rejecting intentionalism and functionalism, Cooren uses speech act theory to argue that organizations are made in communication, thus distinguishing his most pronounced communication-deterministic model of communication in organization from my own.

3. See Vincent Mosco and Catherine McKercher, *Laboring Communication* (Lanham, Md.: Rowman and Littlefield, 2008). They argue that the dependence of corporate capitalism on new information technologies and the presence of a skilled workforce makes knowledge workers powerful not because of their agency as communicators, but because of their capacity to interrupt the flow of information by withholding their labor. See also Michelle Rodino-Colocino, "Laboring under the Digital Divide," *New Media and Society* 8 (2006): 487–511.

4. Dana L. Cloud, "Fighting Words: Labor and the Limits of Communication at Staley, 1993 to 1996," *Management Communication Quarterly* 18 (2005): 509–42; Dana L. Cloud, "Laboring under the Sign of the New: Cultural Studies, Organizational Communication, and the Fallacy of the New Economy," *Management Communication Quarterly* 15 (2001): 268–78; see also Dan Schiller, *Theorizing Communication: A History* (New York: Oxford University Press, 1996).

5. See the review of this literature in David R. Seibold and B. Christine Shea, "Participation and Decision-Making," in *The New Handbook of Organizational Communication*, eds. Fredric Jablin and Linda L. Putnam (Thousand Oaks, Calif.: Sage, 2001), 664–703.

6. For a review of literature on critical approaches to organizations and power, see Dennis Mumby, "Power and Politics," in *The New Handbook of Organizational Communication*, eds. Fredric Jablin and Linda L. Putnam (Thousand Oaks, Calif.: Sage, 2001), 585–624; Carole Pateman, *Participation and Democratic Theory* (Cambridge: Cambridge University Press, 1976); Mohammed A. Auwal, Michael J. Papa, and Arvind Singhal, "Organizing for Social Change within Concertive Control Systems: Member Identification, Empowerment, and the Masking of Discipline," *Communication Monographs* 64 (1997): 219–49; Paul Bernstein, "Necessary Elements for Effective Worker Participation in Decision Making," *Journal of Economic Issues* 10 (1976): 490–522.

7. See J. Straub, George Cheney, L. Spiers, Cynthia Stohl, D. DeGooyer, and Susan Whalen, "Democracy, Participation, and Communication at Work: A Multi-Disciplinary Review," in *Communication Yearbook* 21, ed. Michael E. Roloff (Thousand Oaks, Calif.: Sage, 1998), 35–91; Stanley Deetz, *Democracy in an Age of Corporate Colonization* (Albany: State University of New York Press, 1992); George Cheney, *Values at Work* (Ithaca, N.Y.: Cornell University Press, 1999); Cynthia Stohl and

George Cheney, "Participatory Processes/Paradoxical Practices: Communication and the Dilemmas of Organizational Democracy," *Management Communication Quarterly* 14 (2001): 349–406; Auwal et al. "Organizing for Social Change within Concertive Control Systems"; Bernstein, "Necessary Elements for Effective Worker Participation in Decision Making."

8. Stohl and Cheney, "Participatory Processes/Paradoxical Practices," 382.

9. Carole Pateman, *Participation and Democratic Theory* (Cambridge: Cambridge University Press, 1976), 68; emphasis in the original.

10. Ibid., 73.

11. See Bonnie Brennen, "Lockouts, Protests, and Scabs: An Examination of the Los Angeles Herald-Examiner Strike," *Critical Studies in Media Communication* 22 (2005): 64–81; Deepa Kumar, "Mass, Class, and Democracy: The Struggle over Newspaper Representation of the UPS Strike," *Critical Studies in Media Communication* 18 (2001): 285–302; Deepa Kumar, *Outside the Box: Corporate Media, Globalization, and the UPS Strike* (Urbana: University of Illinois Press, 2008); Enid M. I. Sefcovic, "Cultural Memory and the Cultural Legacy of Individualism and Community in Two Classic Films about Labor Unions," *Critical Studies in Media Communication* 19 (2002): 329–51.

12. See David A. Carter, "The Industrial Workers of the World and the Rhetoric of Song," *Quarterly Journal of Speech* 66 (1980): 365–74; David Carlone, "The Contradictions of Communicative Labor in Service Work," *Communication and Critical/ Cultural Studies* 5 (2008): 158–79; Mark L. Knapp and James C. McCroskey, "Communication Research and the American Labor Union," *Journal of Communication* 18 (1968): 160–72; Mari Boor Tonn, "Militant Motherhood: Labor's Mary Harris 'Mother' Jones," *Quarterly Journal of Speech* 82 (1996): 1–22.

13. See Stephen Fineman, ed., *The Emotional Organization* (Hoboken, N.J.: Wiley-Blackwell, 2007); Melissa Gregg, "Learning to (Love) Labor: Production Culture and the Affective Turn," *Communication and Critical/Cultural Studies* 6 (2009): 209–14; Sarah J. Tracy, "Becoming a Character for Commerce," *Management Communication Quarterly* 14 (2000): 90–128; Rodino-Colocino, "Laboring under the Digital Divide"; Loril Gossett, "Falling through the Cracks: Control and Communication Challenges of a Temporary Workforce," *Management Communication Quarterly* 19 (2006): 376–415; Loril Gossett, "The Long-Term Impact of Short-Term Workers," *Management Communication Quarterly* 15 (2001): 115–28; Karen Ashcraft and Dennis Mumby, *A Feminist Communicology of Organization* (Thousand Oaks, Calif.: Sage, 2003). For a microanalytical approach of working-class language, see Paul Drew and John Heritage, eds., *Talk at Work* (Cambridge: Cambridge University Press, 1992).

14. Paul Buhle, *Taking Care of Business: Samuel Gompers, George Meany, Lane Kirkland, and the Tragedy of American Labor* (New York: Monthly Review Press, 1999).

15. Cheney, *Values at Work.*

16. Dennis K. Mumby, "The Political Function of Narrative in Organizations," *Communication Monographs* 54 (1987): 113–27.

17. Stohl and Cheney, "Participatory Processes/Paradoxical Practices," 352.

18. Kevin Real and Linda L. Putnam, "Ironies in the Discursive Struggle of Pilots Defending the Profession," *Management Communication Quarterly* 19 (2005): 91–119; Linda L. Putnam and Tricia S. Jones, "Reciprocity in Negotiations: An Analysis of Bargaining Interactions," *Communication Monographs* 49 (1982): 171–91.

19. Real and Putnam, "Ironies in the Discursive Struggle of Pilots Defending the Profession," 98.

20. Ibid., 105; see also Linda L. Putnam, "Contradictions and Paradoxes in Organizations," in *Organizational Communication: Emerging Perspectives*, ed. Lee Thayer, vol. 1 (Norwood, Mass.: Ablex, 1986), 151–62; and Angela Trethewey, "Isn't It Ironic: Using Irony to Explore the Contradictions of Organizational Life," *Western Journal of Communication* 63 (1999): 140–67.

21. Paul Willis, *Learning to Labor: How Working Class Kids Get Working Class Jobs* (New York: Columbia University Press, 1977), xiii.

22. Ibid., 2.

23. Ibid.

24. Ibid., 178.

25. Karl Marx, "Eighteenth Brumaire of Louis Napoleon," 1852, *Marxists.org*, http://www.marxists.org/archive/marx/works/1852/18th-brumaire/ch01.htm (accessed June 5, 2005).

26. Originally articulated by Marx, this distinction was taken up by a succession of Marxists interested in the role of discourse, intellectuals, and political organizations (i.e., parties) in the production of class-consciousness and organization; Karl Marx, "Strikes and Combinations of Workers," in *Collected Works*, vol. 6 (London: Lawrence and Wishart, 1987), 211; see also Georg Lukács, *History and Class-Consciousness*, trans. Rodney Livingstone (Cambridge, Mass.: MIT Press, 1972), 168. See also Georg Lukács, *A Defense of History and Class-Consciousness*, trans. Esther Leslie (London: Verso, 2000); Oskar Negt and Alexander Kluge, *Public Sphere and Experience*, trans. Peter Labanyi, Jamie Owen Daniel, and Assenka Oksiloff (Minneapolis: University of Minnesota Press, 1993).

Conclusion: The Beginnings and Ends of Union Democracy

1. Robert J. Samuelson, "Is Organized Labor Obsolete?" *Newsweek*, February 28, 2011, http://www.newsweek.com/2011/02/28/is-organized-labor-obsolete.print.html (accessed March 19, 2011).

2. Jacob S. Hacker and Paul Pierson, "The Wisconsin Union Fight Isn't about Benefits. It's About Labor's Influence," *Washington Post*, March 4, 2011, http://www.washingtonpost.com/opinions/the-wisconsin-union-fight-isnt-about-benefits-its-about-labors-influence/2011/02/28/ABH5L0N_story.html (accessed March 20, 2011).

3. John Logan, "Is This the End for Organised Labour in the US?" *guardian.co.uk*, March 11, 2011, http://www.guardian.co.uk/commentisfree/cifamerica/2011/mar/11/us-unions-wisconsin (accessed March 19, 2011).

4. Art Preis, *Labor's Giant Step: The First Twenty Years of the CIO: 1936–55* (New York: Pathfinder Press, 1964).

5. United States Department of Labor, "Union Members Summary," *Bureau of Labor Statistics,* January 22, 2010, http://www.bls.gov/news.release/union2.nro.htm (accessed August 17, 2010).

6. Irving Bernstein, "The Growth of American Unionism," *The American Economic Review* 44 (1954): 301–18.

7. Leo Troy, *Distribution of Union Membership among the States, 1939 and 1953* (Cambridge, Mass.: National Bureau of Economic Research, 1957).

8. William W. Stafford, "Disputes within Trade Unions," *Yale Law Journal* 45 (1936): 1248–71; emphasis in the original.

9. Ibid., 1259.

10. Lee Sustar and Nicole Colson, "Raising the Stakes at Republic," *Socialistworker. org,* December 9, 2008, http://socialistworker.org/2008/12/09/raising-the-stakes-at-republic (accessed June 16, 2010).

11. United States Department of Labor, "Labor Force Statistics from the Current Population," *Bureau of Labor Statistics,* http://www.bls.gov/cps/ (accessed September 5, 2010).

12. Louis Uchitelle, "The Wage That Meant Middle Class," *New York Times,* April 20, 2008, WK3.

13. Wendy Kaufman, "Boeing's Earnings a Tool in Machinists' Strike," *National Public Radio Morning Edition,* October 23, 2008, http://www.npr.org/templates/story/story.php?storyId=96019332&ft=1&f=1001 (accessed December 4, 2008).

14. Quoted in Chris Isidore, "Boeing Strike Another Hit to Economy," *CNNMoney .com,* September 12, 2008, http://money.cnn.com/2008/09/12/news/economy/boeing_impact/index.htm (accessed December 4, 2008).

15. David Robertson, "Strike at Boeing Will Cost Aircraft Maker $100m a Day in Lost Revenues," *Times of London,* September 8, 2008.

16. Christopher Hinton, "Machinists' Strike against Boeing Enters Third Week," *MarketWatch,* September 19, 2008, http://www.marketwatch.com/story/boeings-shortfall-grows-as-strike-enters-third-week (accessed August 1, 2010). At the same time, however, the 2008 contract did not prohibit outsourcing of work on the 787, which has more foreign content than any other Boeing plane. "The reality is that it would have been cheaper to keep a lot of this work in-house," columnist Michael Hiltzik wrote. "Boeing executives now admit that the company's aggressive outsourcing put it in partnership with suppliers that weren't up to the job." Unionists had been calling attention to these pitfalls over a period of years; Michael Hiltzik, "787 Dreamliner Teaches Boeing Costly Lesson on Outsourcing," *Los Angeles Times,* February

15, 2011, http://www.latimes.com/news/columnists/la-fi-hiltzik-20110215,0,1160131. column (accessed March 19, 2011).

17. Micheline Maynard, "Earnings Drop 38% at Boeing as Machinists' Strike Wears On," *New York Times*, October 23, 2008, 10.

18. Tom Jenneman, "Suppliers Months Away from Ramp-up after Boeing Strike Ends," *American Metal Market*, November 4, 2008.

19. Christopher Hinton, "Boeing Reaches Tentative Contract with Engineers," *MarketWatch*, November 14, 2008, http://www.marketwatch.com/story/boeing-reaches-tentative-contact-with-21000-engineers (accessed August 1, 2010).

20. Chang-Ran Kim, "Boeing Strike May Have Global Impact; Suppliers Worried," *National Post*, September 9, 2008, FP12.

21. Sharon Smith, *Subterranean Fire: A History of Working-Class Radicalism in the United States* (Chicago: Haymarket, 2007).

22. Ibid., 319.

23. Aronowitz, quoted in ibid.

24. Michael Schiavone, *Unions in Crisis: The Future of Organized Labor in America* (Westport, Conn.: Praeger Press, 2007), 61; Kim Moody, *U.S. Labor in Trouble and Transition* (London: Verso, 1997); Kim Moody, *An Injury to All: The Decline of American Unionism* (London, New York: Verso, 1988).

25. Julius J. Getman, *Restoring the Power of Unions: It Takes a Movement* (New Haven, Conn.: Yale University Press, 2010), 19.

26. Ibid., 309. Note that Early takes issue with Getman's narrative regarding the evolution of UNITE HERE as marked by increasing top-down control; Steve Early, *The Civil Wars in U.S. Labor: Birth of a New Workers' Movement* (Chicago: Haymarket, 2011).

27. Paul Buhle, *Taking Care of Business: Samuel Gompers, George Meany, Lane Kirkland, and the Tragedy of American Labor* (New York: Monthly Review Press, 1999).

28. Ibid., 16.

29. Among the upstart struggles, 2003 saw strike victories by workers at Yale University and at Chicago sanitation companies. The victorious, 100-day-long, 2007–2008 strike on the part of the Writers Guild of America prompted the *Financial Times* of London to exclaim, "Workers of the New World, Unite!"; John Gapper, "Workers of the New World, Unite!" *Financial Times*, December 13, 2007. Jose Rivera summed up a new sense of agency on the part of a workforce that used to consider itself atypical and privileged: "The studios may be feeling like, 'Oh, my God, they're storming the barricades!' And this is just the tip of the iceberg. Every time I go out, my 15-year-old son says, 'Dad, are you gonna stick it to the Man today?' So, it's like, 'All right, I guess I am sticking it to the Man'"; Jay Fernandez, "Scriptland: Strike Plucks a Political Nerve," *Los Angeles Times*, December 19, 2007, E1. At Spirit Airlines, a 2010 pilots' strike grounded flights in the struggle for pay in line with industry standards; Julie Johnson, "Spirit Airlines Labor

Strife Could Set Tone for Other Carriers," *Chicago Tribune,* June 11, 2010, http://www.
chicagotribune.com/business/ct-biz-0612-spirit-20100611,0,1561195.story (accessed
June 16, 2010). In San Francisco in June 2010, municipal workers voted down concessions, threatening a strike; Associated Press, "SF Muni Union Votes against Labor Concessions," *San Diego Union-Tribune,* June 12, 2010, http://www.signonsandiego.com/
news/2010/jun/12/sf-muni-union-votes-against-labor-concessions/ (accessed March 19,
2011). In March 2010, Minneapolis custodians—most of them immigrants and people of
color—organized by the Service Employees International Union (SEIU) won huge gains
in job security, work hours, pay raises, and health insurance by threatening to strike;
Peter Rachleff, "A New Script for Labor in Minnesota," *Socialistworker.org,* March 17,
2010, http://socialistworker.org/print/2010/03/17/new-script-for-labor (accessed June
16, 2010). Graduate students at both the University of Illinois at Chicago and New York
University have been engaged in the fight for graduate employees; Scott Jaschik, "Show-
down on Grad Unions," *InsideHigherEd,* April 28, 2010, http://www.insidehighered.
com/news/2010/04/28/nyu (accessed June 16, 2010). Hotel workers in San Francisco,
organized by UNITE HERE Local 2, have been waging boycotts and rolling strikes
of major hotels across the city; Carl Finamore, "Taking on the San Francisco Hilton,"
Socialistworker.org, January 7, 2010, http://socialistworker.org/2010/01/07/taking-on-
the-hilton (accessed July 8, 2010). At Shaw's supermarket in Massachusetts, 310 United
Food and Commercial Workers (UFCW) members waged a strike in 2010 that shut
down the company's distribution center; Eric Rehder and Chris Murphy, "On Strike at
Shaw's," *Socialistworker.org,* March 17, 2010, http://socialistworker.org/2010/03/16/on-
strike-at-shaws (accessed July 8, 2010). Longshore workers in Los Angeles are striking
at the time of this writing for wage and pension increases, and construction workers are
on the move in Chicago; Andrew Dalton, "La Port Clerk Strike Goes on Despite Holiday
Talks," *Associated Press,* July 6, 2010; Duaa Eldeib and Mick Swasko, "Concerns Rise as
Strike Continues," *Chicagotribune.com,* July 6, 2010, http://www.chicagotribune.com/
news/local/ct-met-construction-strike-07-20100706,0,2528464,print.story (accessed
July 8, 2010); see also "Labor Dispute Threatens Two U.S. Major Ports," *iStockAnalyst,*
July 10, 2010, http://www.istockanalyst.clm/article/viewiStockNews/articleid/4296223
(accessed February 9, 2011).

30. For example, the nearly five-month 2004 strike of 59,000 grocery workers in
California and elsewhere against the retailers Safeway, Vons, and Pavilion ended
tragically with concessions; Lee Sustar, "The Labor Movement: State of Emergency,
Signs of Renewal," *International Socialist Review* 34 (March–April 2004), http://www.
isreview.org/issues/34/stateofemergency.shtml (accessed August 1, 2010). The December 2005 New York City Transit Workers' strike was the largest display of labor's
power in more than twenty-five years, but the Transit Workers Union (TWU) called
an abrupt halt to the strike, taking concessions on wages and health care; Leia Petty
and Jen Roesch, "The Strike That Shut Down New York," *Socialistworker.org,* January
6, 2006, http://socialistworker.org/2006-1/570/570_06_NYCTransit.shtml (accessed

February 9, 2011). Most significant, the TWU International came out publicly against the strike of Local 100, which includes a third of the union's members.

31. Pushed by the formation of the rank-and-file caucus, thousands of unionized nurses in Minnesota struck fourteen Minneapolis hospitals in June 2010, demonstrating the kind of initiative that can revitalize the labor movement; Caralyn Davis, "Minnesota Labor Update: Federal Mediator Tries to Head Off Extended Nurses Strike," *FierceHealthFinance,* http://www.fiercehealthfinance.com/story/minnesota-labor-update-federal-mediator-tries-head-extended-nurses-strike/2010–06–23 (accessed June 24, 2010); Peter Rachleff, "Minnesota Nurses' Rx for Union Revival," *Socialistworker.org,* June 17, 2010, http://socialistworker.org/2010/06/17/nurses-rx-for-union-revival (accessed July 8, 2010); Lee Sustar and Sal Rosselli, "Rebuilding a Fighting Labor Movement," June 17, 2010, http://wearemany.org/a/2010/06/rebuilding-fighting-labor-movement (accessed July 8, 2010). In the Chicago Teachers Union (CTU), reformers in the Caucus of Rank and File Educators (CORE) mounted efforts to win control of the union and press it to stand up against school closings and the evacuation of public resources by charter schools; Lee Sustar, "A New Day in the Chicago Teachers Union," *Socialistworker.org,* June 14, 2010, http://socialistworker.org/print/2010/06/14/new-day-for-chicago-teachers (accessed June 16, 2010); Lee Sustar, "Shock Waves in the CTU," *Socialistworker.org,* May 25, 2010, http://socialistworker.org/print/2010/05/25/shock-waves-in-the-ctu (accessed June 16, 2010). Karen Lewis overcame threats, scapegoating, and corrupt elections—and won. In the United Auto Workers, rank-and-file challenger Gary Walkowicz challenged Ron Gettelfinger for the position of international president, the first challenge of its kind in eighteen years; Nick Kottalis, Gary Walkowicz, Cathy Abney, and Dewayne Jackson, "Letter to Workers at Dearborn Truck Plant," *Soldiers of Solidarity,* June 14, 2010, http://www.soldiersofsolidarity.com (accessed June 16, 2010). SEIU President Andy Stern went on the run in 2010 after resigning his post (after fourteen years) amid rumors of embezzlement of pension funds; Warner Todd Huston, "Andy Stern: Union Chief Fleeing Ahead of Illinois Indictment?" *Chicagonow.com,* April 26, 2010, http://www.chicagonow.com/blogs/publius-forum/2010/04/andy-stern-union-chief-fleeing-ahead-of-illinois-indictment.html (accessed June 16, 2010); Ezra Klein, "SEIU President Offers a Look Ahead Before Stepping Down," *Washington Post,* April 18, 2010, http://www.washingtonpost.com/wp-dyn/content/article/2010/04/17/AR2010041702554_pf.html (accessed June 16, 2010). Reformers in a large Teamsters local at UPS in Laguna, California, won their campaign in May 2010; Edgar Esquivel, "Turning Up the Heat in Local 952," *Socialistworker.org,* May 10, 2010, http://socialistworker.org/2010/05/10/turning-up-the-heat (accessed July 8, 2010). Teamsters also took on Waste Management in Seattle; Darrin Hoop, "Taking on Waste Management in Seattle," *Socialistworker.org,* April 23, 2010, http://socialistworker.org/2010/04/23/taking-on-waste-management (accessed July 8, 2010). Mott's workers have conducted what is so far the longest strike in the history of the Rochester, New York, area. SEIU is also on the run in northern California as reformers won all of the officer

positions in Local 1021; Larry Bradshaw, "Sweeping Victory for SEIU Reformers," *Socialistworker.org,* March 9, 2010, http://socialistworker.org/2010/03/09/sweeping-victory-for-seiu-reformers (accessed July 8, 2010). Educators for a Democratic Union in San Francisco went up against entrenched teachers' union leadership in order to make, in the words of one activist, a "union that fights for all its members—and that doesn't change our working conditions without the full consultation of the membership and ratification by membership vote"; Andy Lisbon, "Union Reform Challenge in S.F.," *Socialistworker.org,* March 18, 2009, http://socialistworker.org/2009/03/18/sf-union-reform-challenge (accessed August 1, 2010).There is a list of union reform groups and efforts in U.S. and Canadian unions at http://www.xpdnc.com/links/poliup.html.

32. For example, in June 2010, 2,500 Boeing Machinists in St. Louis voted to strike to protect workers' pensions. Machinists in Charleston, South Carolina, filed an NLRB complaint against the company for its retaliation against workers after the 2008 strike; Dominic Gates, "Machinists File Unfair Labor Charge against Boeing over Charleston," *Seattle Times,* June 5, 2010, http://seattletimes.nwsource.com/html/businesstechnology/2012034258_boeing05.html (accessed June 16, 2010). In May 2010, 2,000 Boeing workers in Long Beach, California, struck, shutting down the production line for the C-17.

33. Early, *The Civil Wars in U.S. Labor,* 291–303. Also notable among the upstarts has been a group of nurses in California who revolted in 2010 against an SEIU union takeover to form a new health care union called the California Nurses Association.

Interviews and Archival Sources

Interviews April 9–14, 1998, Wichita, Kansas

Keith Thomas, UDC
Shelley Thomas, spouse of Keith
Kelly Vandegrift, UDC
Gary Washington, UDC
Madeleine Meuller (pseudonym), ally of UDC
Sean Mullin, UDC
Arlene Hoaglan, ally of UDC
David "Bones" Smith, UDC
Mike Burleigh, Local 834 organizer
Mary Johnson, Local 834 treasurer
David Robertson, past District 70 president
Sherri Hood, women's committee, delegate to District 70
Denise Harris, delegate to District 70
Garland Moore, vice president of Local 834, president of Wichita Area Union Council
David Eagle, Local 834 president
Molly McMillin, aviation reporter for *Wichita Eagle*

Interviews July 10–14, 1999, Wichita, Kansas

Keith Thomas
Harry Thornton
Robert Holl
Billy Carton
David "Bones" Smith
Gary Washington

Molly McMillin
Harold Schlectweg, organizing director, SEIU Local 13, Wichita
Dick Ziegler, Boeing spokesperson (by phone)

Interviews July 25–August 1, 1999, Seattle/Everett, Washington

Tom Jackson, New Crew
Don Grinde, New Crew
Tom Finnegan, New Crew
Stan Johnson, ally of New Crew
Tom Jackson, New Crew
Rick Herrmann, New Crew
William Sapiens, New Crew
David Mascarenas, New Crew
David Clay, Machinists for Solidarity/Take It Back
Jackie Boschok, IAMAW District 751, Local F, district council
    delegate and union steward
Curtis Thorfinson, career guide developer, IAM/Boeing Quality
    through Training Program (appointed)
Roy Moore, IAMAW-Boeing joint Health and Safety Institute (appointed)
Virginia Roberts, IAMAW education director
Sue Moyer, IAMAW education director
"Joe," gay Boeing worker
Ronnie McGaha, administrative assistant to the district president, District 751
Ron Eldridge, District 751 president
Dick Schneider, aerospace coordinator, lead negotiator
Peter Conte, Boeing spokesperson (by phone)

Interview July 17, 2001, Wichita, Kansas

Keith Thomas

Archives: David Mascarenas

Newspaper coverage of New Crew, IAMAW elections
New Crew election materials (flyers, letters, etc.)
History of 1919 Seattle General Strike

Archives: Don Grinde

Video: Crane operators, Everett
Photographs: Union history, union people, work in plant
Strikes, 1995–2008

Personal journal
Correspondence
Email messages
Radio interviews
Flyers
Newsletters
T-shirts
Buttons

Archives: Keith Thomas

Photographs: Detroit newspaper strike 1994, Boeing events 1989–2008, UDC people
Floormikes (email newsletters), 1997–1999
Correspondence, June–July 2006

Index

DANA L. CLOUD is an associate professor of communication studies at the University of Texas, Austin, and the author of *Consolation and Control in American Culture: Rhetorics of Therapy.*

The University of Illinois Press
is a founding member of the
Association of American University Presses.

———————————————————

Composed in 10/13 Adobe Minion Pro
with Avenir display
by Jim Proefrock
at the University of Illinois Press
Manufactured by Sheridan Books, Inc.

University of Illinois Press
1325 South Oak Street
Champaign, IL 61820-6903
www.press.uillinois.edu